The Essential Guide to Home Networking Technologies

ISBN 0-13-019846-3

90000

9 780130 198464

Essential Guide Series

**THE ESSENTIAL GUIDE TO
DATA WAREHOUSING**

Agosta

**THE ESSENTIAL GUIDE TO
TELECOMMUNICATIONS,**
SECOND EDITION

Dodd

**THE ESSENTIAL GUIDE TO
NETWORKING**

Keogh

**THE ESSENTIAL GUIDE TO DIGITAL
SET-TOP BOXES AND INTERACTIVE TV**

O'Driscoll

**THE ESSENTIAL GUIDE TO
HOME NETWORKING TECHNOLOGIES**

O'Driscoll

THE ESSENTIAL GUIDE TO COMPUTING:
THE STORY OF INFORMATION TECHNOLOGY

Walters

**THE ESSENTIAL GUIDE TO
RF AND WIRELESS**

Weisman

The Essential Guide to Home Networking Technologies

GERARD O'DRISCOLL

PH PTR

Prentice Hall PTR, Upper Saddle River, NJ   07458
www.phptr.com

Library of Congress Cataloging-in-Publication Data

O'Driscoll, Gerard.
    The essential guide to home networking technologies / Gerard O'Driscoll.
        p. cm.—(Essential guide series)
    ISBN: 0-13-019846-3 (pbk. : alk. paper)
    1. Computer software. 2. Home computer networks. 3. Computer software. I. Title. II.
    Essential Guide series (Prentice-Hall, inc.)
    TK5105.7.O34 2000
    004.6—dc21   00-037307

Acquisitions Editor: *Michael Meehan*
Editorial Assistant: *Linda Ramagnano*
Manufacturing buyer: *Maura Goldstaub*
Art Director: *Gail Cocker-Bogusz*
Interior Series Design: *Meg Van Arsdale*
Cover Design: *Bruce Kenselaar*
Cover Design Direction: *Jerry Votta*

All terms mentioned in this book are known to be trademarks or service marks and are the property
of their respective owners. Use of a term in this book should not be regarded as affecting
the validity of any trademark or service mark.

Prentice Hall books are widely used by corporations and government agencies
for training, marketing, and resale.

The publisher offers discounts on this book when ordered in bulk quantities.
For more information, contact Corporate Sales Department,
Phone: 800-382-3419; FAX: 201-236-7141;
E-mail: corpsales@prenhall.com
Or write: Prentice Hall PTR, Corporate Sales Dept., One Lake Street, Upper Saddle River, NJ 07458.

Printed in the United States of America
10 9 8 7 6 5 4 3 2 1

ISBN 0-13-019846-3

Prentice-Hall International (UK) Limited, London
Prentice-Hall of Australia Pty. Limited, Sydney
Prentice-Hall Canada Inc., Toronto
Prentice-Hall Hispanoamericana, S.A., Mexico
Prentice-Hall of India Private Limited, New Delhi
Prentice-Hall of Japan, Inc., Tokyo
Pearson Education Asia Pte. Ltd.
Editora Prentice-Hall do Brasil, Ltda., Rio de Janeiro

This book is dedicated to my loving wife, Olive, and our six-month-old daughter, Aoife (thanks for the early morning wake-up calls!).

To my caring and hardworking parents, Liam and Mary O'Driscoll of Skibbereen, County Cork, Ireland.

To my brothers—Owen, who is about to take "the plunge," and Brian, who continues to enjoy the rock 'n' roll lifestyle.

Finally, to the rock gods and beer men in the electronic production class of 1988.

Contents

17 OSGi *301*

Foreword

HOME NETWORKING: THE CONVERGENCE POINT FOR PERVASIVE COMPUTING ....

In early 1998, the term "home networking" emerged on the IT scene as the newest buzzword in the growing lexicon of hot, new-generation technologies. Yet with the increased hype and media exposure came confusion as consumers struggled to figure out exactly what home networking was and how it would affect their lives.

With Jetsons-like images of robotic butlers and voice-activated appliances, the spin-savvy journalists quickly positioned home networking as the new revolution. The pragmatists, on the other hand, focused on more immediate and practical benefits, like sharing files between multiple computers without having to retrofit an entire home with new wires. Consumers remained confused and largely unresponsive.

Almost overnight the traditional home automation and control technologies, like X-10 and CEBus—which existed long before the media blitz—were thrown into the mix with a new breed of technologies that touted the ability to use phone lines, wireless RF (radio frequency), and AC powerlines for high-speed data networking in the home. At the same time, the expansion of broadband connectivity started bringing continuous, high-speed Internet access to individual households.

Still, home networking meant little to the consumer, and the response was lukewarm.

Why?

While interconnecting PCs is a useful and welcome solution for many people, the truly revolutionary potential of home networking lies in its ability to extend the Internet directly into the hands of everyday consumers. Making Internet access available everywhere hints at what many people are calling *pervasive computing*.

When the pervasive computing movement is in full force, it is only a question of time before all of the electronic devices within the home have some type of embedded intelligence that can share high-speed data. And with their new brains comes the impulsive need to communicate, not only to other smart devices but more important to the people who are using them.

The home network is the convergence point of the next generation of digital devices with the next generation of digital infrastructure. It is a key strategic technology that will enable the new-breed information appliances to connect to, and communicate over, the rapidly expanding digital telecommunications network.

The large service providers and network operators—including telcos, cable companies, ISPs, and electric utilities—have now begun positioning themselves around the home network market, contemplating the next strategic move that could determine their success or failure.

For technology companies, the increasingly competitive environment depends on the strength of the connection to the customer. It's not so much a question of new or better technology, but rather an issue of survival for a company. For these players, the home network represents a critical link in the connectivity puzzle—a way to extend the Internet not just to PCs but to all of the smart devices that will soon exist within the home.

In this sense, it's true that the vision of pervasive computing—essentially the vision to provide consumers a seamless connection to the Internet from any time, at any place, through any device—will not only change the way we view technology, but it will fundamentally change the way we live. Companies realize that the stakes are high, and they'll do just about anything to own a customer.

Consumers are, and ought to be, hesitant about using new technologies.

The Essential Guide to Home Networking Technologies covers some of the most important issues involved in bringing the vision of pervasive computing to fruition. Mr. O'Driscoll has lent his expertise to create this "must have" reference book for anyone who wants to better understand the technologies, business drivers, and industry players that are shaping this quickly growing and constantly evolving market.

This guide will help consumers to wade through the coming onslaught of digital promises and focus on being digitally connected.

Ian O'Sullivan
Director of Strategic Marketing
Enikia, Inc.

Preface

Many consumers access the Internet, e-commerce stores, and e-mail accounts from the comfort of their homes. The home networking business is now only beginning and is expected to soar in the next couple of years as more and more households around the world connect to the Internet. Many large IT and telecommunication companies are planning to offer a range of new products that will allow entertainment devices and PCs scattered around your household to "talk to each other." Allied Business Intelligence estimates that the home networking equipment marketplace will grow dramatically to reach $2.4 billion by 2005.

Simply put, a digital home network is a cluster of audio/visual (A/V) devices, including set-top boxes, TVs, VCRs, DVD players, and general-purpose computing devices such as personal computers. Companies that are involved in the home networking industry need to convince consumers that the new technology can help them save time, make organizing activities more convenient, and can even entertain them. With the steady rise in high-speed access to the Web and the proliferation of households with multiple PCs, the need for home networking solutions has increased dramatically in recent months. Several companies and organizations have responded to this need by developing standards and affordable solutions for consumers. The creation of open standards is an important catalyst for creating high-growth consumer markets. Adopting such a strategy will allow the home networking market to grow faster, without interruption, and will keep consumers confident that the products they buy today will continue to be viable solutions for the future.

Because no single technology fulfills all of the application requirements of the home network, multiple technologies will be deployed at different times, each addressing the needs of unique market segments. Several technology development efforts are currently underway to support the application requirements of the home network. Organizations like HomePNA and HomeRF are primarily focused on the networking of PCs and peripheral devices together. In parallel to these developments, groups, companies, and technologies such as HAVi, UPnP, HomePnP, LonWorks, Digital Harmony, and Jini are actively promoting software systems for networking PCs, home control, and entertainment systems together. In parallel to these in-home technology developments, an industry group called OSGi is working to define and promote an open software standard for connecting the coming generation of smart appliances with commercial network service providers. This book unravels the benefits, technical details, and features of all of these.

What Will I Learn?

After reading this book, you should be able to:

- Understand the core computing models that are used to run digital applications across an in-home network.
- Recognize the companies and organizations that are developing technologies for the home networking marketplace.
- List and explain the broadband technologies that are used to connect home networks to the Internet—DSL, HFC, wireless cable, satellite, and powerline wide area networks.
- Understand phone-line technologies and the standards group that has been established to promote this technology—Home Phoneline Networking Alliance.
- Explain how powerline technology allows home networking users to transmit data over the existing AC infrastructure.
- List and explain the most popular powerline technologies—Enikia, X-10, CEBus, and Inari.
- Outline in detail the high-speed serial technologies that promise home users the ability to easily connect electronics devices such as digital TVs, cameras, cable set-top boxes, and stereo equipment to each other and to PCs.
- Understand the basic principles of wireless based home networks (RF and IR).
- List and explain the industry initiatives that are developing interoperable wireless in-home appliances.

- Learn about the various types of residential gateways that connect the broadband local loop to the in-home network (cable modems, digital set-top boxes, personal video recorders, DSL modems, and home servers).

- Explain the core services that are required to support the smooth operation of an in-home network.

- Describe in detail the most popular home networking middleware and API solutions—HAVi, Jini, UPnP, Digital Harmony, OSGi, and HomePnP.

- Explain content protection and watermarking technologies in a home networking environment.

KEEPING UP TO DATE AND CONTACT DETAILS......

Since the home networking universe expands at an astonishing rate, this book can only provide a time-dated snapshot of the entire industry. Industry groups and organizations are constantly developing technological solutions that will allow people to be able to connect and communicate at any time from anywhere. To stay in tune with the evolution of home networking technologies, please visit the set-tops family of Web sites at http://www.set-tops.com. If you have comments or suggestions about this book, feel free to drop me a line at the following address: gerard@set-tops.com. Time permitting, I'll try my best to get back to you within a week of receiving your e-mail.

Who Should Read This Book?

This book assumes some degree of knowledge about general networking and Internet concepts. It is intended for a wide range of computing professionals who are interested in learning about the myriad of home networking standards and technologies that are currently available. These include:

- Small-business owners and remote telecommuters who want to implement and manage an in-home networking system.

- Members of the software development community who are conceiving and developing applications for the emerging home networking industry.

- Business development executives, system integrators, and technical managers who want to learn about the capabilities of the various types of home networking technologies.

- Executives in cable companies, broadcast, terrestrial, and satellite providers who want to build revenue streams and profits through the deployment of home networks at their customers' premises.

- Anybody who wants to understand the options before selecting a particular technology for networking their in-home appliances.

- IT engineers, researchers, or strategic decision-makers who want to understand the value of the new digital economy.

- Personnel engaged in the convergence industries, including infrastructure operators, device manufacturers, content publishers, and service providers.

Acknowledgments

When any book is written, there are a number of people in the background who help an author to make publication deadlines and make the book a success on the world stage. I would like to thank the staff at Prentice Hall for having the vision to see the need for this book, and the professionalism to follow through and publish the world's first book on this new industry. In particular, my executive editor Michael E. Meehan and Jane Bonnell gave me much needed advice and encouragement to complete the book. A special thanks to Ian O'Sullivan, Jeff Gray, Jim Reeber, David Healey, and Bob Dillon of Enikia, who generously developed content on powerline technologies for this book. Furthermore, Ian has devoted a large amount of personal time to this project and has also provided me with some extremely valuable information about the home networking industry. Staff at the following companies were enormously helpful in reviewing and providing input for this book: Niklas Orup at Ericsson; Paul Shumate and Bill Hagen at IEEE; Bill Bane at Mercer management consultants; Eric McIntyre at Tzolkin Corporation for allowing me to use excerpts from hpna.com; Bob Dolin and Reza Raji at Echelon; Alec Saunders at Microsoft; Bengt Christensson and Olof Larsson at Axis Communications; Bill Woodcock and Bill Manning at ISI; Brent Miller at IBM; Cyrus Namazi at AMD; Alan Walbeck and Todd Green at Intelogis; Edwin Gib Blair at Media Fusion; Bernardino Camba at Domosys; Melissa Pereira at A+R Partners; and Matt Campbell at Axicom. People from various international home networking organizations have been extremely helpful. In particular I would like to thank Rodger Lea and his team at HAVi; John Barr at OSGi; Salim AbiEzzi at UPnP; Craig McAllister at EPRI; Kurt Scherf at Parks Associates; Cindy Stevens, Glyn Finley, and Matt Swanston at Consumer Electronics Association (CEA); P. S. Vishwanath at CEBus Industry Council (CIC); and Joel Di Girolamo at Video Electronics Standards Association (VESA).

A special and sincere thanks to Andrew Liu, Barry Bonder, Ben Manny (Chairman of HomeRF), Jim Lansford (now working at Mobilian.com), and Susan Lubeck at Intel for providing me with invaluable technical information on the exciting home networking technologies that are being developed by Intel architecture labs.

Thanks also to Todd Green at Inari for supplying me with a white paper on the company's powerline networking technologies. Also Wayne Caswell was a great help to me in explaining the positioning of the main wireless technologies.

Additionally I would like to thank David Smith at ShareWave for submitting a detailed white paper on high performance wireless home networking. Also thanks to Kevin Negus for organizing the submission of a number of papers explaining Proxim technologies. A special thanks also goes to Greg Bartlett and his team for developing the chapter on Digital Harmony technologies. The following people have also helped me to develop content for this book, and I sincerely thank all of them: Julie Haywood and Ron Zimmer at CABA; and Craig McAllister at EPRI. Andrew Wajs at MindPort provided me with some expert advice on copyright and watermarking technologies.

Most of all I would like to thank my wife, Olive, for her support in completing this book.

Further Reading

http://www.microsoft.com/homenet/—*Microsoft white papers*

http://www.cedmagazine.com/ced/9903/9903a.htm—*David ller*

http://www.usb.org

http://www.dell.com/r&d/whitepapers/wpwan.htm—*DSL*

http://www.3com.com/technology/tech_net/white_papers/503042.html—*DSL*

http://www.dtcp.com/dtcp_tut.pdf

http://www.techweb.com/wire/story/TWB19980220S0006

http://www.dvcc.com/dhsg/HTML_May_cptwg_present/

http://www.trl.ibm.co.jp/projects/s7730/Hiding/dhvgx_e.htm

http://www.sony.com/SCA/press/feb_19_99b.html

http://www.bluetooth.com/document/default.asp?page=overview

http://www.homerf.org/aboutHRF/

http://www.news.com/News/Item/0,4,40713,00.html?st.ne.fd.gif.d

http://www.cebus.org/

http://www.cemacity.org/gazette/

http://www.x10.org/

http://www-3.ibm.com/pvc/nethome/networking.shtml—*Brent Miller of IBM*

http://www.home.com—*Excite@Home product information*

http://www.rr.com—*Road Runner details*

http://www.cebus.org/hpnp/778899/HPnP10.pdf—*Home Plug & Play specification*

http://www.zdnet.com

http://www.vesa.org/

ADSL Status Update white paper from Intel Architecture Labs.

ShareWave white paper on high performance, wireless home networking and the Whitecap protocol.

The Information Economy Derivative Markets Model and The Introduction to Powerline Technologies white papers by Ian O'Sullivan at Enikia Incorporated.

http://engmgt.com/wwp.html—*White paper on wireless LANs, developed by Wade H. Shaw*

http://www.proxim.com/wireless/index.shtml—*Useful hyperlinks on various wireless technologies.*

http://www.osgi.org—*Version 1.0 of OSGi specification*

Research paper from Intel called "Emerging Trends in Home Computing"

The Design and Implementation of HomeRF: A Radio-Frequency Wireless Networking Standard for the Connected Home by Jim Lansford at Intel and Paramvir Bahl at Microsoft Research.

"Understanding Home Phoneline Networking"—*A technical overview by Intel Corporation*

About the Author

GERARD O'DRISCOLL is a graduate of the University of Limerick, where he earned qualifications in Electronics and Information Technology. He has held various managerial and business development positions in Ireland. Currently, he is the head of New Interactive Services at Irish Multichannel—a leading provider of digital TV, Internet, and telephony services. He is responsible for developing and delivering a range of interactive TV and Internet-based services to the company's customer base. He is also the author of *The Essential Guide to Digital Set-top Boxes and Interactive TV.*

1 Convergence and the Information Economy

In this chapter...

$\mathbf{T}$he development of the Internet-based global telecommunications infrastructure is converging with that of local networks. The distribution and exchange of products and services, a kind of digital commodity, will soon exist in a frictionless, bidirectional, instantaneous environment. This revolution has the potential to redefine the fundamental basis of the world economy.

This opening chapter[1] is a serious attempt to fast-forward five or ten years and model the digital information and communications marketplace. Sections of this chapter examine the possibilities for a technological platform that will interconnect homes, and all the devices in them, into a cohesive system—one that empowers people to work, live, and communicate more effectively. We'll look at underlying social, cultural, and economic forces that act on the marketplace. It's a story about technological convergence, infrastructure development, and marketplace demand that will create a platform for the digital content, devices, and services of the information economy.

THE PERVASIVE COMPUTING VISION....................

As technology experts continue to hail the arrival of the "digital revolution" and the "information era," average citizens wait for the realities of these promises to touch their daily lives. Some consumers don't realize it, but there may already be many computers in their house; they just don't call them computers. There are microchips in refrigerators, microwaves, TVs, VCRs, and stereos. With all of these processors, the concept of *pervasive computing* has emerged. This is a vision for the future where people will be able to connect and communicate at any time from anywhere, using new *information appliance* devices.

As opposed to the general-purpose PCs of today, information appliances will be small, inexpensive consumer devices, optimized to perform a specialized set of user-centric functions, such as a portable Internet phone that has personal e-mail and Web-browsing capabilities. The vision of pervasive computing is to interconnect all devices via a globally integrated, ubiquitous network. The goal: to increase the efficiency and enhance the leisure time of the consumer. This promises greater empowerment for individual citizens.

---

1. This chapter is abstracted from a report developed by Enikia titled "The Information Economy Derivative Markets Model: A Technology Value Chain for the Digital Economy," December, 1999.

HISTORIC PRETEXT FOR THE INFORMATION ECONOMY ....

Just as the invention of the steam engine sparked the industrial revolution of the 1800s, the computer has brought about a revolution equal in social, political, and economic significance. Marked by the ability to process and manipulate data and, more important, the knowledge that it embodies, the information revolution is truly changing the ways in which value is created in our global economy.

Data, in the form of digital bits, is quickly becoming the basis for a new type of economic product—a virtual commodity that drives the continuing demand for the communications infrastructure and computing devices that comprise the massive Information Technology (IT) industry. The importance of digital data as the basis for the information economy can be best understood by comparing it to the commodity that provided the impetus for our civilization's earliest advancements: water. The development and success of history's great civilizations, like the Egyptians, Romans, and Moors, was largely determined by their superior ability to control the flow of water. Infrastructure technologies, like aqueducts and reservoirs, were developed to harness the power of water, which, in turn, provided the basis for other societal advancements of the agrarian era. Crop irrigation enabled the ability to produce surplus food supplies. Food surpluses enabled greater divisions of labor that eventually evolved into the complex systems of global economic commerce that we experience in modern society.

In this historical context, water could be considered the most essential element of the physical economy, serving as the underlying foundation of both the agrarian and industrial revolutions. Now, as we move into the digitized world of the information economy, digital content is playing a similar role in driving our economic advancement.

A MARKET MODEL FOR THE INFORMATION ECONOMY ....

The typical ancient Egyptian probably could never have envisioned a water distribution system like the ones we have today, where almost any person can access and control water from different devices throughout their homes. Likewise, it may be difficult to imagine a future where any person could access information and communicate with other people from any electric device used in the home. Yet by following this historic precedent, we can imagine how such a system of infrastructure and devices will inevitably develop around the control and distribution of our new economic commodity: digital content. Over time, derivative markets of the information economy will devel-

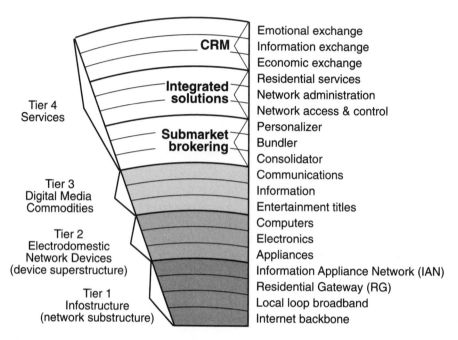

Tier 4
Services

Tier 3
Digital Media
Commodities

Tier 2
Electrodomestic
Network Devices
(device superstructure)

Tier 1
Infostructure
(network substructure)

CRM

Integrated
solutions

Submarket
brokering

Emotional exchange
Information exchange
Economic exchange
Residential services
Network administration
Network access & control
Personalizer
Bundler
Consolidator
Communications
Information
Entertainment titles
Computers
Electronics
Appliances
Information Appliance Network (IAN)
Residential Gateway (RG)
Local loop broadband
Internet backbone

Figure 1.1
Information Economy Derivative Market Model (IEDMM)

op around the systems and products that create value by delivering digital content and services to the home. Figure 1.1 shows a perspective of the derivative market tiers as they relate to creating value for the residential consumer.

The following section gives a more detailed overview of each of the IEDMM tiers.

INFORMATION ECONOMY DERIVATIVE MARKET MODEL (IEDMM)—OVERVIEW ....

Tier 1—Infostructure

Tier 1 represents the substructure of the physical system. It enables the delivery of digital content and services to the consumer. Infrastructure providers, like cable operators, telcos, and ISPs, will play the key role in deploying these substructure systems. These substructures offer pervasive Internet connectivity to the mass market by combining the following components.

Internet Backbone System

The Internet backbone system is the globally integrated, packet-based data network that will provide the Quality of Service levels (QoS) to support the distribution of digital content among users. This physical system will integrate a wide variety of industrial technologies including servers, routers, satellites, and fiber-optic cables to facilitate the instantaneous, bidirectional flow of data to locations throughout the world.

Home Infostructure

By combining broadband Internet access with a residential gateway and an in-home Information Appliance Network (IAN), the home infostructure portion of the network substructure brings the Internet to ubiquitous access throughout the home. We will examine the components of a typical home infostructure in the next section of this chapter.

Tier 2—ENDs

Consumers will experience the pervasive computing revolution when intelligent Electrodomestic Network Devices (ENDs), also called *information appliances*, become available in the mainstream marketplace. This market tier creates value by rendering digital media commodities and services to the consumer.

By connecting to the Information Appliance Network, each END can not only interoperate with other devices, but also provide residents with access to Internet-based services. The technical architecture of this new breed of information appliances is described in the next section of this chapter.

Tier 3—DMCs

Digital Media Commodities (DMCs) are the virtual products of the information economy. In technical terms, DMCs are the different forms of digital content that can be rendered into a format that a human can perceive. Movies, songs, text, graphics, phone calls, reference information, or any other type of content, when rendered into a digital format, all become DMCs. Tier 1 and Tier 2 create value by providing the technological platform on which the Tier 3 and Tier 4 derivative markets can function. Although these higher market tiers generate greater margins in the value chain, they function as derivative markets because their ability to generate value depends on the existence of the underlying tiers. For example, the technology now exists for content publishers to distribute music titles from the Internet directly to residential PC users. But this new distribution method depends on having a home infostructure, as well as inexpensive next-generation ENDs (in the form of a music server and networked speakers), to penetrate the mass market. Tier 3's value is generated through the development and distribution of digital content that, when marketed to consumers, takes the economic form of digital media commodities (DMCs). These virtual products fall broadly into three categories: communications, information, and entertainment titles.

Communications

The following list includes some of the different DMCs within the communications category:

- Voice (local and long-distance Voice over IP)
- Video conferencing
- White board (collaborative communications)
- Text chat
- Entertainment (such as live telecasting, multiuser gaming, etc.)

Information

The following lists include some of the different types of applications within the information category.

Public Information (News, Events, and Research) • Intelligent agents can search, filter, retrieve, organize, and administer public domain information oriented toward individually specified user profiles.

Information delivery (output) may come in a variety of forms, ranging from in-home news printers to custom-cast telereporting. Examples of public information content include weather, traffic, current events, economy and finance, classifieds, reference, editorials, and emergency and crisis information.

Personal Information (Secured System) • Sophisticated databases and intuitive user interfaces can combine to form personal information management systems that will help control and store personally relevant content that changes over time with respect to user interaction. Here is a list of different types of information stored on the home networks of the future:

- E-mail correspondence and content sharing
- Personal and family scheduling
- Coordination of events, schedules, and personal, intrafamily information
- Administrative account management

- Database management for multiple personal accounts (insurance programs, medical records, utilities, vendor billing accounts, etc.)
- Identity records and authentication information
- Social Security, passport, driver's license, birth certificate
- Real estate property management
- Home, car, electronics, appliances (warranties, insurance, maintenance information, etc.)
- Financial management system
- Banking (savings, checking, debit cards)
- Asset management (credit, loans, investments)
- Cash flow (paycheck income, bills, taxes, etc.)

Entertainment Titles

The following list includes the different user applications for digital titles, listed with respect to the different media formats:

- Television programs (taped or archived programming)
- Video (video on demand, DVD downloads)
- Music (streaming audio, CD or MP3 downloads)
- Gaming
- Text
- Hypermedia
- Images and graphics

Tier 4—Services

Tier 4 of the economic model is comprised of different value-adding activities: coordinating the resources in the submarkets, bringing new breeds of services to the consumer, and managing the customer-vendor relationship. The following sections, on submarket brokering, integrated solutions, and customer relationship management, explain some of the services within the context of this new information-based economy.

Submarket Brokering

Brokering activities create value by *consolidating*, *bundling*, and *personalizing* the resources of Tiers 1 through 3. By doing this, they increase the efficiency of the market channels between multiple submarket vendors and the individual consumer. The broker effect offers customers consolidated, turnkey solutions that better meet the complex demands of the information-era marketplace. By consolidating, bundling, and personalizing, brokers add significant value to the market channel. They give the customer the benefits of greater selection and lower prices. Although each of these broker functions represents a distinct value-adding activity, the specific manner in which enterprise may capitalize on the broker effect is still unclear. A vertically integrated vendor, involved at each level of the market tier, will likely perform their own brokering services internally, thereby capitalizing on all of the brokering efficiencies to generate greater profits and to secure better market positioning against competitors.

Consolidating Services • By aggregating the products and resources of the underlying tiers, the market broker gains price advantages and optimizes selection variety for its customer base in the following ways:

- **Scale economies**—Brokers consolidate the products/services from multiple vendors for mass-market resale.
- **Competitive sourcing**—Flexible vendor agreements enable brokers to always receive the most competitive price among multiple vendors.
- **Variety optimization**—Brokers can offer the greatest selection of product and service options to their customer base by exploiting the wide qualitative range to be found in the multitude of specialized source vendors.

Bundling Services • Bundlers combine complementary products and services into synergistic value-adding bundles. They specialize in perceiving and executing the opportunities that maximize value by achieving the most economically synergistic product and service combinations. Offering multiple services and/or turnkey, integrated product and service solutions creates customer loyalty and raises competitive entry barriers by increasing the costs for the customers to switch providers.

Personalizing Services • The provider of personalizing services generates value by redistributing the consolidated product and service bundles to target market segments. They specialize in understanding taste and need profiles. In this step, the broker adds value by differentiating the features of final product and service offerings to best meet the customer's individual needs and specialized preferences.

Integrated Solutions

Integrating the *network access and control* and *network administration* activities provides a platform for network operations. Through this platform, independent service vendors can offer an entirely new generation of information-era *residential services* to the consumer. Let's take a closer look at integrated solutions and how they create value for users of in-home networks and generate new business models for service providers.

Network Access and Control Services • This service category includes the value created by the network access and control functions that are performed from within the home and from remote locations. This empowers the consumer to automate their ENDs and to monitor and control their home network remotely via the Internet. It may also involve the participation of a centrally organized entity that standardizes the access and control functions as a public service for the general population.

Such a network access and control "provider" could serve as the trusted gatekeeper to the home environment, through which private vendors must pass to access the consumer (see "Network Administration Services" and "Residential Services"). Conceptually, this entity will function similarly to public utility companies. But instead of providing electricity or local phone services, they will provide home network access and control services that may include the following:

- Network access security and authentication
- Device automation; heating, ventilation, and air conditioning (HVAC); lighting control
- Telemetry/meter reading (gas, water, and power)
- Device status assessment and network query
- Energy management (load shedding, demand-side management)

Network Administration Services • Network administration services include any activity that makes the operation of the home network environment simpler for the consumer. The value proposition primarily involves masking the network's technological complexity and automating the maintenance of the overall home environment.

The consumer may select among different, competing network administration service providers, similar to how they select among competing long distance phone service providers. The network administration service provider will work with the network access and control service providers similar to how the long distance companies work with the local phone companies.

With the information obtained from the network access and control service providers, the network administration services provider offers user-level technical support for maintaining the substructure (home infostructure), and managing the complex array of service contracts and warranties for the multitude of ENDs provided by different manufacturers. The network access and control services, combined with the following examples of network administration services, will integrate to form the network operations platform needed to deliver the next generation of residential services.

- Operational administration and technical support
- Device maintenance and servicing
- Device warranty management
- Bandwidth management and network optimization
- Remote network configurations and network maintenance

Residential Services • The residential service providers will be independent vendors who integrate their service-based core competency around the new business model of the information era. The residential service providers will include both new and existing business entities that can access the submarket resources (via brokers) and use the network access and control and network administration functions as a powerful platform to deliver their services to the consumer.

The traditional, industrial-era businesses of today will need to evolve their business models to maintain a long-term competitive position in the information economy. For them, success will involve a rapid strategic repositioning that enables them to use the new technologies of the underlying market tiers as competitive tools to become more consumer-centric. This involves a shift in the consumer "turf" from the public marketplace to the private home, where many competitors will vie for consumer attention and loyalty. These vendors will need to learn how to compete in the domain of the consumer, which involves more proactive marketing efforts and greater sensitivity to individual consumer needs.

No longer will vendors be able to wait for customers to walk through the front doors of their offices and shops requesting service. Consumers of tomorrow will be able to relax in the comfort of their homes and choose among multiple vendors who actively seek *them* out. Intelligent agents will empower consumers to compare prices in ways that will eliminate false margins and force vendors to compete based on stricter performance metrics. The vendors that survive the transition will quickly realize how to use *information* and *emotion* to attract and retain the consumer of the information-era marketplace.

New participants will also emerge in the residential services sector to exploit the many market opportunities that cannot yet be foreseen. Many businesses that currently operate in the professional services sector, like health care and finance, will realize the opportunity to extend their market reach directly into the home by leveraging the systems and products of the underlying market tiers of the new economic model. Traditional industrial-era businesses will develop new information-era business models that leverage their fundamental service-based core competencies. The following list includes a few examples of possible home-service businesses that may soon emerge.

- Remote home monitoring (security, disaster, and emergency services)
- Home health care
- Energy management
- E-commerce (virtual retailing), banking, and financial management
- Civic management services
- Distance learning

The following case scenario exemplifies how one part of an industrial-era service sector (the health care industry) might realistically make the transition into a next-generation residential service provider.

Residential Services Case Scenario: Home Health Care • A hospital can capitalize on its core competency of health care, but extend its market scope into the residence with new information-era service offerings.

Their core competency is providing health care. A hospital could augment its service offering by using the Tier 1 infostructure (as a universally compatible communications platform), the Tier 2 ENDs (like a bedside video monitoring camera or a customized patient-diagnostic device), and the Tier 3 DMCs (in the form of voice, video, or information content). By integrating elements from each market tier around its health care expertise, the hospital can create a new type of value-added service like *home patient monitoring*.

Yet, the scenario for this residential service, and the limitless possibilities for others like it, can only exist once the underlying market tiers have been developed. Again, this emphasizes the significance of the derivative market effect in determining the outcome of the emerging information-era business environment.

Customer Relationship Management (CRM)

Customer Relationship Management (CRM) is the most important level of the value model because it involves the final interface and resource exchange with the consumer. The CRM level represents a relationship-management activity, where the CRM provider acts as the contact point through which the consumer can access the resources of the various submarkets.

The strategic importance of managing this relationship is obvious, as the CRM provider acts as the gatekeeper to the systems, products, and services of the composite market model. Additionally, the CRM brand recognition enables the provider to represent many different submarket players in the eyes of the consumer, giving them perhaps the most powerful negotiation position of all the different market makers. The CRM level demonstrates the critical importance that brand recognition and customer loyalty will play within the information economy business models. As the final level in the information economy derivative markets model, the CRM level is characterized by both the highest margins and the highest degree of personalization.

The complexity of the information-era economic system will extend far beyond the conceptual scope of this IEDMM model. It will no doubt include value-adding market segments that were not considered in this discussion. Ultimately, it remains impossible to completely predict a future that, in hindsight, always appears so simply obvious.

THE HOME INFOSTRUCTURE SOLUTION ....

In simplified terms, the home infostructure is the underlying "technology pipe" through which Internet-based business will deliver digital content and services to the many intelligent information appliances within the home. In a way, it is like the plumbing system that brings water to the home and distributes it throughout the house. But instead of different types of faucets and showerheads that allow you connect to and control the water in the plumbing system, you will use different devices that connect to and control the data of the network system.

The home infostructure represents the technological solution that will bring the vision of pervasive computing to fruition in the domestic marketplace. The home infostructure will serve as an economic conduit that connects the next generation of Internet-based vendors with consumers located in the comfort of their own homes.

There are four distinct technological components of the home infostructure, which must be deployed as an integrated and interoperable system in order for it to successfully penetrate the mainstream marketplace: the broadband local loop, the residential gateway, the Information Appliance Network, and electrodomestic network devices (Figure 1.2). Let's now examine these components in more detail.

Broadband Local Loop
(Home Internet Connectivity)

Analysts in the Yankee group (http://www.yankeegroup.com) predict that broadband deployment (via high-speed digital technologies) will reach about 6 million total subscribers by the year 2002. But this figure remains relatively small, considering that there are over 100 million households in the United States. Current xDSL and cable subscribers represent *early adopters* who fit the following profile:

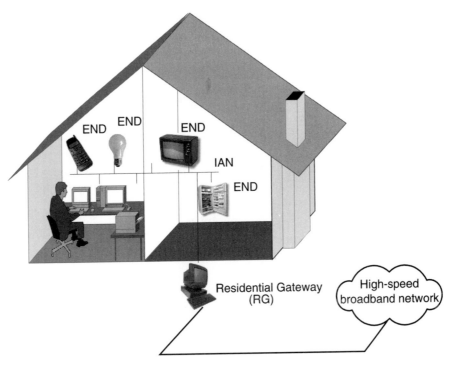

Figure 1.2
Components of the home infostructure

- They live in a geographic region where the service is available.
- They have the financial resources to subscribe to high-speed services.
- They have the interest and technological savvy for using such services.

Some of these early adopters will participate in the first generation of converged voice and data network applications that will include Voice over IP (VoIP) telephony, e-commerce, and multiplayer gaming. Over time, as the penetration of broadband connectivity reaches a critical mass of subscribers, more advanced applications such as video-conferencing, media distribution, and home health care will emerge. Yet mainstream adoption of broadband technology will only happen when:

- The network user interface masks the complexity of the underlying technology, offering an ease-of-use comparable to traditional domestic appliances (like telephones and VCRs) as opposed to the desktop PC.

- The service providers offer a single-point-of-contact for network installation, maintenance, administration, and customer interface activities. This may include billing consolidation for multiple services that will be scaled for each consumer's individual application needs.

Integrating the broadband local loop, the residential gateway, and the Information Appliance Network into a home infostructure represents such a solution that will expedite mainstream adoption of the technology. The market players that will drive this convergence include device OEMs, content developers, and service providers who all benefit from having an end-to-end platform to access the consumer from the Internet. The functional requirements and enabling technologies for the broadband local loop component are shown in Table 1.1.

Table 1.1   Functionality and Enabling Technologies for Broadband Access

Functional Requirements	Enabling Technologies
High speed (>1Mbps)	xDSL
Persistent connection	Cable
Bidirectional communications	Powerline
Simultaneous multiuser support	Wireless
Quality of Service (QoS) scaling	Satellite

The next chapter will examine this home infostructure component in more detail.

Residential Gateway (RG)

The residential gateway (RG) is the interface device that connects the broadband local loop to the in-home network, effectively bringing a bi-directional communications channel to every networked device in the home.

Since it serves as the centralized access point between the home and the outside world, the RG represents an important strategic technology. Additionally, the gateway serves as the convergence point that will bridge the different broadband and LAN (local area network) technologies. The value proposition for the gateway to connect the local loop connection with the in-home LAN can be seen differently from the perspective of the players in each industry.

The Broadband Player Perspective

Home networking technology will take the "last mile" broadband pipe and extend it to the "last inch." This would significantly increase the value of broadband service by distributing it to a multitude of intelligent devices (which could run multiple network applications simultaneously) instead of having it terminate at a single PC.

The Home Network Player Perspective

Broadband connectivity will enable all of the devices on the home network to also have high-speed access to the Internet. While providing a stand-alone solution for interconnecting all of the consumers within the home may be somewhat valuable, the ability to connect all of the consumer's devices to the Internet is truly revolutionary. Another important function of the RG will be to serve as the access platform through which service providers can remotely deploy services to the home from the Internet. Service providers will also use this platform for control, query, and network administration functions. With integrated security features, the gateway will also facilitate authorized access to the home by other third-party service providers (such as a home health care provider). Additionally, the gateway serves as the technological bridging point for the integration of subnetwork systems. One of the key cost considerations for deploying the home infostructure involves the technical persons who must perform on-site installation or maintenance services. A key optimization criterion for the home infostructure hardware technology, and particularly in the gateway device, includes the ability to upgrade the hardware and software with minimal need for on-site technical service. Ideally, the gateway that is integrated into the home infostructure would operate on a standardized, open platform interface that can accommodate upgrades remotely (software) or in a plug-and-play fashion (hardware) that will facilitate modifications in the home infostructure as the broadband technologies continue to evolve over time. Chapter 9 will examine the various types of devices that are competing for a share of the residential gateway marketplace.

Information Appliance Network (IAN)

The Information Appliance Network (IAN) is the high-speed in-home data network that distributes an Internet connection to ubiquitous access points. The IAN provides interconnectivity for all electrodomestic networked devices (ENDs) within the home premises. A wide variety of technologies exist for interconnecting devices within the home, but no single technology meets all of the requirements for the diversity of applications that will be created. While traditional 10base-T/Cat5 Ethernet systems offer a robust and proven solution, most consumers do not have the time, interest, or knowledge to rewire their homes. Fortunately, the emergence of "no new wiring" technologies offers prospects for solving the mass-market home networking issue. The new technologies include wireless, phoneline, and powerline solutions. Since each solution presents distinct benefits and drawbacks, many organizations are beginning to suggest that all of these technologies will exist in a multilayered home network architecture.

Electrodomestic Network Devices (ENDs)

ENDs are best described as a set of intelligent processing tools used in domestic network environments. They include all appliances, electronics, and computers that have both embedded intelligence and the ability to communicate with other devices. Also referred to as *information appliances*, these intelligent devices will have the ability to communicate and interoperate using the in-home network. In cases where the in-home network is connected to a broadband local-loop, these devices will be able to connect to the Internet. This will enable the use of new applications (perhaps proving more important than the devices themselves), such as remote network administration and Web-based home control and automation. The grouping of ENDs encompasses a broad spectrum of devices that tend to fall into one of the following categories:

- **Appliances**—Devices that create value primarily though *physical processing* features (mechanical functioning)
- **Electronics**—Devices that create value through both *physical and logical processing* features
- **Computers**—Devices that create value primarily through *logical processing* features (digital intelligence)

Many mainstream consumers lack the technological savvy to install and maintain their own home infostructure, or have little time to invest in its upkeep. Professional technical support, while available, can be expensive and, due to lack of branded services, is often perceived as untrustworthy. As a result, the infostructure for the home-use market remains comparatively underdeveloped. From a business perspective, the home infostructure serves as an economic conduit through which digital content and services can be delivered directly to the ENDs that consumers use. Since each home is a center of economic activity, the home infostructure represents a powerful new tool for businesses to reach the consumer. Mass-market deployment of the home infostructure turns all homes into commercial endpoints that Internet-based vendors will use to deliver new forms of product and service value. Once deployed to the mass market, the home infostructure solution will interconnect individual homes, and the devices contained within, on a globally integrated data network. At the time of writing this guide, there are many different technologies emerging for each of the home infostructure components. The remaining part of this book will examine these technologies in detail.

HOUSEHOLD ARCHITECTURE ISSUES ....

The architecture of a home network presents unique challenges that even complex business networks have yet to address. Three primary forces will govern the household superstructure architecture:

- **Structure variance**—The configuration of ENDs will vary greatly from home to home.

- **Usage variance**—The application use for each END will vary greatly.

- **Client-server dynamic**—A network architecture will be comprised of multiple client-server relationships across all levels of network environment. The household architecture issues are important because they relate to the technical requirements that the Tier 1 infostructure must support.

Structure Variance

While the Tier 1 infostructure (Internet backbone and home infostructure) provides a universal technical architecture for all consumers, the Tier 2 ENDs superstructure will vary greatly with respect to the needs and preferences of each household. This is why industry-wide standards for the Tier 1 infostructure will be so important. It is essential to establish robust yet flexible technical specifications for substructure technologies. These specifications must optimize the substructure to ensure interoperability and consistent functionality for the multitude of ENDs that will occupy the consumer space in an infinite variety of combinations and configurations.

Because no two households will own the exact make, model, and quantity of ENDs, the superstructure will vary greatly across the demographics of the home user market. The technical features of the ENDs and the configuration architectures within each home will prove much more unpredictable than business network environments. Developers of the supporting substructure systems (Tier 1) must be aware of this fact. This represents one of the most important conceptual requirements for the home network, especially since it must operate in an automatically configured "plug-and-play" way.

Usage Variance

Not only will the physical superstructure vary greatly between homes, but the applications and usage patterns within the home will prove equally unpredictable. This is relevant when comparing the computing usage of traditional business environments with the possible usage scenarios for a networked home.

Business environments consist of straightforward network applications that workers use in a fairly consistent and homogeneous nature. For example, common network applications for business users include Internet browsing, database queries, e-mail, multimedia correspondence, and file sharing. In contrast, the usage patterns in the next generation of home networks will be much more complex and unpredictable. Consider that any END sold to a consumer might have embedded intelligence and network communications capabilities. For example, a manufacturer might sell a networked washing machine with embedded intelligence that will sense malfunctions, automate repair servicing, and synchronize its operations schedule with the electricity provider for optimal pricing.

In most cases, the consumer will be unaware of the technological underpinnings of such a system. The purchaser will not consider that "doing their laundry" also entails running "computer applications." They only care that the washing machine offers valuable new features that will lower utility bills, increase the ease-of-use, and assist during malfunctions by automatically dispatching a service request.

This scenario conveys the fundamental value that the pervasive computing vision offers, where technology and computing give way to the tangible benefits and practical forms of consumer value (like saving money and simplifying work).

Imagine if this scenario is extended to the entire spectrum of ENDs, including all of the appliances, electronics, and computers within the home. Also consider that the variety and complexity of these user applications will increase over time as OEMs leverage them to differentiate their products and achieve continual competitive advantages. Although the possible outcomes of this trend are not within the scope of this discussion, substructure developers must consider the implications of usage variance during their development phases.

Client-Server Dynamic

In their evolution toward a distributed computing environment, the design and function of ENDs will eventually reflect a client-server dynamic. While this architecture may resemble the client-server system of business environments, it will be redesigned to accommodate the unique needs of pervasive home computing. New devices will be sensitive to cost and to the limited technical know-how of the home user. The distribution of digital content from source devices (*front-ENDs*) to the rendering client (*back-END*) is a distinguishing feature of evolved devices. In a sense, back-END devices are the servers, while front-END devices are the clients.

The client-server dynamic achieves greater computing efficiency by centralizing shared resources into single, multipurpose devices. These devices process and distribute digital content to a multitude of thin clients, creating a cost-effective technology solution that scales easily depending on individual consumer needs.

The client-server dynamic will engender multiple client-server relationships at different levels across the network environment. In some cases, the client device might be a platform-independent END that renders content. But other devices might play the dual role of both client and server, depending on their technical relationship to other devices.

For example, a home music server, which might become a future standard for storing music titles (replacing your CD collection), could act as both a client and server in certain network architectures. Consider a scenario where the music server interfaces with the residential gateway to download titles from an Internet-based music vendor. Then the server stores the files directly to a storage device. The music server could, in turn, support multiple speakers by connecting to a powerline-based IAN. The powerline IAN would supply both the power to the run the amplifiers (embedded in the speakers) and the data for the music titles.

Music would be streamed on demand (through a touchscreen control interface) from the server, via the IAN, to multiple networked speakers.

The streamed data would travel between the devices via the AC electrical connections using powerline Ethernet transceivers. In this way, the front-END speakers could render the sound data through an embedded decompression engine that corresponds with the data storage format of the back-END music server (most likely MP3 or other compression technology). Figure 1.3 shows this conceptual architecture where the speakers and touchscreen take the form of next-generation front-ENDs. The home music server takes the form of a back-END, which interfaces with an Internet-based commerce server via the residential gateway, to download newly acquired titles. This model demonstrates the possibility for new architectures that developers could achieve when considering the home infostructure during the design processes of next-generation ENDs.

An alternative to this architecture is for music content to stream from an Internet-based source directly to the home's front-ENDs (thin-client speakers) via the home infostructure. In reality, both of these architectures may be practical entertainment applications for the home.

The client-server dynamic simply dictates the fundamental principle of efficiency for network computing environments. The distributed media system poses the possibility for a more efficient architecture by inserting the home music server between the Internet servers and the front-END speakers.

This creates a redundant, multilevel client-server architecture. In this case, the redesign involves decoupling the distribution media (CD or MP3 source) from the display, control, and playback technology, using the IAN to interconnect them in a distributed computing architecture.

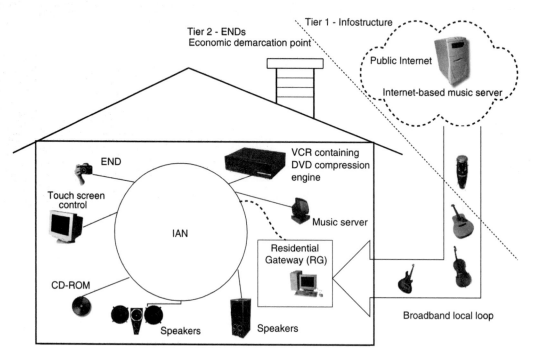

Figure 1.3
Distributed media system

In this case, a distributed computing architecture is more efficient because it reduces unnecessary traffic that may cause a bottleneck on the Internet, or through the home infostructure, each time a user wants to hear a song. It may be better to use the home infostructure for single-use downloads to a local device, like the back-END home music server, which then supports the user's media-rich application needs, using the higher-bandwidth features of the IAN.

Ultimately, the redundant client-server dynamic cannot determine which architectures will prove most viable in the marketplace. However, the concept can be applied as an analytic tool to help determine how to achieve greater efficiencies at multiple levels of the network architecture.

SUMMARY ....

At present we are in a global socioeconomic transition period, changing from an industrial-based *analog* economy to an information-based *digital* economy. The impetus for this transition has been fueled by four converging trends:

- The global deregulation of the communications and utility industries.

- The decreasing costs and increasing power of silicon intelligence (microchip processors).

- New communications technology, like broadband local loop connectivity and in-home networks, that will bring high-speed Internet access to residential consumers.

- The adoption of the Internet as a commercial channel.

The growth of the emerging economy will be driven primarily by a new breed of digitized products and services, including:

- Virtual products, called digital media commodities (DMCs), which consist of digital content in a variety of different formats, including *communications*, *information*, and *entertainment titles*.

- Service-based activities that are built on the development, distribution, and transmission of the DMCs to consumers.

More than just a connection to the Internet, the home infostructure serves as the technology platform that will enable an entirely new generation of user applications, including voice and video communications, e-commerce, personalized news, home security and automation, utilities resource management, and entertainment title distribution. The home infostructure holds significant economic importance to businesses because it serves as a hyperefficient, mass-market distribution platform that can deliver digital media content and value-added services directly into the hands of the consumer.

Home infostructure will be enabled by three distinct technologies: broadband local loop connectivity, residential gateways, and in-home networks. The technology components that constitute the home infostructure are being developed by many different companies and deployed by disparate industries. These include the long distance telcos, ISPs, electric utilities, satellite operators, and cable operators, in addition to many new start-ups and international technology consortiums.

While the information economy derivative market model is not a definitive answer for predicting what will suddenly appear on the day that the marketplace finally matures, it presents a solid framework for evaluating business models and technological trends. This model offers a very broad and comprehensive view of the market so individual entrepreneurs can sharpen their business focus and understand the value of establishing strategic partnerships.

The consumer marketplace, and the society of people that lies behind it, is more organic and unpredictable than can be pinned down through theoretical models or scientific calculations. But by identifying the underlying forces of the market system and understanding the nature of its chaotic tendencies, decision makers and business leaders will be better equipped to deal with the evolving competitive challenges that their organizations will face.

2 Fundamentals

In this chapter...

The integration of computer chips into the next generation of everyday devices is one of the major factors that is driving the emergence of home networks. Our cars have had them for years; now our children's toys, our kitchen appliances, and our living room entertainment systems have computing power that rivals earlier desktop computers. In addition, the emergence of wireless networking technology has allowed these computer-enabled devices to become network-connected. The result is very powerful and useful systems of in-home devices cooperating to simplify everyday activities. This chapter introduces you to the core computing models that are used to run digital applications across an in-home network. We briefly examine the underlying protocols that are used in a home networking environment. We also look at the types of companies that are associated with this new industry. Let's begin this chapter by defining a home network.

WHAT IS A HOME NETWORK?..............................

For years, the electronics industry has awaited the arrival of home automation. What was envisioned was a new generation of controls that would change our lifestyles forever. As we start the 21st century, technologists, business strategists, and market planners are rapidly dismantling the old vision of home automation and replacing it with a more practical concept for developing and selling electronic products and PCs that work together. The newly defined concept is *home networks*. Home networks embraces home theatre, home office, intelligent appliances, smart objects, and telecommunications (the products and systems that present content and information to the consumer), as well as the whole-home and subsystem controls (security, heating/cooling, lighting, and energy management) traditionally associated with home automation. The underlying theme for the home networks of the new millennium is to connect everyone and everything.

CONSUMER REQUIREMENTS..................................

The end users of a home network drive a different set of requirements than traditional enterprise network environments. These requirements include:

- **Ease of use, low complexity**—Unlike an enterprise network, there is no network system administrator or IT department in the home. As a result, home networking must be easy to use and simple to install. A home network must be "invisible," providing seamless operation with little or no user intervention or maintenance.

- **Reliability**—Home networks must be reliable. The network needs to resolve interference from other home networking devices as well as common household appliances, such as microwave ovens and cordless phones.

- **Scalability**—As consumers begin to buy home networking products, scalability must be considered, even with their first purchase. Scalability results in a lower lifetime cost to the consumer. Buying a network device is not a point product purchase; it establishes the foundation for an entire home network. Consumers who make informed decisions will avoid purchasing technology that will soon be obsolete. A home network needs to maintain interoperability and accommodate future applications to protect the consumer's initial investment.

- **Standards compliance**—Industry standards are crucial for enabling mainstream consumer adoption of home networking products.

- **No new wires**—Consumers do not want to run hundreds of feet of cables around their home.

- **"My home is my castle"**—The customer owns the data and decides who gets access to certain parts of this data.

BASIC CONCEPTS..

At its most basic level, a home network consists of a computer and a consumer audio-visual (A/V) device connected to each other by a cable so that they can share data. Home networks today let you share information and computer resources, and enable online communication. The underlying structure for a home network consists of interconnected clusters of digital appliances. Typically, there will be several clusters in your house, with one per floor or possibly one per room.

So why would we want to network various types of electronic devices? First, let's consider what it would be like if a digital camera you purchased was not connected to a network. It would operate in what is called a stand-alone environment. In this environment, sharing files would become time consuming. You would have to copy your picture files on to a floppy disk and print them out to share them. Most people are not happy with this situation, and are now connecting their digital cameras to networks that are designed for entertaining people in their homes.

For computers and A/V devices to form a network, they need to be connected by a transmission medium. You can use cable and/or wireless transmission media. They also need an adapter that connects them to the network medium—this is known as a network interface card. Within a home network, devices that provide shared resources are known as servers, and digital appliances that access the shared resources are known as clients. Many multimedia and data applications that run on your in-home network are based on the client-server networking model. In this model, a member of your household sends small messages to a server, requesting data and services. In response, large amounts of data are sent from the server to the client. Some examples of in-home client-server applications include:

- High-speed Internet and Web access
- Digital imaging
- Remote access to storage devices
- Interactive video content
- Distribution of music around the house

Home networks require appropriate software to interconnect in-home appliances. This can be a dedicated network operating system (NOS) or an operating system that incorporates networking software—for example, Windows 2000 Professional. This software integrates the network's hardware components and maintains the connection between the client home devices and the server.

The servers that run on an in-home network are optimized to service requests from clients. Additionally, servers can be used to protect your family from questionable content that has been downloaded and stored locally. Home networks start out small, with perhaps two computers and a digital set-top box connected together, but they tend to grow in size over time, with the addition of new consumer A/V devices.

HOME NETWORKING INDUSTRY ....

In a recent study, Parks Associates, a research firm based in Dallas, Texas, found that the total end-user market value for data and entertainment networks (including integrated wiring systems) is projected to follow this path:

2000—$0.7 billion
2001—$1.3 billion
2002—$2.4 billion
2003—$3.3 billion
2004—$4.5 billion

What these figures say is that people will probably be investing in home networking at an ever-increasing rate. Lab research and development, market research, product sales and marketing, and, most important, public uptake will expand through the next five years—and beyond.

These growth predictions have encouraged many large companies to collaborate in projects that promote the convergence between personal computers, digital television, and consumer A/V platforms. The strategy is being adopted to ensure that PCs and A/V equipment do not continue to evolve and develop on separate paths. Many people believe that the time has come for the computer and consumer A/V device manufacturers to shake hands and get on with the job of helping people build and deploy home entertainment centers. These new centers will deliver a range of new and exciting in-home applications including:

- Multiple members of one household having simultaneous access to high-speed Internet-based services.
- Controlling A/V devices such as VCRs, camcorders, and stereos from a single location in the house.
- Home monitoring, which allows you to use a television screen to keep an eye on visitors to the house, or on young babies sleeping in their bedrooms.
- Unification of all types of devices, including desktop PCs, DVD players, digital set-top boxes, stereos, VCRs, and high-speed Internet connections.

All kinds of manufacturers—from entertainment and home security to PC and networking companies—have latched onto the home networking market because it allows them to create a whole new set of consumer products. Investment supporting home networking technologies continues from established companies and venture capitalists. Software and hardware makers will profit from this home networking revolution, but so will content providers, telecommunications carriers, developers, and IT consultants. Figure 2.1 shows the major participants. This figure offers a quick overview of companies and standards groups that are current leaders within their fields.

With the technology explosion in computers, Internet, and communications, it is much more difficult than ever to sort through the deluge of raw information and glean useful knowledge. During my research work into this new industry, I came across two organizations that are following home networking trends and working to foster its growth, CABA and EPRIsolutions, Inc.

CABA

CABA (Continental Automated Buildings Association) is a not-for-profit industry association that promotes advanced technologies for the automation of homes and buildings in North America. Its mission is to encourage the development, promotion, and pursuit of automation in homes and buildings. It is among CABA's goals to provide the necessary information for people in the home networking and home and building

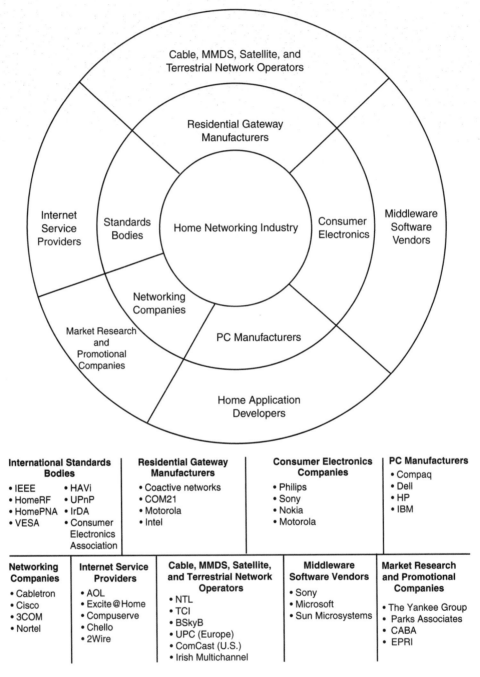

Figure 2.1
Home networking industry overview

automation industry (dealers/installers, builders/developers, manufacturers, governments, energy utilities, telecommunications companies) to be educated and kept up-to-date on advances. To facilitate and develop collaboration within the industry, CABA provides the following initiatives to its members.

CABA's Initiatives

CABA and Parks Associates have co-hosted an annual home networking and residential gateways conference since 1997, the CONNECTIONS Conference. The gathering is traditionally a two-day event, with a day of workshops preceding it. The conference features a showcase area for home networking industry representatives to "strut" their stuff and to provide delegates with a firsthand look at new technologies and initiatives.

The conference is international in scope, with delegates from all over the world and presentations appealing to, and covering, an international perspective. There are traditionally 300 to 500 participants at this event, and it has become known as one of the best meetings at which to hear the latest and to meet the players of the home networking industry.

Resources and Publications

There are a number of publications provided by CABA to their membership that have positioned the association as an information source within the home networking industry:

- The *CABA Home and Building Automation Quarterly* delivers news of the industry four times a year. With regular features concentrating on new products and services, home and building automation, and a full complement of "observations and opinions," the publication is the successful flagship of the CABA library of resources. Updates on various home networking technologies also appear in each issue, with the chairpersons or representatives of companies providing the latest news of their developments.

- The CABA Information Series is a collection of white papers on protocol and standards issues.

- CABA Event Reports are synopses of conferences, workshops, and trade shows. In response to this, CABA sends writers to cover session events and compiles a document that is then mailed to member companies.

- Through CABA's Web site (http://www.caba.org), all documents noted are available and searchable, though portions of the site are restricted to members only.

Standards Committee

The CABA Standards Committee acts as an ongoing discovery group for standards
and protocol issues. They do not write standards but rather provide a forum for standards
and protocol groups to share common concerns and to discuss issues of common
interest. Where there is a need, subcommittees are established to delve more
deeply into an issue. In Canada, for example, regulations that may adversely affect the
use of powerline carrier products are undergoing review and change. A subcommittee
was established, and the group is providing input to the federal government for consideration.
The CABA Standards Committee is predominantly North American,
though it is open to participants from around the world.

EPRIsolution's Networked Home Services

EPRIsolutions, Inc., a subsidiary of EPRI (Electric Power Research Institute), is a
leader in the home networking industry. EPRI and EPRIsolutions offer convenient and
relevant technology surveillance services, coupled with interactive Web-based access
to specialists and experts inside and outside the utility industry (see http://
www.epri.com). Focus and custom EPRI analysis is provided in several key areas and
is updated with about 100 new items weekly:

- Protocols and technical standards, converging technologies and commercial
  activity in powerline, phone, RF, and cable media.
- Products and vendors of commercially available systems, including integration
  and management services.
- Projects, market assessments, economic analysis.

In addition, EPRIsolutions supports implementation of practical solutions in
several ways:

- **Networked homes technology surveillance**—Energy companies (for example)
  serving residential and small commercial customers need to determine
  which new technologies can be quickly put to use to serve those
  customers. A "technology watch" service follows the emerging areas of
  home networks, external access networks, and gateways; smart appliances;
  and converging information and control management technologies.
- **Intellectrics Webcast Conference Service**—The Intellectrics Webcast
  Service provides a remote, highly scalable, thin client "virtual concert
  hall" for meetings, training sessions, and distant conferences.
- **Home automation builder guide**—High-level overview of technologies,
  applications, installation and support services. The continually updated

Builder Guide covers key issues in design, construction, applications and services, price and product availability, and references to qualified installers and technical support. The Guide is intended to provide both high-level background as well as necessary collateral for energy companies to support modern local new building practices to help their customers "future proof" their homes.

- **Mobile home automation showcase**—EPRIsolutions has prepared specifications, designs, and collaboration arrangements for mobile demonstration centers, custom built from a large recreational vehicle, to promote high-speed broadband communications, home networking, smart appliances, customer care services, and other value-added applications. Available as a time-share lease on a monthly basis, the mobile showcase demonstrates the value of external network access and internal control, and will connect to distant stationary demonstrations via the Internet. The mobile showcase is a year-round Web site as well as a hands-on laboratory for local time-share.

- **Community network projects**—These projects involve the deployment of full Internet services to entire communities, giving the "have nots" a chance to catch up to the "haves." EPRIsolutions has crafted a Web site full of localized content, and using existing PCs plus TV set-top boxes (phone and cable access) making the two-way access very easy for all users to publish as well as subscribe to custom content. EPRIsolutions operates turnkey "local net" projects in collaboration with key stakeholders (content, infrastructure, customer and users, and financial sponsors) who share equity in the new business operations.

For more information, see EPRI's Web site at http://www.epri.com

PROTOCOLS

Simply plugging an A/V device or a standard desktop PC into a home network does not guarantee successful communications between devices on your in-home network and the Internet. All devices on a home network need some type of network *protocol* software to instruct them on how and when to transmit signals across the network.

To achieve a reliable transfer of data across your home network, the protocol needs to identify errors, apply compression techniques, and decide on the following:

- How the sending device will inform the receiving device that it has finished sending data across the home network.
- How the receiving device will inform the sending device that it has received the correct data.

- The structure of the addresses that are assigned to devices on your home network.
- How the data is to be sent across the home network, one bit at a time or one block of bits at a time.

There are a variety of standard protocols from which to choose. Each option has particular advantages and disadvantages. For instance, some are faster than others but may not be as reliable. To help you understand how A/V devices and computers communicate with each other, we explore some of the most popular home networking protocols in the following subsections.

TCP/IP

The TCP/IP (Transmission Control Protocol/Internet Protocol) suite is a widely implemented internetworking standard protocol for linking computers together on the Internet. All home networks that require broadband connectivity to the Internet will need to install this protocol.

As the name suggests, TCP and IP are two separate protocols that have been tightly woven together for the purpose of transmitting data in an efficient manner. The main responsibility of the TCP is to break the data into packets, the IP delivers these packets to the correct location, and the TCP reassembles the packets on the receiving end. TCP/IP was originally developed in the early 1980s by the Advanced Research Projects Agency (ARPA) in the United States. Since its inception, TCP/IP has become the de facto communications protocol for transferring files across the Internet.

The TCP/IP communications model is a conceptual model composed of four layers that are stacked on top of each other, each specifying particular network functions (see Figure 2.2). Data is passed down the model from one layer to the next on the sending device, until it is transmitted over the network by the network access layer protocols. Each layer in the communications model adds control information (such as addresses and error correction digits) to ensure proper delivery. At the remote end, the data is passed up the communications model to the receiving application.

The four layers of the TCP/IP model are:

- Network access layer
- Internetwork layer
- Transport layer
- Application layer

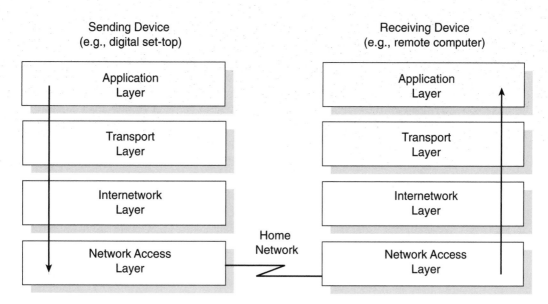

Figure 2.2
TCP/IP communications model

The network access layer defines the functions that coordinate the transmission of digital bits on a home network. It is concerned with getting data across a specific type of physical network. It defines physical network structures (topologies), mechanical specifications, and electrical specifications for using the transmission medium.

The layer above the network access layer is called the *internetwork layer.* Its primary objective is to move data to specific network locations over multiple interconnected independent networks called internetworks. This layer is used to send data over specific routes to its destination. IP is the best-known protocol located at the internetwork layer, which provides the basic packet delivery service for all TCP/IP networks. The IP protocol implements a system of logical host addresses called IP addresses. The protocol layer just above the internetwork layer is the *transport layer.* It has been designed to hide the intricacies of the home network structure from the upper-layer processes. Standards at this layer provide for the reliability and integrity of the end-to-end communication link.

Obviously, if a cable breaks, for example, the transport layer cannot ensure delivery of the data. If data is not delivered to the receiving device correctly, the transport layer can initiate retransmission. Alternatively, it can inform the upper layers, which can then take the necessary corrective action. TCP is the most important protocol employed at this layer of the TCP/IP communications stack.

The top layer in the TCP/IP communications model is the *application layer.* This layer provides the services that you use to communicate over the in-home network. These services include file transfers, access control, and printing capabilities. TCP/IP protocols were designed to solve several complex problems related to message delivery in widely distributed computer networks such as the Internet. Home networks are generally more well-contained and predictable environments compared to the Internet. From recent developments in the industry, it is quite obvious that TCP/IP will play an increasingly important role in relation to in-home networks. This can be seen from the following trends:

- Real-time A/V streams like audio, video, and voice will come to the home via the Internet and need to be delivered to in-home information devices.

- More and more devices in the home will need access to the Internet.

ATM

The abbreviation ATM stands for *asynchronous transfer mode.* ATM is a high-bandwidth, low-delay technology that is very suitable for deployment on home networks. It allows a variety of rich multimedia applications and services (video, data, voice, etc.) to be supported on a single network. Unlike TCP/IP, ATM is a cell relay technology capable of very high speeds. It divides all information to be transferred into blocks called cells. These cells are fixed in size—each has a header with five bytes and an information field that contains forty-eight bytes of information. The information field of an ATM cell carries user data, whereas the header contains information relevant to the functioning of the ATM protocol.

ATM requires the installation of dedicated hardware devices in your home. ATM also requires a high-speed, high-bandwidth medium such as fiber optic cable for optimal operation. For many home users, this may not be a practical measure.

ATM offers many benefits for those who decide to make the investment. These benefits include:

- Bandwidth is allocated on a demand basis and so ATM is particularly suitable for applications whose transmissions are of a bursty nature.

- The use of relatively small cells and high transmission rates (typically >240 Mbps) enables ATM to support a wide range of digital services. ATM can support such demanding applications as real-time video and multimedia services.

- ATM is a scalable technology—it can adapt to networks of different sizes and topologies. ATM can be scaled from low-speed (56 Kbps) to high-speed video and multimedia-based home applications.

With the proliferation of digital technologies in our homes, storage of multimedia information in different rooms is becoming increasingly important for entertainment purposes. ATM is an ideal protocol for accessing and retrieving this information from any part of your house.

The ATM protocol model is composed of three distinct layers (see Figure 2.3):

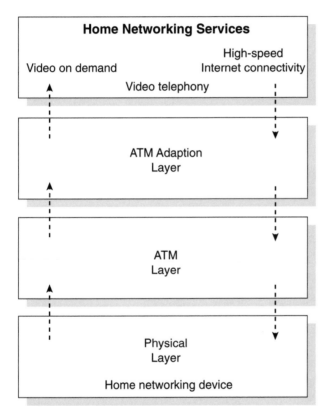

Figure 2.3
ATM protocol model

1. The ATM adaption layer
2. The ATM layer
3. The physical layer

Each layer provides services to the layer above it, in a manner similar to the Open System Interconnection (OSI) networking model. The ATM adaption layer is responsible for implementing the interfaces between higher-level services and the ATM home network. It accepts data from high-level network services and converts them to a form suitable for transmission over ATM. It operates on the information content of the ATM cells.

The ATM layer supplies the networking functions for the transport and delivery of cells. This layer decides how and when cells will be sent and supplies a suitable header for each one. The physical layer is concerned with delivering the cell stream to and from the actual transmission medium. It defines the interface with the transmission media and manages the rates of transmissions across the network. ATM does not rely on any specific type of physical transport medium; it's compatible with existing physical architectures, including coax, twisted pair, and fiber optics.

SUMMARY ....

Many companies have begun manufacturing products and offering support services for the home networking industry. All home networks are based on the two popular network models found in the corporate IT world—peer-to-peer and client-server systems. ATM is currently the fastest and most efficient protocol that is available to users of home networks. It has the ability to simultaneously transport data, video, and voice at real-time speeds between different rooms within your home. It is a fully scalable communications solution and is suitable for all types of advanced broadband applications. It is, however, a very expensive technology and it will be a long time before we see ATM networks being deployed within the walls of our homes. In the immediate future, we do see ATM being used as a technology that will provide broadband Internet access to users of home networks. TCP/IP will be a fundamental building block in supporting the entertainment services that run on the home networks of the future.

3 Residential Broadband Internet Technologies

In this chapter...

Over the past couple of years, the Internet has become an inescapable part of our lives. It has been around in one form or another since the late 1960s. In the last few years it has caught the imagination of millions of people around the world, with the number of people connecting to the Internet doubling every six months. The Internet's best-known feature is the World Wide Web (the Web). The resources available on the Web include text, graphics, video, audio, and animation. Unfortunately, many people that access the Web experience the frustration of endless waiting for information to download to their computers. You probably started accessing the Web with a 14.4K modem, and then upgraded to a 28.8K device. Now we are seeing the mass deployment of 56K modems, which is still not enough to satisfy our demands for speed. Everybody is in agreement that doubling analog modem speeds every year is no longer a feasible strategy. The days of impatiently waiting for Web pages are about to end, with large companies like AT&T, Microsoft, America Online, Yahoo!, and Cisco spending billions of dollars to bring the broadband revolution to our homes.

Simply put, residential broadband technologies will provide us with the conduit we need to access advanced services such as rich multimedia content, video on demand, and private networking services. A significant benefit of these technologies is that the link between your home network and the Internet is always on, which means users don't have to log in each time they access the Net. With an always-on connection, the Internet can become an integral part of our lives and will allow each of us to develop a Web style that is unique.

Forrester Research is projecting that at least twenty million American homes will have a broadband connection by the end of 2003. There are several rival technologies that are competing with each other to deliver these services to our doorsteps. This chapter will present an overview of the main rivals.

DIGITAL SUBSCRIBER LINE (DSL) TECHNOLOGIES...

Up to a couple of years ago, the plain old telephone system in conjunction with a standard modem offered us the most convenient means of accessing information on the Internet. Due to the explosive growth of people connecting to the Internet using this system, it has become less convenient for accessing data.

This is mainly because the existing telephone infrastructure was designed for voice signals only. It was never intended to carry digital information due to its sensitivity to external noise sources and attenuation losses over long distances. The demands on the system from a typical phone call are very different from the resources that are required to support a connection to the Web.

Voice-optimized networks usually need to handle less than ten percent of their total number of possible users at any one time. One of the reasons for this is that the average duration of a voice call is between four and five minutes. And as network usage follows well-known patterns over time, resources can be allocated efficiently according to probabilistic models.

The patterns of usage of a typical data network are very different from those of a voice network. For one thing, users typically remain connected to the Internet for longer periods of time. So when you open a circuit to access the Internet, that circuit may remain open for a lot longer than a normal telephone conversation. During this time, the network resources for that circuit are unavailable for voice calls. The increased level of Internet access combined with the very nature of this data traffic has prompted telecommunication companies and large carriers to deploy a new class of technologies known as Digital Subscriber Lines (DSL).

DSL lines carry voice, video, and data at multimegabit speeds over standard telephone wires. DSL services can achieve much higher bit rates than traditional analog modems. Depending on the exact type of DSL service being used, bit rates from about 1.5 Mbps to 51 Mbps can be achieved. The family of DSL services are collectively referred to as xDSL. Bellcore Laboratories in the United States developed the first xDSL services in the late 1980s. During this time period, telecommunications companies were planning to compete directly with cable television providers for the video-on-demand market.

To do this, they needed a cost-effective way of making high-capacity connections to the homes of subscribers. Video-on-demand was expected to generate large revenues for its providers.

So DSL was created as a way of providing video-on-demand over copper wiring. But this application was never fully developed or implemented properly.

There are six different types of xDSL services available to home network users:

- Asymmetric DSL (ADSL)
- Lite ADSL (LADSL)
- Rate-adaptive DSL (RADSL)
- Symmetric DSL (SDSL)
- High-bit-rate DSL (HDSL)
- Very-high-bit-rate DSL (VDSL)

Rather than boring you with the details of all of these flavors, we decided to concentrate our efforts on explaining the technologies that are most relevant to the home networking market—ADSL.

ADSL is the most popular of all the new DSL technologies. It was designed for the local loop or last mile of copper from the telephone company's central office to your home. It has many benefits for people who have in-home networks and are looking for a broadband connection to the Internet. First and foremost, ADSL will allow you to download data to your network at speeds that are comparable with Ethernet standards. So you can expect a service that is up to 100 times faster than your existing dial-up connections, and over 25 times faster than Integrated Services Digital Network (ISDN). Second, the technology uses your existing phone line, so you can simultaneously use a telephone line for both data transmission and voice calls.

Unlike a cabled TV environment, you will not experience the slowdown or degradation of performance due to sharing the media. The ADSL equipment is relatively easy to install. Once your home network is connected to an ADSL broadband connection, you have the convenience of having an "always-on access" to the Internet. Typical test trials of ADSL show downstream data transmission rates of between 6 and 8 Mbps and upstream rates between 640 and 800 Kbps. These factors are dependent on line length and the capabilities of the modem that is connected to your in-home network. As a rule, any home networks within a range of three miles of the central office will receive a good ADSL service. Data rates will start to degrade when the distance between your home and the telecommunication provider's central office is greater than three miles.

Apportioning the line bandwidth asymmetrically helps to achieve high data rates. An ADSL circuit has three different information channels:

1. A plain old telephone service (POTS) channel
2. An upstream channel with a capacity of up to 1 Mbps
3. A downstream channel with a capacity of up to 8 Mbps

The frequency within the POTS channel is used for normal voice communications over your broadband connection.

The second type of channel associated with an ADSL is the upstream channel. It is considerably smaller than its downstream channel and bit rates can range from 16 Kbps to 1 Mbps. Upstream rates can be set to be compatible with standard U.S. and European digital rate hierarchies.

The upstream channel is in fact a duplex channel, but is usually configured for upstream transmission only. This is why ADSL is called an asymmetric xDSL service. ADSL technology is ideal for a range of different interactive services, however due to its asymmetric nature it is not well-suited to people who want to use their home networks for video conferencing purposes.

The downstream channel can be used to deliver Internet content and rich video-on-demand services to digital appliances connected to your in-home network at very high speeds (around 150 times the speed of a standard dial-up connection).

This all sounds great; what about the drawbacks associated with ADSL? First and foremost, the deployment of these services is very slow. Availability has been a major stumbling block to DSL sales. Although there have been many successful trials, telephone companies are finding it difficult to finance the rollout of these services to the mass market. Second, the costs of splitters and modems tend to be fairly high.

DSL Standardization and Interoperability

Standards and interoperability are two sides of the same coin, and both are critical to achieve any mass market.[1] This has been proven for a number of different markets, such as VCRs, cellular phones, set-top boxes, and DVD drives. The same model applies to the DSL market. Standards and interoperability conformance enable the following:

- Uniform services and products in the marketplace
- Lower cost services and products
- Consumer confidence in purchase
- Better consumer understanding of technology
- Portability of a product to different service regions
- Service provider and PC OEM confidence in the equipment supplied to end customers
- Widespread availability of central office equipment from a number of different vendors
- Widespread availability of consumer equipment from a number of different vendors in retail stores and from PC OEMs
- Competitive environment leading to innovation and differentiation on price points, product features, and design

The consumer DSL market is in a transitional period typical of emerging markets. To meet significant consumer demand for high-speed Internet access, DSL service providers have begun to offer proprietary DSL solutions. Because interoperable standards-based products are still in a developmental phase, DSL service providers are deploying these full-rate ADSL solutions based on noninteroperable American

---

1. This section has been adapted from Intel's "ADSL Status Update," Intel Architecture Labs, September, 1999.

National Standards Institute (ANSI) T1.413 solutions or proprietary Carrierless Amplitude Modulation (CAP) technology, in "pairs." This means that the central office line card modem in the Digital Subscriber Line Access Multiplexer (DSLAM) and the DSL modem at the customer's home come from the same manufacturer to ensure interoperability. Also, service providers must supply these modems with DSL service because consumers cannot obtain the proprietary DSL modems through traditional channels such as retail stores or PC OEMs. Until recently, DSL service providers deployed noninteroperable ANSI T1.413, commonly known as full-rate ADSL service, with a *splitter*, which requires a visit to the customer premises. A splitter is a physical component that is used to filter and forward incoming signals. Now they are beginning to use a nonstandard splitterless full-rate implementation with distributed micro-filters, making DSL equipment customer-installable. In the short term, this is a positive step because it simplifies DSL installation and hastens DSL service delivery to customers. However, over the next year, standards-based DSL product development will reach the stage at which it can be regularly deployed. Unfortunately, consumers and businesses relying on non-standards-based full-rate splitterless products will continue to experience interoperability problems. Meanwhile, *G.lite* and *G.dmt* (see below) products will become widely available and provide the same advantages of high transmission bandwidth and easy consumer installation as their full-rate non-standards-based counterparts, but will have several added benefits. The next section of our guide will discuss these two standards in more detail.

G.dmt

G.dmt ADSL technology uses existing phone lines between the central office and customer residences to provide always-on, high-speed Internet access at rates up to 8 Mbps downstream and up to 2 Mbps upstream. G.dmt was approved as an International Telecommunications Union (ITU) standard on June 22, 1999 and has two implementations: splittered and splitterless (see Figure 3.1).

Splittered G.dmt is the implementation the DSL industry is attempting to simplify because it requires a technician visit, or "truck roll," to the customer premises to install a splitter device and rewire the existing phone lines in the home. The splitter acts as a filter to separate the existing telephone service voice signals from the ADSL data signals, which prevents interference between the two signals while allowing simultaneous analog phone and Internet access use. Splittered G.dmt may be a useful broadband alternative for power users who require extremely fast data speeds, are willing to pay significantly more for these faster rates, or are not comfortable installing DSL equipment themselves. However, the service provider truck roll prerequisite is expensive and limits scalability, thus preventing mass-market subscriber volumes. Splitterless G.dmt is a relatively new implementation of ADSL. Instead of a technician-installed splitter,

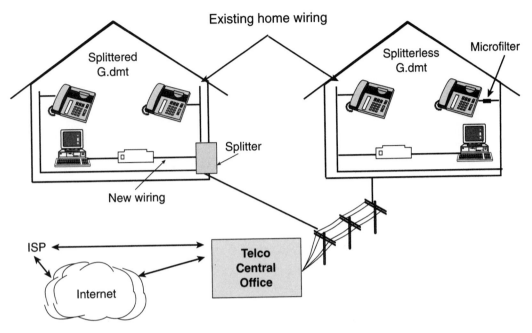

Figure 3.1
Splittered G.dmt versus splitterless G.dmt

splitterless G.dmt allows consumers to use small, easy-to-install devices between phone jacks and all customer premises equipment, like telephones and fax machines. In the short-term, the splitterless G.dmt will allow DSL service providers to avoid the truck roll in their DSL deployments and to capture modest numbers of potential broadband customers. For these reasons, DSL service providers are moving to this splitterless implementation of G.dmt and will be using splittered G.dmt on a more limited basis. In the long-term, splitterless G.dmt will allow DSL service providers to provide higher-speed service that is customer-installable and interoperable. However, in the interim, substantial roadblocks to mass market DSL volumes will exist from factors such as higher pricing, lack of product interoperability, and data transmission performance at longer loops not even reaching speeds up to 1.5 Mbps.

G.lite

G.lite is a consumer-focused version of ADSL capable of providing data over existing phone lines at rates of up to 1.5 Mbps downstream and 512 Kbps upstream. Like G.dmt, G.lite was approved as an ITU standard on June 22, 1999.

However, compared to G.dmt or proprietary ADSL solutions, G.lite was specifically designed, from a technical standpoint, to eliminate the telephone company truck roll. Because G.lite offers high-speed, always-on Internet access at a low cost and with convenient installation, it will be the mass-market vehicle for unlocking the broadband market for DSL services. From the name, you can probably deduct that the deployment of this technology on your home network does not require a POTS splitter. In terms of speed, G.lite runs at a slower rate than the complete ADSL solution. If the data rates are not enough to satisfy your hunger for bandwidth, G.lite provides you with an evolution path to migrate over to full rate ADSL. The effort to introduce G.lite has been spearheaded by an industry group called the Universal ADSL Working Group. Its charter is to support and expedite the development of a worldwide G.lite standard.

If you are looking for more technical detail on the G.lite standard, visit the following URL: http://www.uawg.com/index2.html.

Benefits of G.lite

The advantages of G.lite will lead to faster DSL subscriber ramp rates; in turn, this will benefit consumers, PC OEMs, equipment vendors, and DSL service providers. In addition to the high data transfer rates of up to 1.5 Mbps downstream and up to 512 Kbps upstream (sufficient for typical consumer needs), the advantages of G.lite include:

- Faster time to market with highly interoperable and integrated products
- Lower equipment costs for DSL service providers and consumers
- Lower power consumption and heat dissipation, lowering operational costs
- Higher port density, allowing more subscriber lines per DSLAM
- Equivalent loop reach performance to G.dmt

Faster Time to Market with Interoperability • The retail channel requires standards-based interoperable DSL products for wide distribution. A wide retail channel presence for DSL products increases the availability of, and promotions for, DSL equipment to consumers. Consequently, consumer awareness of DSL service will multiply, driving subscriber signups and product purchases. G.lite will lead to faster time to market for DSL products that meet those retail channel requirements. Because cable modems will soon be available in the retail channel, G.lite modems will provide the DSL industry with a compelling competitive product and service presence. Otherwise, consumers shopping in retail stores and online will select the only broadband service they know about and can buy products for—cable. G.lite will enable the acquisition of those broadband customers and their service revenue streams into the future. Most vendors are currently developing products based on the G.lite and G.dmt standards. Interoperability of these products, however, is not guaranteed and requires much cooperation and collaboration between vendors. Vendors have been working through ADSL Forum-sponsored industry plugfests and private bilateral testing to advance interoperability for G.lite and G.dmt products. Different interpretations of standards are resulting in products that work well with some DSL products but are incompatible with others.

Lower Equipment Costs • Equipment costs are minimized for key DSL stakeholders on several levels. DSL service providers shift the cost of Customer Premises Equipment (CPE) subsidization to consumers and reduce central office equipment costs with more space- and power-efficient G.lite equipment.

High Port Density • Port density refers to the number of subscriber connections that can be managed by a line card in a DSLAM. Because of its more efficient size requirements, G.lite can double or triple the number of subscribers served by a DSLAM. This means that DSL service providers can reduce their capital investments and improve their bottom lines by serving more customers from a central office.

Real Products • Nearly 40 companies showed how DSL technology improves speed for e-mail, telecommuting, e-commerce, and entertainment at the 1999 Consumer Electronics Show in Las Vegas. In addition, 12 leading equipment vendors demonstrated interoperable products based on the G.lite standard.

Widespread Deployment of DSL

The consumer DSL market is currently in a transitional phase, common to emerging markets. To break through this transitional period and enable a mass market for DSL services, the DSL industry needs to deploy standards-based and interoperable G.lite equipment. Equipment vendors have been working together to ensure that this fully interoperable G.lite equipment is developed. DSL service providers and PC OEMs will then integrate those products into their consumer offerings. Both G.dmt and G.lite are beneficial to the DSL industry and are not mutually exclusive. Large companies like Intel believe that G.lite offers several key advantages to the main stakeholders, particularly because of its progress in interoperability. G.lite technology will be the first to enable PC OEMs to distribute standards-based DSL modems widely in the retail channel across service regions and to allow DSL service providers to scale their subscriber bases for anticipated consumer demand. G.dmt will eventually provide an attractive sell-up opportunity for higher bandwidth once the consumer has subscribed to and experienced DSL service. By the end of 2000, it is envisioned that millions of consumers will be enjoying Internet experiences enhanced by the speed and efficiency of broadband service. G.lite has the potential to be the catalyst that makes this vision a reality for the mass market; thereafter, G.dmt will allow DSL consumers to enjoy greater bandwidth well into the future.

From a commercial perspective, the DSL broadband marketplace is expected to become a booming business in the next couple of years. Companies like Microsoft are investing heavily in the sector. In addition to large deals in 1999, many phone companies have started to offer DSL service to their customers as an alternative to fast Web access through a cable modem. Most companies involved with delivering the service admitted that the customer demand for high-speed DSL Internet connectivity was phenomenal. At the time of going to press, start-ups, ISPs, and established phone companies had begun waiving their access fees for customers who sign up for the new DSL services.

HYBRID FIBER-COAX (HFC) TECHNOLOGIES ....

Hybrid fiber-coax (HFC) technology refers to any network configuration of fiber-optic and coaxial cable that may be used to redistribute a variety of broadband entertainment services. These broadband services include telephony, interactive multimedia, high speed Internet access, video-on-demand, and distance learning. The types of services provided to consumers will vary among cable companies.

Many of the major cable television companies in the United States, Europe, Latin America, and Southeast Asia are already using it. Networks built using HFC technology have many characteristics that make it ideal for handling the next generation of communication services. First and foremost, HFC networks can simultaneously transmit broadband analog and digital services. Additionally, HFC meets the capacity and reliability requirements of new digital data services. HFC's expandable capacity allows network operators to add services incrementally without major changes to the overall plant infrastructure. HFC is essentially a "pay as you go" architecture that matches infrastructure investment with new revenue streams, operational savings, and reliability enhancements. The HFC network architecture consists of fiber transmitters, optical nodes, coaxial cables, and distribution hubs. The architecture of an HFC system required to deliver data services to a home network is illustrated in Figure 3.2.

From the diagram, we can see that the signal is transmitted from a central location in a star-like fashion to the fiber nodes using fiber-optic feeders. The fiber node, in turn, distributes the signals over coaxial cable, amplifiers, and taps throughout the customer service area. The size of the customer service area can range from 500 to 2000 home networks.

HFC networks are two-way systems that are capable of communicating with a home network at speeds of 40 Mbits per second and above. To achieve these high speeds, a signal leaving the network operator's premises needs to be compressed and modulated using a technique called QAM (Quadrature Amplitude Modulation). This method of formatting a signal improves the rate at which information can be broadcast over the HFC network to the home network.

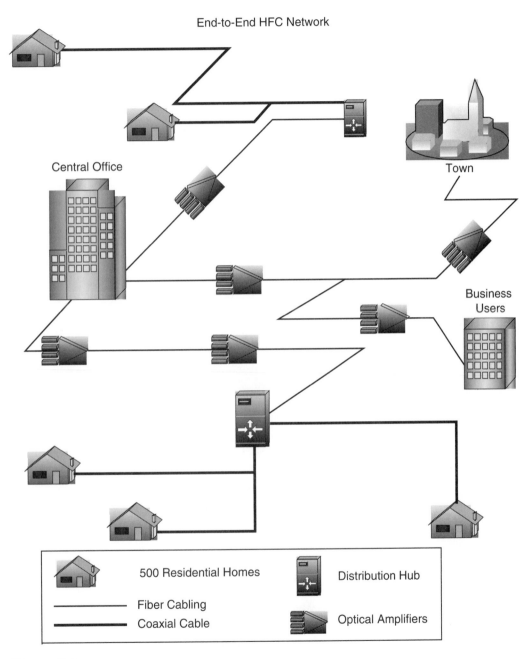

Figure 3.2
Architecture of a typical HFC network

For cable companies, the combination of HFC with home networking technologies is expected to be the next big money spinner. Income sources will come from installations, equipment rentals, and service support. Additionally, many of the senior executives in the cable TV industry are planning to generate huge profits through the provision of value-added interactive TV applications. For example, Canada's largest operator, Rodgers Cablesystems, is rolling out home data networks to its subscriber base. This lead is expected to be followed in the near future by other large cable operators such as AT&T, Cox Communications, and Time Warner.

WIRELESS LOCAL LOOP.....................................

Originally developed to support telephony traffic, the *local loop* of a telecommunications network now supports a much greater number of subscriber lines transmitting both voice and Internet traffic. The term "local loop" is widely used to describe the electrical circuit between consumers and the local telephone company. The national carriers no longer have exclusive access to the local loop and are facing stiff competition from cable and satellite companies. AT&T, for instance, is spending billions of dollars on upgrading their cable TV networks.

Early in 1999, a new horse entered the race to take control of the local loop—wireless technologies. The battle commenced when two U.S.-based phone giants, MCI WorldCom and Sprint, each started buying up wireless cable companies. This was the beginning of an ambitious campaign to shift away from video programming to high-speed Internet services. Wireless local loop (WLL) is a relatively new service that is used by telecommunications companies to carry IP data from central locations on their networks to small low-cost antennas that are mounted on their subscribers' roofs. Wireless cable Internet access is enabled through the use of a number of distribution technologies, including the multichannel multipoint distribution system (MMDS) and the local multipoint distribution system (LMDS).

MMDS

Analog-based MMDS began in the mid-seventies with the allocation of two television channels for sending business data. This service became very popular, and applications were made to allocate part of the ITFS (Instructional Television Fixed Service) band to wireless cable TV. Once the regulations had been amended it became possible for a wireless cable system to offer up to thirty-one 6-MHz channels in the 2.5 to 2.7 GHz frequency band. During this timeframe, nonprofit organizations used the system to broadcast educational and religious programs. In 1983, the Federal Communications Commission (FCC) allocated frequencies in both of these spectrums, providing 200 MHz bandwidth for licensed network providers. The basic components of a digital MMDS system providing broadband connectivity to a home network are shown in Figure 3.3.

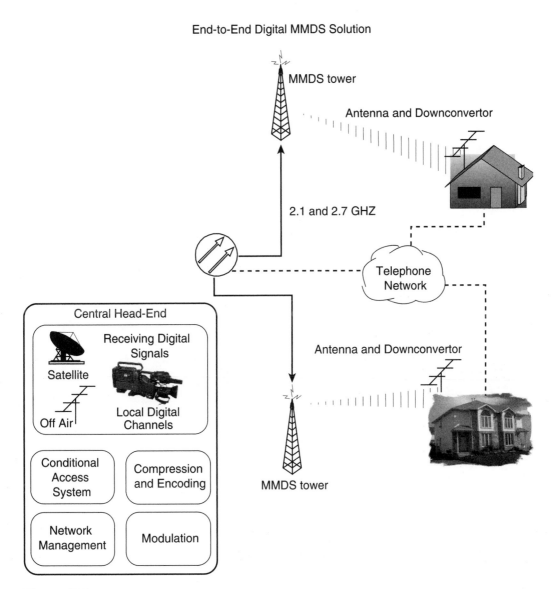

Figure 3.3
MMDS broadband connectivity

An MMDS broadband system consists of a head-end that receives data from a wide variety of sources including Internet Service Providers (ISPs) and TV broadcast stations. At the head-end the data is processed, converted to the 2.1 and 2.7 GHz frequency range and sent to microwave towers. QAM is the most commonly used format used in sending data over an MMDS network, however some operators use a modulation format called Coded Orthogonal Frequency Division Multiplexing (COFDM). This format operates extremely well in conditions likely to be found in heavily built- up areas where digital transmissions become distorted by line of sight obstacles, such as buildings, bridges, and hills. The signals are then rebroadcast from low-powered base stations in a diameter of 35 miles from your home place. Signals are received with home rooftop antennas.

The receiving antenna has a clear line of site to the transmitting antenna. A down converter, usually a part of the antenna, converts the microwave signals into standard cable channel frequencies. From the antenna the signal travels to a gateway device where it is routed and passed onto the various devices that are connected to the in-home network. Today, there are MMDS systems in use all around the United States and in many other countries including Australia, South Africa, South America, Ireland, and Canada.

LMDS

LMDS uses microwave frequencies in the 27 to 31 GHz frequency range to send and receive broadband signals, which are suitable for the transmission of video, voice, and multimedia data. Digital LMDS has been commercially deployed and is being used to deliver video programming and a plethora of Internet- and telephony-based services to consumers. The system architecture for LMDS is similar to the MMDS system. The reception, processing, and broadcasting of data are the same. The signals are then re-broadcast from low-powered base stations in a 4 to 6 mile radius of your home. Signals are received using six square-inch antennas, which can be mounted either inside or outside of your house. As with the MMDS, the signal travels to the gateway device, is formatted, and is passed to one of the consumer or PC devices connected to the home network.

The LMDS frequency allocations in the United States were auctioned off to the highest bidders in 1999. The auctions raised about $45 million—not very much when you consider it gives the winners the ability to compete with the local telephone company, the local cable company, and Internet service providers.

SATELLITE ....

Communication satellites are, in effect, orbiting microwave relay stations, located about 35,000 km above the surface of the earth, used to link two or more earth-based microwave stations. Communication satellite providers typically lease some or all of a satellite's channels to large corporations, which use them for long-distance telephone traffic, private data networks, and distribution of television signals. Leasing these huge communication "pipes" can be very expensive, therefore they are not suitable for the mass residential marketplace. Consequently, a new suite of services, called the direct broadcast satellite (DBS) system, has been developed to provide consumers with a range of high-speed Internet access services.

A DBS system consists of a minidish that connects in-home networks to satellites with the ability to deliver multimedia data to a home network at speeds in excess of 45 Mbps. This speed can only be achieved when downloading content, however. To upload or send information to the Internet, the system uses a slow telephone connection. Satellite systems normally use the Quadrature Phase Shift Keying (QPSK) modulation format to transmit data from the dish in the sky to the minidish on the roof.

BROADBAND POWERLINE AREA NETWORKS ....

For many years, power companies have had the ambition to use electrical distribution networks for communications and data transfer. The first patent on technology for sending signals over powerlines was in 1899. However, a realistic technology for providing high-speed, two-way communications has until recently been just a dream of utilities. That dream is now becoming a reality. The idea is simple: The utilities' existing infrastructure of stout copper lines, long-distance cables, and in-house wiring has the potential to become a ubiquitous communications platform. Every electrical outlet in every building could become a port to the ultimate communications network. However, electrical grids do the job they were designed to do. They were not originally intended to transmit data.

Inherent characteristics of power networks confounding communications efforts include: low impedance, no specific topology, multitudes of fuses and circuit breakers, and transformers that scrub encoded signals from the voltage wave. Despite these problems, the energy industry insists on seeking a way to use the power grid as a broadband communications platform. The major advantage to power networks is that they are ubiquitous, and the largest capital outlay for any communications network *is* the network.

A powerline communications system must be designed to overcome these inherent obstacles. To become reality, a system will need both the appropriate technology and a critical mass of demand to make the solution cost-effective.

Opportunities and Applications

The primary motivation for power companies to pursue a powerline communications solution is the desire to harness the technology for remote meter-reading, load management, and network administration. However, in an era of deregulation, there is a new interest in using "spare bandwidth" to enhance value. Added-value applications could be in the area of customer service enhancements, such as non-energy-related services like voice, video, or data transmission.

Other potential applications include:

- Load switching
- Remote tariff setting
- Prepayment systems
- Remote connection and disconnection
- Monitoring supply quality, outages, voltage levels, and disturbances
- Monitoring for tampering and theft
- Load research, including detailed load profiles for future tariffing schemes
- Multiutility metering

Such applications represent only the meter-related possibilities of a powerline carrier system. Various applications require different supporting communication systems performance. For some, a simple broadcast-level system could be sufficient. However, most will require two-way communications with individual meters. Certain applications, such as prepayment, demand a secure and reliable system. Other applications may be supported by a system with relatively limited responsiveness. For example, meter reading for billing purposes may only require one successful communication in a given 24-hour period. In principle, there is every reason for a powerline communications system owned and operated by an electricity supplier to be capable of directly addressing individual appliances on a customer's premises.

Strengths and Weaknesses of Powerline Communications Technology

Powerline communications technology enjoys several important strengths. The power grid is an ideal communications platform, as it is the most extensive wired network, its analog signals are additive, there are no topology limitations, and it has a powerful duplex dynamic in the AC field (as opposed to telephony's DC pulses). Based on robust, modern, and organized engineering, it offers a permanent online connection and is inexpensive thanks to an existing infrastructure. Lately, certain energy companies involved with powerline communications projects have seen shareholder value increase. The main weakness of powerline communications is that it is still in the developmental stage, pursued by a fragmented industry lacking standards.

Powerline Communications Technology Efforts Around the World

Canada

Ontario Hydro • "Smart Utility Operations" is Ontario Hydro's powerline communications concept. Their focus is on developing monitoring and communications for rural distribution stations and developing a communications system to improve information processing and delivery to operations personnel in the field.

West End Networks • In 1995, Nor.Web invited West End Networks (WEN) to participate in their powerline communications test. WEN had been testing a product to provide high-speed interactive communications over cable TV networks using fiber-optic and coaxial cables. WEN's protocol technology was considered particularly suitable for the powerline communications environment. The goal for WEN technology is to provide individual customers with potential bandwidth of up to 2 Mbps.

France

Electricité de France • In 1994, EdF carried out studies that indicated strong customer interest in services such as demand-side and energy management. Although interest in energy management services by residential customers was high, their actual knowledge of their own load and cost profiles was very limited. EdF is attempting to introduce a service to improve customer knowledge of their own use.

Germany

Bewag • Bewag, in collaboration with the University of Paderborn, has tested powerline technology products designed for service over local and in-building wiring. This could make each power socket a communications port. Based on a Code Division Multiple Access protocol as used in wireless telephony networks, the Bewag product is still in the design and test stage.

EnBW • Energie Baden-Wurttemberg (EnBW) and Nor.Web are working in southern Germany on a project to deploy digital powerline technology.

RWE • RWE, in cooperation with telecommunications network provider Alcatel, recently announced a breakthrough on a powerline communications technology. Following the announcement, both companies' stock rose. RWE has been working on pilot tests to determine technical and economic feasibility of using the low-voltage grid for both telephony and data transmission. The German energy company regards powerline communications as a strategic asset, which will be especially valuable in a deregulated energy market. RWE is promoting an "Open Powerline Platform" to be achieved by cross-European cooperation among utilities, suppliers, and developers.

Siemens • Siemens' system for energy meter data management, called SEMMS, can be used for power supply measurement or optimization of processes and cost accounting. Based on flexible communication, the system has standard protocols for: telephone, low-voltage grid, radio, broadband cable, standard field bus, and mobile data recording.

Italy

Enel • Enel has developed a system they call SITRED for two-way communication using distribution power networks as data transmission media. SITRED features remote power distribution control and remote meter reading.

Netherlands

ECN, KEMA • KEMA is studying software applications technologies for the standardization and integration of powerline communications protocols. ECN, the national energy research foundation of the Netherlands, is developing tools to support energy customer policy.

Edon • Edon is working on a digital powerline technology trial.

Sweden

ABB (Sweden/Switzerland) • ABB's Panorama system for distribution and demand-side management is based on powerline communications for data transfer. Through improved grid coupling, the medium voltage distribution line carrier is completed. The local area network at the household level provides two-way communication for load management, meter reading, and other services.

Stockholm Energi • Stockholm Energi is cooperating with Nor.Web to establish a telecommunication services group.

Sydkraft/EnerSearch • EnerSearch, a joint venture between Sydkraft and IBM Utility, is conducting research on a program called Information Society Energy System (ISES). The goal of ISES is to encompass the whole spectrum of powerline communications product tests. Sydkraft has completed a feasibility demonstration, and is currently planning for a market introduction program. Within the ISES program, a technology called Homebots has been developed for large-scale decentralized electric load management. This is based on intelligent software agents representing electrical equipment and appliances. These agents communicate over the low-voltage grid to optimize energy use efficiency and cost.

Vattenfall • Vattenfall is working with Electrolux to provide home management services over the low-voltage network.

United Kingdom

Nor.Web • In 1992, British power distribution company Nor.Web achieved a breakthrough in powerline communications systems. Using the power distribution network, the utility implemented the world's first telephony and data trial for 25 domestic customers. A year and a half later, the trial was operating these services at over 99% reliability. This technology cannot, however, pass signals through transformers.

RMS • The RMS PowerNet system, evaluated by a number of utilities in Europe, has remote meter-reading capability. The biggest installation is being completed in the U.S. in Perth and Fort William, where 2000 meters are being installed. Similar systems are also being constructed in England, Sweden, Germany, and Malaysia.

United States

Enikia • Enikia has a "power strip" style device with ports to connect computers to the Internet. They run Ethernet-speed communications over the existing powerline network in a home.

EPRI • As described in Chapter 2, EPRI is researching a communication system to transmit data between customers and utilities using powerlines.

IBM • IBM has developed an Intelligent Distribution Automation and Management (IDAM) system, based on a modular structure with proprietary interfaces among the system's individual components. The main system components are: the Multi Functional Node (MFN), the interface on the customer side; the Concentrator and Communication Node (CCN), which manages multiple MFNs; and the Operation and Management System (OMS) that manages the total network. The system is mainly intended for remote meter reading, distribution, automation, and customer services.

Intellon • Intellon manufactures chip sets for use in powerline communications modems.

Inari • Inari has a product that sends data communications over in-building wiring. The "Passport" device is connected to a computer or printer port and enables printer sharing and local area networking within a home or office. The device is plugged directly into the electricity mains, converting the data and transmitting it at about 5.6 MHz. Unable to send transmissions through transformers, the application is not designed for use over external power distribution cables.

Broadband Powerline Technology Providers

Most of the companies we encountered during our research into powerline technologies were focussed on supplying products for consumers who want to use their in-home electrical wiring system for networking purposes (these technologies are covered in Chapter 6). On the wide area powerline front, a company called Media Fusion is developing a comprehensive suite of technologies to support powerline infrastructures.

About Media Fusion

Media Fusion, incorporated in February, 1998, is a company dedicated to the development, deployment, and management of a very low-cost infrastructure that reliably provides infinite bandwidth and speed for the transmission of voice, video, and data over electrical power grids. Using its unique, proprietary technology, Media Fusion is poised to facilitate the use of the most extensive global network—the electrical power grid—to surmount the "last mile" problem, the primary obstacle to the delivery of advanced telecommunications capabilities to urban, suburban, and rural consumers, as well as to provide initial and expanded telecommunications capabilities and data services to developing countries. While designed for use in the U.S. market, its technologies can be easily adapted to comply with electrical and communications requirements in foreign countries.

SUMMARY ....

Worldwide use of computers and new appliances that allow people access to the Internet from the comfort of their homes are the major driving forces behind the development and implementation of broadband technologies. The spread of broadband connections that provide lighting-fast Internet services is seen as a key factor in encouraging the proliferation of home networking technologies.

Nowadays, applications such as Internet access and high-speed remote access to storage media require more data capacity than traditional telecommunications services can provide. Replacing copper wiring with fiber optic-cabling is one way of delivering this capacity to your home, but the associated technology is expensive. So the focus over the past few years has been on deploying new technologies on existing network infrastructures. As a result, the telecommunication companies developed a technology called DSL that transforms ordinary phone lines into high-speed digital lines for ultrafast Internet access. The family of DSL technologies ranges from ADSL to VDSL. This chapter focussed on two members of this family that have emerged as the services most in demand for home network users—G.dmt and G.lite. Home applications that DSL is suitable for include high-speed Internet access and large file downloads.

Cable, wireless cable, and satellite companies have also done a great job in marketing their networks as an infrastructure that can provide home networking users with a variety of broadband Internet services. The new era of digital TV presents these network service providers with an opportunity to deliver profitable Internet-centric services. Cable companies are able to offer an Internet access service to users of home networks at a much higher rate than traditional and specialized ISPs). Wireless operators are also looking at ways of using LMDS and MMDS technologies to boost data rates between our homes and the Internet. At the time of going to press, a number of large companies were investing billions of dollars in their wireless networks to secure their place in the Internet race. Satellite companies are also expected to be major players in the Internet game. With companies like AOL investing billions of dollars in this industry, the future is looking very bright for satellite companies. Energy companies are exploring two-way residential communications to help reduce the cost of providing standard energy-related services, such as itemized billing or demand reduction, as well as to provide nontraditional services, such as diagnostic services and e-mail. Power companies around the world are planning to use their electrical power grids to carry telephone, radio, video, and Internet data to any destination at near light speed. Media Fusion, armed with patents, funding, governmental encouragement, and a laboratory at Stennis Space Center, Mississippi, is poised to emerge as a leading powerline communications technology. Media Fusion, incorporated in February, 1998, is a company dedicated to the development, deployment, and management of a very low-cost infrastructure that reliably provides infinite bandwidth and speed for the transmission of voice, video, and data over electrical power grids. the company's proprietary technology is used by U.S.-based utility companies to deliver advanced telecommunications capabilities to urban, suburban, and rural consumers. While designed for use in the U.S. market, its technologies can be easily adapted to comply with electrical and communications requirements in other countries.

4 Phone-Line–Based Home Networks

In this chapter...

Until recently, home networks depended on special cables (typically requiring professional installation) to link PCs, A/V equipment, and peripheral devices together, which could be expensive and problematic if the hardware components were in different rooms of the house. Now, thanks to recent technological developments, consumers can use their already installed telephone and electrical wiring system to link multiple computers and digital appliances around the house. This chapter examines a number of phone line technologies that promise to deliver the holy grail of home networks without the need to run hundreds of meters of new data cables inside the walls of your house.

MARKET RESEARCH (SPONSORED BY INTEL) ....

As discussed in the preface, the phone-line companies are concentrating most of their energies on homeowners who have mulitple PCs. Following is an overview of research work, sponsored by Intel and carried out by Market Strategies, Inc., into the trend across the world toward multiple-PC households.

There was a time when the idea of one television set per home was considered a luxury. Today, according to a December, 1997, Odyssey study, approximately 76% of all U.S. households have two or more televisions. It can be argued that the PC is following the same pattern. Consider three factors that contributed significantly to multiple TV-set ownership within the home:

- Purchase of a newer, bigger, better television

- Purchase of an additional television to reduce conflicts in the house over TV use

- Purchase of an additional television for use in a second or third room (kitchen, bedroom, etc.)

Replace the word "television" with "PC" in each of the above statements and they fit the multiple-PC phenomenon. After all, rapid advancements in PC technology result in "newer, bigger, and better" every holiday season. PCs undoubtedly take the potential for conflict one step further than television. Unlike TV viewing, which can be a multiperson experience, personal computer use is distinctively personal. In most cases, it is impossible for users to share.

During Intel-sponsored focus group research, one respondent lamented that, because his teenage daughter has replaced the telephone with the Internet for long distance communication with her boyfriend, he had to purchase another computer for his use. Finally, as PC use increases, more home users are likely to demand the convenience of accessing the computers' capabilities from the home office, the kitchen, the bedroom, or wherever they happen to be.

Today's Multiple-PC Home

What does today's multiple-PC home look like? Perhaps less "techy" than might be imagined. Notably, among the hundreds of two-PC household decision-makers that Intel interviewed, few consider themselves early adopters of technology. In fact, in focus group discussions, most indicated a modest level of PC knowledge. What they communicated was that they find the PC a useful, integral part of life—*for more than one member of the household.* Intel also learned the following about these consumers:

- 85% have two or more adult users in the home and 50% have at least one child user.

- *The primary* users are typically adults between the ages of 25 and 54.

- Multiple-PC homes don't appear to be a trend of only the highly affluent. Annual household income ranged widely from $20,000 to over $100,000, with the most prevalent income cluster being in the $20,000 to $70,000 range.

The only *significant* difference between these households and one-PC households is the tendency to be connected to the Internet. According to research Intel conducted in May of 1998, 86% of multiple-PC homes have Internet access, compared to 47% reported for single-PC homes in a January, 1998, Odyssey study. Notably, this access is used by nearly everyone in the home. Ninety-eight percent of adults and sixty-nine percent of children who use a PC in these households report being on the Internet at least once per month.

Getting the Most From Your PCs

If you buy a PC for everyone in the house, all PC-related conflicts are over, right? Well, maybe. In a number of Intel-sponsored focus group discussions across the United States, one issue was apparent: Home consumers don't consider the PC a standalone device any more than businesses do. To get the most value from their computers, home users need to be able to access PC resources (like printers and Internet access) from any PC they are working on. For most home consumers, multiple PCs in their homes only partially address their needs. To get full use of their PCs, these consumers have turned to a variety of methods. A very small percentage of U.S. multiple-PC homes have actually installed a traditional office network. Other consumers have purchased additional printers and/or Internet access accounts and phone lines for their additional PCs. Those who haven't made such purchases (the majority) are grudgingly living with makeshift solutions, like running floppy disks from the nonprinter-connected PC to the printer-connected PC, and simply waiting for the Internet-connected PC to be available before accessing their favorite Web site. While most felt they could live with such compromises, when presented with an easy home networking option, the majority indicated they would jump at the chance to take it.

But Few Are Networked Today

Nearly 18 million consumers have more than one PC in their home. At least half of these have indicated they would be very interested in a solution that would give them the major benefits of a home network. Why aren't multiple-PC consumers flocking to retailers for the currently existing network-in-a-box solutions? Two reasons:

First, consumers perceive a network as difficult to install and maintain. Intel's study showed that 50% of multiple-PC household decision-makers use a networked PC at work. Among those who don't use a Local Area Network (LAN), focus groups indicate that they are very familiar with someone who does. These people are not strangers to the idea of sharing data and PC resources on an office network. But familiarity has bred contempt. Throughout Intel's investigation of the multiple-PC home, few discussion topics were as lively or emotional as those surrounding consumers' impressions of office networking:

"The network is always going down."

"It takes a whole department to run the network."

"Networking is a hassle."

All of these are similar to the types of responses heard across the United States from consumers who have (or plan to have soon) at least two PCs in their homes—a fairly PC-literate group. Few argued the overall benefits of networking, but all perceived the cost of those benefits (in hassle and frustration) to be very high. Almost none felt compelled to pay that high a price to install a traditional network in their home.

The second reason multiple-PC owners aren't rushing to install home networks is practicality: Most don't want to drill holes in their walls to install network wiring. The option of stringing loose wire from room to room across the carpets or hardwood floors leaves something to be desired from an interior design standpoint.

Enter Telephone-Based Home Networking

Existing telephone wiring is an excellent medium for networking PCs within the home without adding new wires. The average multiple-PC household in the United States has four to five telephone jacks, and most are near existing PCs. Phone lines also provide a secure environment for data transmission.

HOME TELEPHONE NETWORKING CHALLENGES ....

Creating a technology that can deliver high-speed networking in the multiple–PC home is a challenging task. Commercial networks are designed from the ground up to minimize noise and interference. High-speed, corporate networks typically use fiber-optic, twisted pair, or coaxial cables that are dedicated to that single use.

Most homes, on the other hand, don't have dedicated, high-speed network wiring, and the cost and labor required to install such wiring is well above the threshold of interest for the typical homeowner (as well as for many small-business owners). So, the first requirement of a home network solution is that it allow homeowners to share PC resources without installing additional wiring. Phone-line networking meets this requirement by using the existing home telephone wiring to transmit data. But because home phone lines weren't designed for high-speed data transmission, phone-line networking technology must address the following issues:

- **Random wiring topologies and signal attenuation**—The telephone wiring structure within each home is unknown and can change on a day-to-day basis. Rather than the hub structure of many business networks, the home phone-line wiring system is a random "tree," and something as simple as plugging in a telephone or disconnecting a fax machine changes the tree. In addition, the random tree network topology can cause signal attenuation, because open plugs and unterminated devices can cause impedance mismatches and signal echoes and lead to multipath signals.

- **Signal noise**—Appliances, heaters, air conditioners, and telephones can introduce signal noise on the phone wires.

- **Changing transmission line characteristics**—The network must be able to function reliably despite changes that result from someone picking up the phone or receiving a fax, or an answering machine recording a message.

- **Coexistence with other phone line equipment and compliance with FCC regulations**—Phone-line network solutions must use signals with low power levels, which further complicates the task of establishing adequate signal-to-noise ratios. In addition, the phone-line network must work without interrupting existing phone services.

- **Performance**—To meet the needs of today's networking applications, a home network must be highly reliable at speeds of at least 1 Mbps.

- **Telephone jacks**—There are a limited number of phone jacks per home (especially outside the United States). Also, the physical location of those jacks with respect to the devices that need to be networked is another problem.

An organization called the Home Phoneline Networking Alliance (HomePNA) has been established to define standards and technologies that will overcome these technical issues.

ABOUT HOMEPNA...

The HomePNA is a group of more than 130 companies seeking to develop specifications for interoperable, home-networked devices using existing phone wiring. The group was founded in June, 1998 by 11 companies (3Com, AMD, AT&T Wireless, Compaq, Conexant, Epigram, Hewlett-Packard, IBM, Intel, Lucent Technologies, and Tut Systems). Toward the end of 1998 the group created a de facto industry standard when it published an easy-to-use, cost-effective, and proven 1 Mbps home phone-line networking technology as its 1.0 specification. The technology allows computers, peripherals, and other information appliances to connect with each other and the Internet without interrupting standard telephone service. Utilizing existing telephone wiring, it requires no costly or disruptive rewiring of the home. HomePNA members began producing compliant products in December, 1998. In December of 1999, the organization announced the release of its much-anticipated second-generation home phone-line networking technology (HomePNA 2.0). The new specification brings a faster 10 Mbps to phone-line networking, while at the same time maintaining backward compatibility with existing 1 Mbps HomePNA technology. The new technology uses selective portions of the 2 to 30 MHz frequency band to achieve these data rates. The technology foundation for the 10 Mbps HomePNA 2.0 standard is currently based on chipsets from a U.S.-based company called Broadcom Corporation.

In addition to increasing data speeds within the home, HomePNA is working to incorporate their technologies into a range of electronic appliances including: PCs, ADSL modems, cable modems, digital televisions, set-top boxes, and IP-based Web phones. Let's examine each component of a HomePNA-based network and see how they work together.

HomePNA Technical Architecture

Network Transport Technologies

The Alliance has chosen to standardize on Ethernet-based technology, allowing consumers to link devices at speeds up to 10 Mbps over existing home telephone wires. Ethernet is a popular and internationally standardized networking technology (comprising both hardware and software) that enables computers to communicate with each other. Ethernet was developed by Xerox, Intel, and DEC. The Institute of Electrical and Electronics Engineers (IEEE) later standardized it as IEEE 802.3. As a result, people tend to use the terms Ethernet and IEEE 802.3 interchangeably. The fact that IEEE 802.3 has been chosen as a networking technology allows HomePNA to leverage the tremendous amount of Ethernet-compatible software, applications, and existing hardware in the market today. The IEEE 802.3 standard was designed to support the CSMA/CD access method. CSMA/CD stands for Carrier Sense Multiple Access with Collision Detection. Let's briefly explore what this means. On a home network that uses the CSMA/CD access method, the devices can send data at any time—so there's multiple access. When an electronic or PC device has data to send, it listens to the phone line to see if it is busy. The device is sensitive to any carrier on the line—that's why this access method is said to have carrier sense. If there's traffic on the line, the device waits—in other words, it enters *waiting mode*. If the line is free, the station transmits its data immediately. Let's say that another device in another part of the home decides to send data at the same time. In such a case, a collision may occur. Collision detection allows the two devices to detect this event and perform the required recovery. The devices back off for a period of time before retransmitting. Of course, it's essential that the two devices do not back off for the same length of time. If, for example, all appliances on the home network were set to back off and retry after half a second, the same two frames would collide again. To prevent continual collisions, each appliance on the network backs off for a random amount of time. Under the Ethernet standard, information is bundled into a package called a frame. Figure 4.1 shows the home phone-line networking data frame.

A standard Ethernet frame consists of the following six sections of information:

1. **Preamble**—This field is used to establish synchronization between the transmitting and the receiving device.

2. **Destination address**—The destination address identifies the intended receiver of the data frame.

3. **Source address**—The source address identifies the sending device, so the receiving device knows where to direct its response.

4. **Type**—This field indicates the upper-layer (or network) protocol that's using the frame. IP is the most commonly used network protocol for home networks.

5. **Data**—The data field contains the actual data that is been transported across the home network. The size of this field varies from frame to frame. The Ethernet standard specifies that this field must contain a minimum of 64 bytes and a maximum of 1518 bytes.

6. **Frame Check Sequence (FCS)**—This field is used to identify whether there are any errors in the received frame. The transmitting digital appliance performs a mathematical computation, known as a CRC (cyclic re-

Home Phoneline Networking Data Frame
Is Based on Ethernet Standards

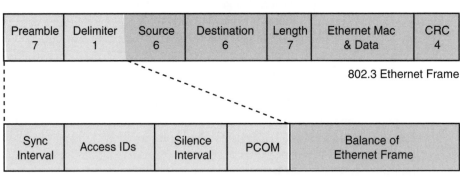

Preamble 7	Delimiter 1	Source 6	Destination 6	Length 7	Ethernet Mac & Data	CRC 4

802.3 Ethernet Frame

Sync Interval	Access IDs	Silence Interval	PCOM	Balance of Ethernet Frame

Home Phoneline Networking Data Frame

├──────Phoneline Header Replacement──────┼───── Unchanged ─────┤

Figure 4.1
HomePNA data frame. (Courtesy of Intel Corporation)

dundancy check) on the frame and stores the resulting value in the FCS field. Because the FCS field contains the frame's CRC value, it's often referred to as the CRC field. The same calculation is performed again by the receiving appliance when the frame is received. If any errors occur, a new frame has to be built and retransmitted. From Figure 4.1, we can see that the home phone-line networking data frame is based on Ethernet standards with a specialized header. Under the Ethernet standard each digital appliance on the home network receives, but does not necessarily process, each frame. First an appliance checks to make sure that the packet consists of at least 64 bytes. If the frame is too short, it is immediately discarded. If the frame is an appropriate length, then the appliance checks the destination address. If the appliance is itself the target address, it copies the rest of the frame into its buffer. Once the frame is in the buffer, the CRC value is calculated and the value is compared with the one stored in the frame's FCS field. If the two values don't match, the receiving appliance assumes that the frame was corrupted in transit, and discards it. If the receiving digital appliance is satisfied with a frame's CRC value, it examines the frame's length field to make sure it is not greater than 1518 bytes. If any errors are detected, the frame is discarded.

An additional requirement of home phone-line networking is the coexistence of multiple services on a single piece of telephone wire. For example, members of the household may need to make telephone calls while other members of the family use the home network for data transfer purposes. One of the most common methods of simultaneously operating multiple data and voice services over a single pair of wires is Frequency Division Multiplexing (FDM). This is a multiplexing technique that assigns each communications service a frequency spectrum that is different from all others. Through the use of frequency-selective filters, devices using one type of service can exchange information without interference from other services that communicate in another frequency band. The home network operates in the frequency range between 5.5 MHz and 9.5 MHz. Passband filters attenuate frequencies below 5.5 MHz very rapidly to eliminate interference with other potential services sharing the wire, such as standard voice communications (which operate in the 20 Hz to 3.4 kHz range in the United States, slightly higher internationally) and UADSL services (which occupy the frequency range of 25 kHz to 1.1 MHz). The chart in Figure 4.2 depicts the spectral usage of three services that can share home phone wiring. POTS, UADSL Internet connectivity, and home phone-line networking share the same line by operating at different frequencies.

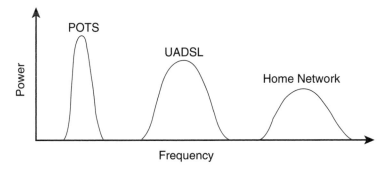

Figure 4.2
HomePNA spectral usage. (Courtesy of Intel Corporation)

Wiring

The Ethernet technology found in corporate office environments was originally designed to support four types of wiring systems:

1. Thick coaxial cable
2. Thin coaxial cable
3. Unshielded twisted pair
4. Fiber-optic cable

These types of expensive cabling systems are not available in most residences. Consequently, HomePNA decided to leverage the existing infrastructure provided by phone wire inside the home. The use of the phone wiring system means that every RJ-11 modular jack in the house becomes a port on the home network, as well as a phone extension. RJ-11 is a standard telephone line connector.

The first HomePNA specification operates at maximum distances of at least 500 feet between nodes on the network and is capable of achieving data rates of 10 Mbps. Each appliance that forms part of the home network is known as a node.

Network Interface Cards

All the appliances on a HomePNA-based network need an adapter to control the I/O to the network. The network interface card (NIC) acts as the physical interface between the appliance and the telephone cable. Without the card, digital appliances would be unable to connect to the network or each other. Network cards are typically connected to each computer or A/V device via an interface slot.

After the card has been installed, the telephone cable is attached to the card's port. Once this connection is made, the computer is physically linked to the home network. All network cards are equipped with onboard microprocessors. The microprocessor is like the card's brain—it is the central point from which the card's various functions are coordinated. The roles of the network card are to:

- Prepare data for transmission
- Send data across the in-home network
- Store data prior to transmission
- Control the flow of data between the digital appliance and the transmission medium

The NIC also acts as a translator. When receiving data, it translates electrical signals from the telephone cable into bytes that the processor in the digital appliance can understand. And when transmitting data, it translates the computer's digital signals into electrical pulses that the telephone cable can carry. A typical HomePNA card will cost you around $100. This card contains the necessary hardware and software routines that are stored in read-only memory that allow you to create a home network using the existing in-home phone wiring system. Some HomePNA certified adapters come with connectors known as RJ-45. These interfaces are slightly wider than RJ-11 connectors and can be used to connect into a sophisticated data wiring system.

Software

As mentioned previously, every device on a home network needs an OS with networking capabilities. Once a NIC is installed in a PC, a driver is required to communicate with other appliances on the network. It is also very important that the driver is configured correctly. If the driver communicates commands to the network card quickly and clearly, the card will operate efficiently. If the card is not configured correctly by the driver, the card will perform less effectively. This will slow up network performance as a whole. HomePNA has decided to use the NDIS driver model that is integrated with most of the Microsoft Windows Operating Systems. NDIS is short for the "Network Driver Interface Specification."

As shown in Figure 4.3, NDIS provides a simplified plug-in driver architecture. At the lowest boundary layer, NDIS contains a driver that is specific to the telephone wiring transmission medium. The layer above this contains a platform-independent

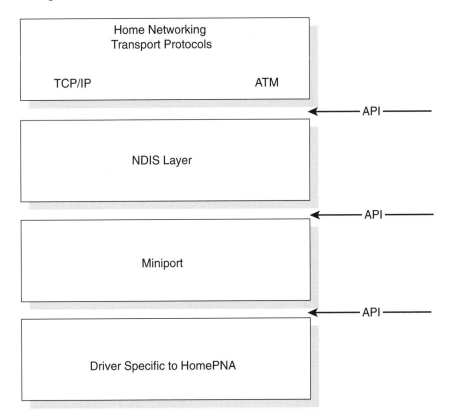

Figure 4.3
NDIS architecture

driver called a miniport. This layer interfaces through a standard Application Programming Interface (API) to the NDIS layer and this layer in turn communicates with the transport protocols that are running across the home network. A major advantage of the NDIS software model is that network cards can be installed in a telephone-based home network without requiring a truck roll from the local service provider.

HomePNA Products

The new HomePNA networking standard has caught the attention of a number of companies and has sparked the launch and deployment of several new products. The following subsections provide specific details about implementations based on the HomePNA standard. Please note that these specifications are subject to continual improvement and hence may have changed since the writing of this book. There is also a high probability that by the time you read this book, many more HomePNA products will have hit retail stores.

HomeRun Products from Tut Systems

Tut Systems is shipping HomeRun products that fulfill the promise of a home networking solution that is easy to install, easy to use, and inexpensive. These products use the telephone wires that already exist inside a home and eliminate the time, costs, and headaches associated with installing new wires. Simply plug any HomeRun-enabled device into an RJ-11 jack to allow it to share a 1 Mbps Ethernet-compatible network with other devices. A HomeRun network supports up to 25 PCs, peripherals, or network devices and connects them across distances of up to 500 feet. With Tut's HomeRun technology, telephones share the same physical wire with the network devices. Voice and data operate simultaneously on the same pair of wires without compromising the voice quality in any way.

HomeRun's 1 Mbps data rate provides the bandwidth necessary for today's home networking applications, such as file sharing, application sharing, and peripheral sharing. HomeRun allows users to share high-speed Internet access devices such as xDSL, wireless, ISDN, and cable modems. With simultaneous Internet access, it is no longer necessary for one person to wait while another finishes accessing the Internet.

Current HomeRun products include:

- HR1000T HomeRun Ethernet Adapter—A stand-alone external adapter that connects any Ethernet device to a HomeRun network.

- HR1000PCI NIC—A network interface card for desktop PCs. The network driver supports Windows 95, Windows 98, Windows NT 3.5.1, and Windows NT 4.0.

In addition to the products listed above, Tut is working with other industry leaders to license HomeRun technology for compatible networking products such as PCs, printers, TV-based browsers, IP telephones, IP cameras, and residential gateways.

3Com HomeConnect Networking Kit

At the beginning of 1999, 3Com teamed up with Microsoft to develop easy-to-use home networking kits based on Ethernet technologies. The 3Com HomeConnect kit includes the hardware and software you need to get your home network up and running. The cables and adapters that are included in the kit are simple to install and plug in. 3Com recommends the following PC hardware and software configuration for installing the kit:

- 486DX/66 Mhz or higher processor
- CD-ROM drive
- Available PCI slot
- Windows 95, 98, or 2000
- 16 MB RAM
- 5 MB of hard disk space
- Modem

HomeConnect home networking kits provide all the necessary hardware and software needed to set up a home network for high-speed Internet access, peripheral processing, and personal file sharing. A HomeConnect kit includes two 10/100 Mbps internal Ethernet network adapters, one five-port 10/100 Mbps dual-speed Ethernet hub, cables, HomeClick software, a Windows 98 Second Edition update, and a collection of Microsoft games.

3Com uses Microsoft HomeClick network software to simplify network setup. HomeClick network software features a step-by-step setup wizard and network center application. With HomeClick software, complex network configuration functions are transparent to consumers, since they are completed behind the scenes. You need only complete a simple series of steps to install a new home network. If necessary, Home-Click network software provides equally intuitive troubleshooting, helping you to pinpoint and correct any errors on your network.

Intel AnyPoint

In September 1998, Intel announced the Intel 21145 Phoneline/Ethernet LAN control-ler, a single-chip, low-cost silicon solution that enables home networking over exist-ing telephone lines. Using this chip, PC and peripheral manufacturers can develop home-networking-capable devices.

On April 6, 1999, Intel announced the AnyPoint suite of phone-line–based home networking products. The AnyPoint network uses regular phone lines within your home to send data between your home PCs. From Figure 4.4 we can see that there is no network wiring to string, no complicated network configurations to tangle with, and you can use your phone normally. PCs on the home network can send and receive data at up to 1 Mbps—fast enough to share most PC resources with ease. At this speed, you can experience the Internet on all connected PCs, without bottlenecks. Be-cause most Internet traffic is intermittent, the speed of your Internet connection is eas-ily shared with all PCs. The 1 Mbps AnyPoint models will support up to 10 PCs, and the 10 Mbps products will support up to 25 PCs. The AnyPoint home network lets you simultaneously share access to the Internet across multiple PCs, even if only one con-nected PC has a broadband Internet connection, like a DSL or cable modem.

In addition to the products described above, large IT companies like Compaq, Linksys, and IBM have also started to ship families of products that are based on HomePNA.

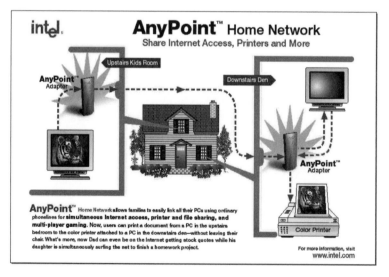

Figure 4.4
Intel's AnyPoint network. (Courtesy of Intel Corporation)

SUMMARY ....

As the number of multiple-PC homes increases, more and more home users are looking for an easy way to network their PCs. With a home network, all PCs have access to the best printer; all PCs can access the Internet at the same time through one Internet account; all PCs can access and share files; and home users can even enjoy multiplayer games. Phone-line–based networking has emerged as one of the most viable, economical approaches to PC networking in the home. Phone lines offer consumers an established in-home wiring system for networking devices in different parts of the house by transmitting data between multiple phone jacks within the home. Phone-line technology currently leads the "no new wiring" technologies in product development (with existing products ranging from 1 to 10 Mbps).

An organization called HomePNA is promoting the adoption of a single, unified phone-line networking industry standard to rapidly bring to market a range of interoperable home networking solutions. Founded in June 1998, HomePNA has grown to include nearly 130 members spanning the networking, telecommunications, hardware, software, and consumer electronics industries. HomePNA has defined a standard specification that simplifies the implementation of a home network over residential phone lines. HomePNA's technology allows computers, peripherals, and other information appliances to connect with each other and the Internet without interrupting standard telephone service. Utilizing existing telephone wiring, it requires no costly or disruptive rewiring of the home. HomePNA utilizes a technology known as Frequency Division Multiplexing (FDM), which essentially divides the data travelling over the phone lines into separate frequencies—one for voice, one for high-bandwidth net access such as DSL, and one for the network data. These frequencies can coexist on the same telephone line without impacting one another.

5 LonWorks Home Control and Automation

In this chapter...

The home automation market is growing at a tremendous pace. There are about 40,000 new homes constructed in the United States each year with a value of more than $1 million, and market research firm Parks Associates estimates that about 80 percent are installing some form of intelligent electronic control system.

So what is home automation? There are numerous answers to this question, but they all are based on one fundamental concept—consumer requirements and expectations have changed dramatically in the past decade. Let's look at a modern home as an example. A fully automated lighting system ties all the lights, dimmers, and switches to an underlying home network. Electricians no longer need to worry about individually wiring switches to lights, and consumers don't have to be concerned about changing lighting requirements within the home. Additional cost savings are also gained by the fact that lights automatically shut themselves off based on occupancy and/or pre-set schedules. In the intelligent homes of the future, your lighting system will harmoniously work with the following subsystems to create new levels of comfort, convenience, and safety:

- Security and alarm system
- Heating subsystem
- Ventilation
- Air conditioning
- Fire alarm subsystem

This chapter describes a popular home automation system called LonWorks. This system includes all the necessary hardware and software components for implementing complete end-to-end control systems.

THE LONWORKS SYSTEM.................................

Echelon Corporation is the developer of LonWorks technology, recognized internationally as a standard for interoperable control networks. The LonWorks system is a networked automation and control solution for the building, industrial, transportation, and home markets.

In a LonWorks network, no central control or master-slave architecture is needed. Intelligent control devices, called *nodes*, communicate with one another using a common protocol. Each node in the network contains embedded intelligence that implements the protocol and performs control functions. In addition, each node includes a physical interface (transceiver) that couples the node *microcontroller* with the communications medium. A microcontroller is best described as a highly integrated chip that has been designed to perform very specific tasks.

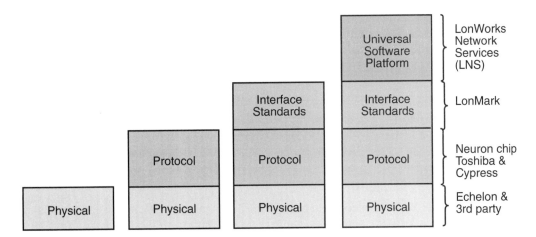

Figure 5.1
LonWorks software components

A typical node in a LonWorks control network performs a simple task. Devices such as proximity sensors, switches, motion detectors, and sprinkler systems may all be nodes on a home network. The architecture of a LonWorks software stack is illustrated in Figure 5.1 and explained in the following sections.

LonTalk Protocol

Devices on a LonWorks-enabled home network use a protocol to communicate with each other. This protocol is known as *LonTalk* and has been approved as an open industry standard by the American National Standards Institute (ANSI)—EIA 709.1.

In addition to the ANSI/EIA 709.1 standard, the following standard bodies also approve Echelon's networking communication protocol:

- The Institute of Electrical and Electronics Engineers (IEEE)
- The American Society of Heating, Refrigeration and Air Conditioning Engineers (ASHRAE)
- Association of American Railroads (AAR)
- International Forecourt Standards Forum (IFSC)
- Semiconductor Equipment and Materials International (SEMI)
- The European Committee for Standardization (CEN)

Protocols today are generally designed to follow the OSI reference model, which encompasses a full set of protocol features, and classifies them according to seven functional categories (referred to as "layers"). The LonTalk protocol implements all seven layers of the OSI model. Features include media access, transaction acknowledgment, peer-to-peer communication, and more advanced services such as sender authentication, priority transmissions, duplicate message detection, collision avoidance, automatic retries, mixed data rates, client-server support, foreign frame transmission, data type standardization and identification, unicast/multicast/broadcast addressing, mixed media support, and error detection and recovery.

The LonTalk protocol offers two principal reliability techniques. Reliable delivery is ensured by true end-to-end acknowledgments, made possible by a full OSI-based protocol. Data integrity is guaranteed by the fact that *all* packet transmissions incorporate a full 16-bit error polynomial (as opposed to parity or a checksum). Additionally, transceivers for difficult media (i.e., with high noise and attenuation) incorporate forward error correction; they are able to detect and correct single-bit errors without retransmission. An integral part of the protocol used in LonWorks networks is its unique media access technique, termed "predictive p-persistent CSMA, with optional priority and collision detection." It provides linear response to offered traffic load, predictable response time for heavily loaded networks, and consistent performance independent of network size.

The LonTalk protocol is embedded in every neuron chip, a microcontroller specifically designed to offer a cost-effective solution for network-enabling and embedding intelligence into home control devices. Each neuron chip contains:

- Three 8-bit, in-line CPUs
- On-board memory (RAM, ROM, and EEPROM)
- At least eleven general purpose I/O pins
- A complete, interoperable implementation of the LonTalk protocol

The neuron chip contains self-test circuitry, three watchdog timers, and a variety of diagnostic features such as a continuous EEPROM memory corruption check.

In addition to neuron chips, the EIA 709.1 control-networking standard allows developers to implement LonTalk on any processor. The neuron chip, which is the enabling technology for, and the core component of, each and every LonWorks node, is manufactured and sold worldwide by Cypress Semiconductor and Toshiba.

LonWorks Network Services Software Architecture

The LonWorks Network Services (LNS) is a powerful platform for installing, upgrading, and interacting with home-controlled networks. The availability of high-quality networks tools is a key benefit of LonWorks technology. A *network tool* is any tool that installs, diagnoses, or maintains devices on a LonWorks network, or that monitors and controls a LonWorks system. These tools make control networks easier to install, operate, and maintain than conventional control systems. The result is lower-cost systems.

End users are demanding more automated tools that are tailored to their application. Automated tools can be viewed as plug-and-play for LonWorks networks. The installer should be able to just physically plug in devices and have them configure themselves with minimal or no user interaction. Failed devices should be easily identified and replaced by a maintenance technician, with replacement devices automatically taking on the application and network configuration of the failed device.

The LNS architecture (see Figure 5.2) provides network services as collections of objects, each with methods, properties, and events. Methods are used to invoke services on objects. For example, methods are used to commission a device or bind a net-

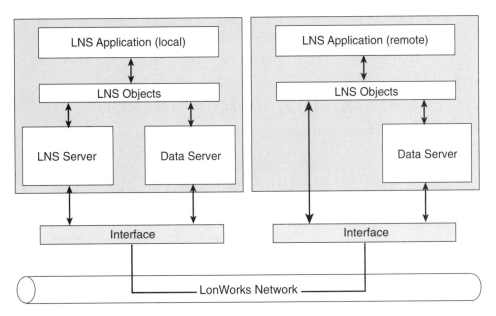

Figure 5.2
LNS architecture

work variable connection. Properties are used to read or write data parameters within objects. For example, a property can be used to get or set the state of a device. Events are used to inform applications of significant occurrences such as the receipt of a service pin message. LNS objects are accessed using a client-server architecture. Clients make network service requests of a server which performs the service and notifies the client when it is complete. Standard network services are provided by a single network services server, but application-specific services can be provided by application servers. Each application may provide its own application server. For example, a building control system may have separate application servers for the HVAC system, lighting system, and security system.

LONWORKS AND THE INTERNET ....

LonWorks control networks can be easily integrated with the Internet. This built-in capability allows for seamless networking between IP-based devices and control devices. Home appliances can be monitored and controlled remotely through standard Web browsers.

Echelon is working with Cisco to ensure the seamless integration of control and data networks. The i.LON 1000 Internet Server is the first product resulting from this partnership, providing level 3 routing between LonWorks networks and IP networks (i.e., the Internet). It also includes a Web server that can be used to provide visual feedback to remote users. Control parameters are served and embedded by the i.LON within the Web pages automatically.

LONWORKS AND OTHER HOME CONTROL INITIATIVES ....

There are currently several industry initiatives intended to enable total home networking. These include Microsoft's Universal Plug and Play (UPnP), Sun Microsystems' Jini, as well as Open Services Gateway Initiative (OSGi).

The LonWorks platform allows these initiatives to incorporate control and automation networking in their suite of offerings. It is clear that including an IP stack or a Java Virtual Machine (JVM) in light-weight devices such as those found in home control and automation networks (e.g., switches) is not practical (for both economical and technical reasons). LonWorks allows these higher-end networks (IP, UPnP, and Jini) to tap into the control networking space and seamlessly interact with light-weight devices.

DEVELOPING LONWORKS HOME CONTROL APPLICATIONS...

There are two development tools available for the LonWorks platform, the LonBuilder and the NodeBuilder. The LonBuilder Developer's Workbench integrates a complete set of tools for developing LonWorks-based nodes and systems. These tools include an environment for developing and debugging applications at multiple nodes, a network manager to install and configure these nodes, and a protocol analyzer to examine network traffic to ensure adequate network capacity and to debug errors. The LonBuilder tool can be assembled in various configurations, with a range of essential and optional tools. The NodeBuilder Development Tool makes it easy and inexpensive for manufacturers to design and test individual nodes for LonWorks-based control networks. It uses a familiar Windows-based development environment with easy-to-use on-line help. For large development teams, the NodeBuilder tool can complement the development capabilities of the LonBuilder Developer's Workbench. Each engineer can use a NodeBuilder tool to develop individual nodes that are integrated and tested as a system using the LonBuilder tool.

LonMark Interoperability Association

Supported by a who's-who of controls companies, the LonMark Association counts among its members not only the manufacturers fuelling the home networking revolution but also the end users, equipment specifiers, and system integrators driving its implementation. The LonMark Association's mission is to enable the easy integration of multivendor systems based on LonWorks networks using standard tools and components. Today over 4,000 companies are using Echelon's LonWorks platform to provide systems and solutions for building, home, industrial, telecommunications, transportation, and other industries. There are over 6 million LonWorks-based appliances installed worldwide. The association provides an open forum for member companies to work together on marketing and technical programs to advance the LonMark standard for open interoperable solutions.

The association has three major functions:

- Promotion of LonMark products and systems as open interoperable control solutions

- Recommendation of design guidelines for interoperable devices based on LonWorks

- Verification of products that meet the LonMark guidelines for interoperability

The association develops and maintains technical design guidelines to help manufacturers build interoperable LonMark products based on Echelon's LonWorks platform. Products that have been verified to conform to LonMark interoperability guidelines are eligible to carry the LonMark logo.

BENEFITS OF LONWORKS TECHNOLOGY...............

Echelon's LonWorks solution is used by OEMs, installers, and service providers to provide better products, systems, and services at a lower overall cost to their customers. Ultimately all players involved, including the homeowner, gain from this open, interoperable platform.

Benefits for Manufacturers

In addition to expanding their market reach, the LonWorks solution offers everything device manufacturers need to embed communications and control technology into home products.

- **Off-the-shelf parts**—Echelon provides small control components and software APIs—a palette of tools and solutions to pick and choose from—and they're ready to be designed into home products from thermostats to television sets.

- **Low cost**—Advanced manufacturing techniques have lowered the cost of every part. Increasing volume means neuron chips are low-cost now and will continually come down in price, thanks to the combined usage by the aggregate markets.

- **Quick time to market**—Fast and easy-to-use development tools save months of development time and lead to increased revenue because products get to market sooner.

- **Openness**—In addition to being a de facto standard, with over 6 million LonWorks-based devices installed all around the world, LonWorks technology is endorsed by several standards organizations, including EIA/CEMA.

Benefits for Service Providers

Utility and telecommunication deregulation translates into increased choices for homeowner to pick their services from. Consequently, utility and telecommunication companies are under more pressure to create new revenue streams while simultaneously reducing customer churn. The LonWorks system provides an open platform for new services to be offered by utilities and telcos that can work with the existing and future products from manufacturers.

Benefits for Home Automation Installers

LonWorks uses existing power lines in homes as a dependable and robust communications medium. The result is dramatically lower installation costs.

Benefits for Homeowners

Any product with the LonMark can work as part of a LonWorks control system, no matter who made the product and who installed the system. That includes dishwashers, hot-water heaters, thermostats, security keypads, and air conditioners.

LONWORKS CASE STUDIES ....

Home Appliance Automation

Italy-based multinational Merloni Elettrodomestici, a leading European home appliance manufacturer, offers a new group of home products that use Echelon's LonWorks system to communicate with one another in the home and through the Internet to the outside world. The Ariston Digital marks the first commercial availability of "smart" appliances that work together to be easier to use, more reliable, and at lower cost to own. The Ariston Digital product family includes refrigerators, dishwashers, washing machines, and other home appliances, as well as a multimedia, interactive, touchscreen home smart monitor that tracks the performance of all domestic appliances, while facilitating access to the Internet.

The use of LonWorks technology makes the Ariston Digital products easy to install and use (plug and play). No complex network configuration is required, and no new wires need to be installed. To connect a new appliance to the network, the homeowner just plugs it in. The intelligence is distributed in each appliance, eliminating the need for a central computer to process the data and control the appliances. All Ariston Digital appliances communicate with each other by exchanging information through the home's power mains using Echelon's powerline communications transceivers, eliminating the need for new wires. Embedded intelligence in each appliance enables each device to be constantly "aware" of how much power is being consumed in the home and to regulate the consumption accordingly to avoid the risk of a circuit overload or blackout. Should a circuit overload threaten, the appliances are able to decide which one should be given priority; for example, the washing machine over the oven.

This built-in intelligence and new sensors developed by Merloni also allow each appliance to supply better performance with lower consumption of resources like power and water. For example, an appliance can lower power costs by shifting its electricity usage to off-peak, lower-cost hours. Ariston Digital appliances communicate to the outside world via the Internet. Each appliance can regularly transmit information to the assistance center on its running conditions or to indicate possible faults, enabling the assistance center to act more rapidly and to provide a more accurate diagnosis of the problem. For example, in the case of a prolonged power outage, the transmission of an alarm can safeguard the food stored in the freezer compartment. Each appliance also maintains and analyzes important status information (washing or cooking cycles, power consumption, repairs, etc.) to optimize its own performance and to perform proactive troubleshooting. This information can also be used by the service center to perform remote diagnostics for any possible repairs quickly and accurately.

Apartment Building Automation

Life in France gets better every day; more and more "smart" apartment buildings are opening their doors. These state-of-the-art complexes provide convenience and safety to multitenant-building dwellers, plus control infrastructure necessary to building management and service suppliers. SILD, a joint venture of Schlumberger Industries and Lyonnaise des Eaux-Dumez, began automating such buildings in 1992. Meeting requirements for automated comfort control, energy management, indoor and outdoor communications, remote meter reading, plus access control and other security features, demanded a flexible, yet low-cost technology. SILD had less than a year to develop and deploy systems, in order to fend off competition from two government-subsidized contenders. LonWorks technology was selected as the basis for the new building control solution, dubbed "TIPI."

The TIPI product line today consists of four different LonWorks-based control modules: a building module, governing the whole building; a technical module, providing remote access to equipment; a doorway module, for access security; and a housing module, to control individual apartment environments. The key element in every module is a neuron chip, integrating three microprocessors, memory, interface electronics, operating system, and a seven-layer communication protocol, to help ensure interoperability among the TIPI building blocks. It all begins with the TIPI housing module, an aesthetically pleasing and user-friendly device installed in individual apartments. This module offers a variety of services such as temperature management, voice messages, a simulated occupancy function, antiintrusion alarm, distress calls, a hands-free intercom, and environmental fault detection, all from a single control point. Outside each building entrance is a TIPI doorway module, a waterproof, fireproof, shockproof, tamperproof unit permitting direct communication with individual apartments. It incorporates a keypad for entering a personal entry code, issuing system commands, and searching residents' names to select and call specific parties. It also houses a closed circuit video camera for remote observation and controls entrance-hall lighting. Individual occupants can determine those persons allowed to enter, as well as selecting free access periods. Such functions contribute to improvements in both resident security and property protection for building owners. The TIPI building module provides the overall system with a centralized data management service and monitoring site. Designed as a rugged, high-availability component, it receives, stores, and sends voice messages for the residents; monitors the building's overall network operation; manages external communication; creates and updates logbooks for the manager, residents, and suppliers; and processes and transmits alarms. The fourth component, the TIPI technical module, allows remote access to such building services as monitoring, network management, and maintenance of technical equipment, often a key to reducing costs and improving comfort and security. Service providers can remotely access heating systems, elevators, utility meters (water, gas, electricity), and the like. Due to the variety in both type and location of such hardware, the technical module is designed as a simple and rugged unit that can be installed close to the equipment yet still be connected to the network. All TIPI services are available from the moment a resident moves in.

The TIPI solution has succeeded in both the new construction and retrofit markets, in traditional residential buildings and those designed for students or the elderly. Its use of LonWorks technology guarantees the flexibility necessary for fast customized designs. It also means being able to keep costs low, staying abreast of technological evolution, and taking advantage of a host of existing peripherals and software programs.

SUMMARY ....

With millions of devices already installed worldwide and thousands of application developers, LonWorks technology is a leading cross-industry standard for the networking of everyday devices in homes, buildings, factories, and transportation systems. LonWorks technology enables the myriad of everyday devices around us—from the light switches in homes, to occupancy sensors in office buildings, to the valves in factories, to the automatic doors in subway cars—to be made "intelligent" and to communicate with one another. In addition, the complete end-to-end networking platform offered allows for extending the home control network beyond the home via the Internet, thereby allowing service providers to leverage the devices in the home by offering new and dynamic services.

6 Powerline-Based Home Networks

In this chapter...

Powerline-based home networking is an emerging technology that allows consumers to use their existing electrical wiring system to link appliances to each other and to the Internet. Home networks that use high-speed powerline technology can control anything that plugs into an outlet, including lights, televisions, thermostats, and alarms. The most popular powerline technologies are explained in this chapter.

INTRODUCTION TO POWERLINE COMMUNICATIONS ....

For several decades, researchers have attempted to use AC powerlines to create a communications network. Since almost all electronic devices already connect to AC powerlines for the electricity they need to operate, it seems only logical to develop a technology that would send data signals over the same wires. Considering that a vast majority of people in the world, even in developing areas, already live in homes with pervasive access to electrical outlets, such a technology would provide a quantum leap forward in the mass-market proliferation of IT and communications products. Using electrical wires seems logical and efficient. Traditional communications networks, such as phone lines, cable television, and computer data networks, use dedicated wiring designed specifically for communicating information. Powerline networks, on the other hand, were designed to deliver electricity, not data signals. This difference is not trivial. The highly variable and unpredictable levels of impedance, signal attenuation, and noise combine to create an extremely harsh environment that make high-speed data transmissions over powerlines very challenging.

The following sections provide an overview of these technical obstacles and present some of the strategies that different developers are using to overcome them. But first, we will define the powerline network and present a background of how this industry has developed.

Industry Background

The powerline is not an ideal environment for data communications. Historically, it has proven much easier to modify the existing phone-line and cable networks for the modern needs of a digital economy. By upgrading portions of those networks with new digital communications equipment, the same copper phone lines and coaxial cable lines can be used for transmitting high-speed data traffic. Although it is easier for companies to upgrade existing wiring, phone and cable wiring is not as widespread as electrical networks, especially outside of the United States. And while phone and cable networks might be effective at bringing Internet access to the home, they do not provide networks *within* the home. In the near future, having ubiquitous access points within the home will be increasingly important, especially with the proliferation of non-PC devices, or *information appliances*. And although wireless technology will be needed for battery-powered mobile devices, the majority of devices in the home remain stationary and connected to the AC powerline network. It is for these reasons that high-speed powerline technology represents one of the most important hurdles in the world of communications and computing. But why weren't powerline technologies available earlier? The next sections explore the powerline network and the inherent obstacles that the medium presents.

Defining the Powerline Data Network

In conventional terms, the powerline connects the home to the electric utility company in order to supply power to the building. But powerline communications falls into two distinct categories: *access* and *in-home*. *Access* powerline technologies send data over the low-voltage electric networks that connect the home to the electric utility provider. The powerline access technologies enable a "last mile" local loop solution that provides individual homes with broadband connectivity to the Internet. *In-home* powerline technology communicates data exclusively *within* the consumer's premises and extends to all of the electrical outlets within the home. The same electric outlets that provide power will also serve as access points for the network devices. Although the access and in-home solutions both send data signals over the powerlines, they are fundamentally different technologies. Whereas the access technologies discussed in Chapter 3 focus on delivering a long-distance solution, competing with xDSL and broadband cable technologies, the in-home powerline technologies focus on delivering a short-distance high-bandwidth solution (10 Mbps) that would compete against other in-home LAN technologies, such as phone line and wireless.

We will limit the discussion of powerline technology to the following definition of the in-home powerline network. The in-home powerline network, shown in Figure 6.1, consists of everything interconnecting through power outlets, including:

- House wiring inside of the building
- Appliance wiring (power cords)
- The appliances themselves (load devices)
- The circuit breaker

POWERLINE MODEM TECHNOLOGY......................

Communicating data over the powerline, just like in any other analog medium, requires some type of modulation device, or modem, that can transmit and receive data

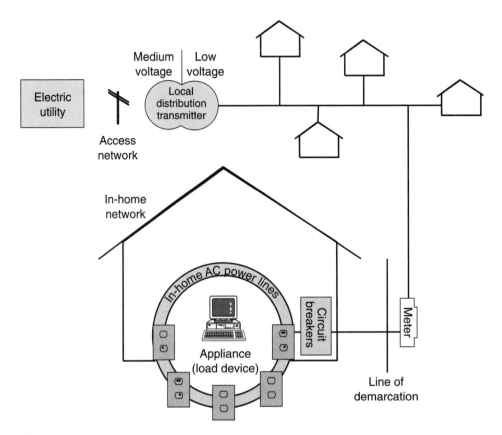

Figure 6.1
In-home powerline network

signals. In order to turn a powerline electric network into a data communications net-work, a transceiver must be used to transmit the data from the device across the pow-erline medium. Thus the transceiver sends and receives digital data in analog form using the electrical outlets that it is connected to.

Similar to other home network technologies, such as phone line and wireless, these transceiver nodes will take the form of microchips that will be embedded direct-ly into next-generation computers and smart devices. But first generation powerline network products will have to provide backward compatibility for devices that were not originally designed for powerline communications.

Wall modules containing powerline transceivers will likely be the first products on the market. These small devices could plug into an electrical outlet and replicate the sockets, similar to a power strip, but with an embedded powerline transceiver. The wall modules couple the device to the electrical network using a standardized communications input interface, like a USB or Ethernet port. This way even traditional devices, like desktop PCs with Ethernet cards, will communicate with one another over the powerline.[1] In such a configuration, different network devices could share data, control one another, and access each other's resources. But to facilitate these applications, the network's communication throughput must be high enough to reduce noticeable time delays, especially when the network environment is noisy. The following section addresses some of the key technical obstacles that have made powerline communications so difficult.

TECHNICAL OBSTACLES OF IN-HOME POWERLINE NETWORKS ....

Typical data and communications networks (like corporate LANs) use dedicated wiring to interconnect devices. But powerline networks, from their inception, were never intended for transmitting data. Instead the networks were optimized to efficiently distribute power to all the electrical outlets throughout a building at frequencies typically between 50 to 60 Hz. Thus, the original designs of electrical networks never considered using the powerline medium for communicating data signals at other frequencies. For this reason, the powerline is a more difficult communications medium than other types of isolated wiring like the Category 5 cabling used in Ethernet data networks.

The physical topology of the electrical network, the physical properties of the electrical cabling, the appliances connected, and the behavioral characteristics of the electric current itself all combine to create technical obstacles.

Signal Attenuation, Impedance, and Appliance Loading

Attenuation describes how the signal strength decreases and loses energy as it transmits across a medium. In the powerline environment, the amount of attenuation that a signal experiences is primarily a function of the signal frequency and the distance it must travel on the wire. However, recent field studies show that attenuation is also affected by other factors, including appliance loading and impedance discontinuities.

---

1. In this case, two computers in a home could be networked together connecting their RJ45 cables from the Ethernet card into two wall modules that would then stream the Ethernet data across the powerline. Later versions would most likely involve embedding the powerline transceiver directly onto the motherboard of the PC, effectively eliminating the need for an Ethernet card and Cat5 cabling altogether. Instead the data would stream over the same cord that the computer uses to draw power.

Distance between Socket Links • As a signal travels across a wire, it inevitably loses energy. Attenuation increases as a function of the distance the signal must travel on the wire. In other words, the signal gets weaker the farther it must travel between the transmitting and receiving devices.

Frequency • Generally, the higher the frequency of the carrier, the greater the attenuation.

Impedance Discontinuities • Impedance refers to the resistance in flow of the alternating current (AC) in an electrical circuit. Impedance discontinuities, caused by wire nuts, switches, wall socket outlets and their appliance loads, create nulls, or spectrum "suckouts." Wall sockets create a problem both as unterminated network points (when there is no device connected) and as appliance loading points (when there is a device connected).

Network Load • The network load is determined by the number and type of appliances that are connected to the electrical network in relation to the network's overall size. All of the electric devices in a consumer's home, like televisions, lamps, washing machines, and other appliances, combine to change the impedance of the network at various points. Even devices that are not operating and consuming electricity still inhibit the network's performance because they load the line both resistively and reactively, causing impedance mismatches that dissipate the energy of the signal as it travels across the network. New impedance mismatches are created every time a device is plugged in or out of the network. All of these factors combine to create the network load, which causes increased signal attenuation across the overall topology of the network.

Real-World Attenuation Scenarios

Overcoming signal attenuation is important for developing marketable products since a consumer may want to network two devices located at opposite sides of their home. If the signal attenuates excessively these devices may not be able to communicate at all, rendering the technology ineffective. But in order to successfully address the problem of attenuation it is necessary to first understand some of the interrelated variables that affect how signals attenuate in real-world environments.

Attenuation as a Function of Network Loading and Home Size

Since attenuation increases with distance, it seems logical to assume that larger homes, with greater average distances between socket links, would present greater attenuation problems. But field research shows that this is not necessarily the case. This is because the powerline networks tend to be less "loaded" in larger homes due to the fact that in larger homes there are more circuits with a similar number of household appliances connected.

For example, imagine a family moving into a home twice the size of their previous home. It is unlikely that they will furnish their home with twice as many appliances as their previous home (they probably wouldn't purchase an additional refrigerator and washing machine). Thus, given the same quantity of appliances, the overall network load per circuit in a larger home may actually be lower than that of a smaller home. As a result, the increase in attenuation caused by distance in the larger home may in fact be offset by the lower levels of each circuit's load.

Attenuation as a Function of Network Loading and Transmission Frequency

Another consideration is that not all signals attenuate equally. For example, a high frequency signal will attenuate more rapidly than a low frequency signal that is transmitted over the same length of wire. The first graph in Figure 6.2 shows that the wire attenuation of a signal (caused by distance) will be greater if the signal is transmitted at higher frequency levels.

As previously stated, appliance loading is a primary cause of signal attenuation. But the amount of attenuation caused by a given appliance load will also vary with respect to the transmission frequency of the signal. The second graph in Figure 6.2 demonstrates that the attenuation from appliance loading actually *decreases* at higher frequencies. This is due to the fact that most appliances have capacitive filters that significantly limit signals in lower frequencies. Therefore, as signal frequency increases above the limits of the capacitive filters in appliances, attenuation caused by appliance loading decreases. The final graph in Figure 6.2 shows a real-world attenuation environment where increased wire attenuation in higher frequencies is significantly offset by appliance load attenuation in higher frequencies.

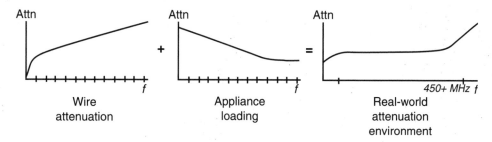

Figure 6.2
Attenuation effects

Interference and Noise Sources

In powerline communications, the term "noise" refers to any undesired signals on the wire that interfere with the data transmission of the original communications signal. The two common types of noise that affect the powerline environment are injected noise, caused by operating appliances, and steady state background noise.

Injected noise

Injected noise (also called impulse noise) results from the switching of inductive loads that produce strong impulses. The worst offenders producing injected noise are devices containing AC motors, such hair dryers, vacuum cleaners, and electric drills. When these appliances are turned on, they saturate the powerline with violent spikes of noise that defeat many communication methods (see Figure 6.3). For this reason, powerline technologies must focus on overcoming injected noise impairments.

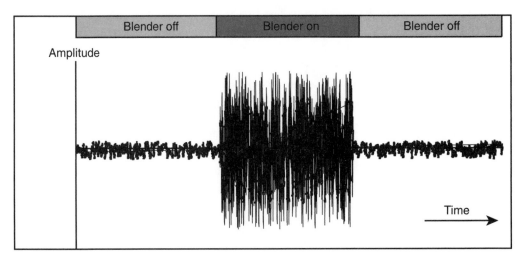

Figure 6.3
Injected noise

Background noise

Background noise (also called ambient or white noise) presents an additional impediment. This quasi-steady state of noise is caused by radio frequency interference (RFI) from noise emitters such as florescent lights that may be operating in the vicinity of the network.

Noise as a Function of Frequency

As with attenuation, the characteristics of noise interference change across different transmission frequencies. But while the attenuation problem increases at higher frequencies, the problem of noise interference decreases (see Figure 6.4). Thus the noise and attenuation problems present inevitable tradeoffs in the selection of an optimal transmission frequency band. Solving this "frequency dilemma" lies at the core of most strategies for developing a high-speed powerline solution.

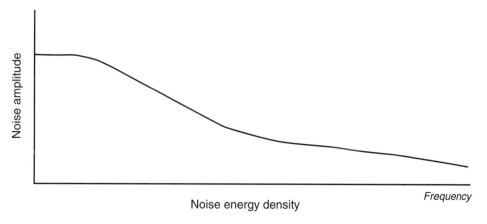

Figure 6.4
Noise as a function of frequency

The Multireflective Effect (Standing Waves)

When a beam of sunlight shines at the surface of water, some of the light will go through the water, and some of the light will reflect off the surface, bouncing in different directions to create the shimmering effect that people see. The fact that the air and water are physically different media causes part of the light beam to reflect back toward the source of the signal.

In powerline networks a similar phenomenon happens to the data signal, known as the multireflective effect. As stated previously, impedance is a measure of the resistance that the signal experiences as it travels across the wire. Just as when some of the light reflects as it passes from air to the water, some of the data signal reflects as it experiences impedance discontinuities on the wire.

The multireflective effect comes into play anytime the signal changes impedance as it crosses a medium. Unterminated network points, changes in the physical wiring structure, and jumping phases at the circuit represent common impedance discontinuities in electrical networks. The multireflective effect presents an obstacle for communications because the portion of the signal that is reflected back along the origination path can interfere with the source signal. In these cases the reflected signal creates a standing wave that may result in a null, or cancellation, of the source data signal.[2]

Fortunately, research has shown that the nulls, which appear as spectrum suckouts across certain frequencies, occur as a function of the network's topology. For example, regulations in electrical coding, like the distance between wall sockets, are consistent across the network. This makes it possible to exploit regularities and statistical characteristics to overcome certain aspects of the multireflective effect.

Demographic Variability of Electrical Networks

Just as homes vary greatly in their size and physical layout, the electrical networks that serve them also vary. The average and maximum distance between wall sockets (and subsequently node devices), the placement of the breaker panel and its effect on phase jumping, and the era of the home's electrical system vary greatly across the demographics of the American and international marketplace. Consider, for example, two homes of equal size (3000 sq. ft.); one is single story and the other is two stories. The average physical distance between outlets, and subsequently the network devices, would be much greater in the single story home, making it more susceptible to the effects of attenuation and the multipath effect. Also consider the difference between a WWII-era American home, that might have an electrical network made from aluminum wiring, and a modern home that uses copper wiring. And, as previously stated, the powerline home network inevitably extends to the power transformer. Thus, the number of homes connected to each transformer presents another consideration that varies greatly across residential demographics.

THE CRITERIA FOR TESTING POWERLINE SOLUTIONS ....

Evaluating the overall effectiveness of a given powerline solution can be difficult, considering the multitude of technical obstacles and different possible approaches for overcoming each of them. The following three criteria are typically used to benchmark the technical performance of a given powerline communications solution. To-

---

2. The multireflective effect illustrates one of the key advantages that networks using dedicated wiring possess. Isolated cabling, like Category 5 for Ethernet, provides consistent impedance across the length of the wire, making the multireflective effect irrelevant.

gether, the bit error rates (BER), the throughput levels, and the latency levels of a given solution provide a solid benchmark for its effectiveness.

Technical Criteria

Bit Error Rate (BER)

The BER quantifies the amount of data lost between the transmitter and receiver when the signal is propagated across the line. BER measurements are particularly important in powerline networks where the harsh noise environment can cause considerable loss of data packets. The BER figures provides a useful measure of the performance of different coding techniques and serve as a good initial indicator of data throughput.[3]

Throughput Levels

Nominal and effective bit rates provide an indication of a technology's overall performance in normal to noisy environments. Because the powerline is inherently so noisy, it is inevitable that the throughput varies with the characteristics of the environment. For example, when a blender (or other brush motor device) is being used it will inject significant noise onto the line, degrading the effective throughput of data. Some technologies might be completely unable to transmit data in such an environment, effectively crashing the network, while others might be able to transmit data consistently, but at much lower throughput levels.[4] This issue is considerable if you extend the blender example to all of the other devices in a home, like hair dryers, heaters, and stereos, that consumers will use without concern for their effect on the performance of the network. For this reason, both nominal and effective bit rate measurements together provide a true assessment of a technology's overall functional performance under both the ideal and noisy environments of the real world.

---

3. Although the effective and nominal throughput levels are typically a function of the Bit Error Rate levels, the level of correlation between them can vary with different technologies. For this reason they are identified as separate criteria, although they tend to be highly interdependent.

4. One of the key requirements for a home network is "dial tone" quality, whereby the network never crashes. Instead the network performance will "degrade gracefully" and bandwidth will scale down in the face of noise offenders. Thus, a high-speed network with a nominal throughput of 10 Mbps must be able to scale down to a lower effective throughput (perhaps to a minimum of 1 Mbps), which could still manage high-priority traffic even with significant environment noise. Quality of Service (QoS) features will be necessary for high-speed networks as a way of prioritizing data between devices that compete for bandwidth. For example, QoS parameters could help ensure that, in a noisy environment, the packets from a voice conversation by one user have priority over the packets of Web page downloads of another user on the same network.

Latency Levels

This metric is used to assess the time lag for data to travel between nodes (transmitter and receiver) on a network. Although the latency requirements for a home network vary depending on the applications needs, a latency level of about 10 milliseconds is necessary to support synchronous (real-time) applications, like voice telephony or video conferencing. Anything greater than this level would cause a noticeable delay that many consumers would likely find unacceptable.

Functional Criteria

While the previous criteria can help determine how effectively a product performs technically, the following attributes may be equally important for vendors and OEMs who need to formulate implementation strategies to deploy the technology into the actual consumer marketplace.

Quality of Service (QoS) Features

In the powerline environment, it is nearly impossible to maintain the throughput with noise levels that fluctuate over time. Even high-speed technologies that might attain 20 Mbps nominal throughput will be significantly reduced during periods when multiple appliances are injecting noise onto the line simultaneously. Even though such occurrences might be rare, a consumer would find it unacceptable if the network crashes. And while they may tolerate slower Web page downloads for a short period, they will not tolerate having their phone conversation break apart. For this reason, it is important that the technology allow quality of service levels to be independently assigned to each device. In this way, the data packets of a voice call would have priority over the data packets from a print job. During times when there is limited bandwidth, the QoS scheme will help sustain the higher priority applications, making the network more reliable and effective from the user's viewpoint.

REMOTE MANAGEMENT FEATURES ....

Many technology proponents believe that home networks will only penetrate the mainstream marketplace once they are deployed by service providers who use them to extend their broadband Internet connection into the home. It is entirely possible that service providers may eventually choose to redefine the lines of network demarcation to actually include the home network itself. Yet for this to happen, the service provider would need the ability to query a network that now extends all the way to the powerline transceivers embedded either into wall modules or into the devices themselves. Remote management features would need to be integrated into the transceivers in order to give network operators and service providers the option of this functionality.

One of the largest single expenses that service providers incur is the "truck roll" of dispatching a technician to the user's home for maintenance. With remote management features, intelligent "wizards" could be used to automatically configure the network and test it at periodic intervals. It would also enable the service provider to remotely query the network from a centralized customer service center. Thus, the more remote management features a powerline technology supports, the more likely it is to be adopted by service providers who are deploying broadband solutions.

IN-FIELD PRODUCT TESTING ....

In-field testing represents an important step in the development of any communications product because it helps to prove the "real-world" viability of the technology. But it is particularly important for powerline technologies, which are specifically designed to overcome the randomness and complexity of the environment.

In essence, the challenge to powerline communications is to design a product that works in an environment that was never intended for such use. In other words, sending a data signal down a copper wire that carries an electrical current is one hurdle. But it is quite a different technological challenge to produce a universal, low-cost powerline transceiver that operates reliably between all sockets links, in all homes, at all times throughout the day.

The following list highlights some of the key obstacles that a powerline technology will encounter during field trials.

Socket Links

The transceivers must be able to establish connections and maintain transmission bandwidth across all combinations of socket links in a given home. This means that signals may have to jump phases at the circuit breaker and reach opposite sides of the home without attenuating significantly.

Time Variability (Appliance Usage Cycles)

The transceivers must be able to maintain transmission bandwidth consistently over the time cycles that correspond with appliance usage. This means that bandwidth transmission must be maintained even as appliance usage varies throughout the day.

Such usage patterns may involve multiple sources of noise being injected onto the network simultaneously. (Imagine the powerline environment in a home with different family members operating a dishwasher, a blender, and a hair dryer at the same time, compared to that same home when everyone is at work or school.)

Household Demographics

The transceivers must operate across the vast majority of homes in the marketplace. This involves significant variability in size, design, and materials used for the electrical network.

Although in the past many developers were able to achieve high-speed data communications in laboratory environments, none of these technologies evolved into consumer products because they were unable to successfully pass through the stage of in-field testing. The following sections cover some of the newest advancements and innovations from developers in the powerline communications industry, which may bring products enabling speeds of 10 Mbps and beyond as soon as early 2001.

ENIKIA INCORPORATED ....

Enikia Incorporated is a privately held company headquartered in Piscataway, New Jersey. A start-up founded in 1997, Enikia quickly established itself as a technological innovator and industry leader by being the first company to publicly demonstrate that high-speed in-home powerline communications was possible. After announcing that its upcoming product line would enable speeds of up to 10 Mbps, Enikia followed up by successfully unveiling its prototype units.

Enikia's product line consists of powerline Ethernet transceiver chipsets that enable data transmission speeds of 10 Mbps and above. Device OEMs purchase Enikia's chipsets or license Enikia's intellectual property in order to embed this technology into intelligent devices. Enikia's solution makes it possible for computers, as well as other "smart" appliances, to communicate with one another over the home's electrical network.

Enikia's Research and Development Efforts

Enikia's technology team invested two years of R&D to realize their vision of an elegant home networking solution that was reliable, inexpensive, and easy for the end user to operate. During the R&D period, Enikia's team conducted in-field studies of the powerline environment, gathering research data from real-world homes throughout the United States and in international locations. These studies provided some of the following discoveries that led to Enikia's novel approach for developing a high-speed powerline solution:

- The powerline is capable of reliably transmitting a signal over a wide range of frequencies.

- Noise impairments on the line can be defeated by adapting data transmission techniques to the changing environment over time.

- A combination of wiring methods can be used to transmit high-speed data signals.

By rigorously studying the effects of noise generators and appliance loading in actual homes, the Enikia team was able to statistically model these real-world environments. This knowledge was then integrated into a protocol, called ACT, which represents the core of Enikia's solution for powerline communications.

The Noise Generator and Appliance Loading Studies

The noise generator studies characterized the properties of injected noise emitted by different generators (such as a hair dryer versus a light dimmer). These studies showed that the continuous noise injected by many appliances creates a strobing effect that equates to periodic noise spikes in the time domain. (See Figure 6.5.)

Enikia was able to statistically model the pulse widths and separation of the spikes and found that the time period between spikes offers an opportunity to transmit data across the line. To exploit this opportunity, Enikia's protocol design takes a traditional Ethernet frame, segments it into small packets, and sends them in the clear time spaces between the impulse noise spikes. On the receiving side, Enikia's protocol then reassembles the segments into the original Ethernet frame, making the segmentation and reassembly process transparent to devices connected to the network.

Enikia also discovered that a combination of different wiring methods could be used. Most powerline technologies use the hot-neutral wires only. But Enikia's studies showed that the hot-ground wires could also be used for transmitting signals, and this in fact often presented a very clean channel for communication.

In the past, higher frequencies were not considered viable for powerline communications, due to the high attenuation levels. But, Enikia's field studies showed that frequencies in excess of 100 MHz can be reliably used for homes up to 5000 sq. ft. In addition, Enikia's technology includes a repeater function that extends the reach of the network.

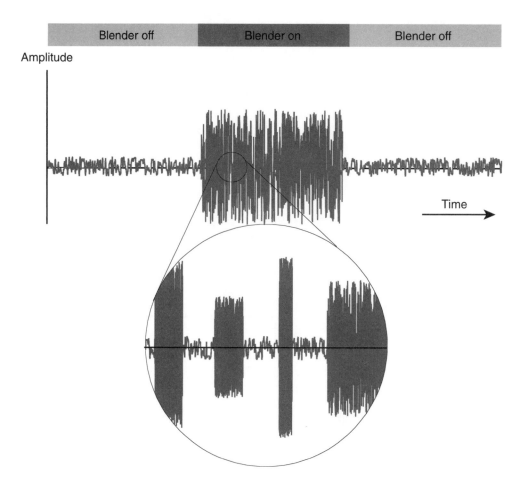

Figure 6.5
Effect of continuous injected noise

In the United States, the FCC imposes limits on the amount of energy that can be injected on the powerline at different frequencies. The main purpose of this is to protect the rights of licensed spectrum users from interference from unintentional radiation. Enikia's signal was tested within the FCC-imposed energy limits and showed that a signal could exist on the powerline in a wide variety of frequencies without interfering with licensed users.

Development of Enikia Core Technology

The beginning of this chapter identified the powerline environment as an extremely difficult communications environment. Background noise from outside interferers, injected noise from in-home appliances, multireflective effects, and widespread signal attenuation are the primary impairments to communications. Enikia engineered a powerline technology, embodied in the following components, that addresses each obstacle and enables high-speed communications even in the harshest environments.

- **The protocol processor**—The protocol processor runs Enikia's ACT protocol and SST token-passing scheme.
- **The DSP modem**—Enikia's DSP modem is comprised of 16 digital channels and employs DBPSK and DQPSK selectively according to channel conditions.
- **The analog RF front end**—Enikia employs a low-cost simple analog design to couple the protocol processor and DSP modem to the powerline.

Figure 6.6 illustrates, and the following sections detail, these major elements of Enikia's technology.

ACT Protocol Overview

ACT stands for Adaptive to Channel and Time. The protocol consists of a frequency dimension, which evaluates the environment and determines the frequencies that provide the clearest path for the signal. It also includes a time dimension, which allows the signal to adapt to the ever-changing conditions on the powerline.

When viewing impulse noise on an oscilloscope, it appears as lightning strikes, where there is a clear space between every impulse. Since the noise is narrow, the network is clear for a time period between the noise spikes. In the same way that WWI planes used to shoot their machine guns time-synchronized with the rotation of their propeller blades, Enikia is able to send short packets through the clear spaces in between the impulse noise strikes. These short bursts of data are delivered very quickly.

The ACT protocol uses an environmental detector called the Received Signal Strength Indicator circuit (RSSI). This circuit aids the transmitter in identifying the beginning of a "clear" time interval as the preferred instance to launch the data across the wire. Thus, the data has a better chance of avoiding noise and maintaining a reliable link.

The ACT protocol also uses techniques to sense the density of noise on the line and adjusts the packet size and error-correction schemes accordingly. Enikia calls

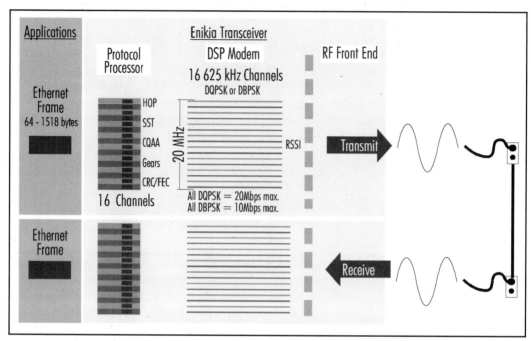

Figure 6.6
Enikia's technology components

these different packet sizes *gears* since they are representative of shifting gears in a car depending on the conditions of the road. By varying the packet size in each gear, the communication throughput is optimized.

Under extreme noise conditions, the ACT protocol employs lower gears containing extensive error correction and small packets to fit in between the noise spikes. As the noise environment becomes less volatile, the ACT protocol shifts to higher, more efficient gears with larger packets sizes and less error correction.

The technology also uses up to 16 channels in parallel over a 20 MHz range. The channels adapt to the changing environment, and only the channels that communicate clearly are used at any given instant. For example, all 16 channels may be communicating at once, delivering a full 20 Mbps between transceivers. But when noise is present, a spike may flow through the 20 MHz range and eliminate the use of a few channels. The ACT protocol adapts the flow of data by eliminating certain channels, changing to a shorter packet length, changing its modulation technique, and slowing the speed of transmission so that a reliable link is maintained.

Enikia employs an additional technique, known as HOP (Historically Oriented Preference), which allows two transceivers with a poor communication link to reroute their signal through a third transceiver. HOP relates to how XCVR A and XCVR B might use another XCVR as a kind of repeater if taking that path offers better communications. HOP uses historical data to make decisions about which path through the network is best. Since powerline networks can vary greatly moment-by-moment or in a certain daily or weekly cycle, keeping this information is valuable.

By frequently evaluating the environment on the powerline, and establishing a mode of communication based on the state of the communications medium, Enikia's ACT protocol succeeds in making the network reliable.

Secure Sparse Token (SST)

The protocol processor also runs a Medium Access Protocol called Enikia's Secure Sparse Token (SST) token-passing scheme for Quality of Service considerations. The SST scheme was specifically designed for the powerline environment due to its quick token regeneration, special priority of token passing, and robustness for real-time data priorities.

Enikia's SST algorithm is based on the IEEE 802.4 token bus protocol, which has been modified by Enikia for the powerline environment.

In general, token bus offers some unique properties that are a good match for the home networking environment:

- Short token-passing times for home networks (characterized by a small diameter)
- Different levels of priorities for data
- Deterministic delay properties
- Contention-free environment
- Reduction in peak signal levels due to lack of contention

In addition, the SST provides several features that are especially desirable and often critical for the home network powerline environment. For example, the SST supports local, small-size (7-bit) addresses, as economical fronts for full-size (48-bit) Ethernet addresses. However, all nodes are aware of both (local and Ethernet) addresses of the other nodes in the network. For networks that use Ethernet hubbing, SST supports full addressing of the nodes that may reside in a network section behind a hub.

Further, to increase the efficiency of communicating nodes on the network, SST allow inactive nodes to drop out of the token passing scheme. This allows only the currently active and communicating nodes to "join" in a conversation, decreasing latency and increasing available bandwidth.

In addition, SST allows the active ring to become totally silent, eliminating token passing entirely, when no node is active. Security is addressed by using very secure three-way handshaking for token passing, and efficiency is addressed by using small control frames (approximately 30 milliseconds).

Digital DSP Modem

Enikia's DSP was designed to accomplish the following objectives:

- Be able to fit symbols in between noise spikes by utilizing fast symbol rates
- Defeat "nulls" by using narrow channel widths
- Utilize a minimum number of channels to achieve low production cost

Taking these criteria into account, Enikia engineered its DSP with channels using swift symbol rates to take advantage of the impulse noise time domain spaces, narrow channels to accept and conquer extremely deep nulls, and a limited number of channels to keep the DSP inexpensive for consumer applications.

Further, the design overcomes narrowband interferers. Most narrowband interference will only affect a single channel, rather than affecting multiple carriers or the entire signal.

The DSP Modem also implements two modulation schemes: DBPSK and DQPSK. These are used selectively according to the varying powerline environments. Under the harshest SNR (signal-to-noise ratio), the modem uses DBPSK because of its high resiliency to noise. But when signal-to-noise ratios improve, the modulation scheme switches to DQPSK for increased efficiency, doubling the potential throughput. Therefore Enikia's technology is able to balance the tradeoffs between throughput and reliability as channel conditions fluctuate. Future versions of Enikia's technology are able to employ even more efficient versions of quadrature amplitude modulation (QAM), allowing more bits per Hz and greater throughput.

Analog RF Front End

Enikia uses a low-cost, simple analog design for its RF front end. Since the DSP is responsible for the channel signal processing, Enikia only had to include a single A/D, D/A in its design. The efficiencies of the ACT protocol allow Enikia to inject low power onto the line, and therefore, the RF front end is able to use these three bands: low band (2 to 30 MHz), mid band (108 to 174 MHz), and high band (216 to 470

MHz). Even though the mid and high bands are more efficient radiators, the low injected power keeps Enikia's signal well within FCC guidelines for such frequencies.

Because of the spectrum available in these three bands, future Enikia products will offer very high throughput communications, allowing multichannel video distribution, and other very high bandwidth applications. Further, since the RF front end's design is so simple and uses relatively few components, it allows easy design of an analog semiconductor.

X-10 ....

X-10 is a communications protocol that allows compatible home networking products to talk to each other via the existing electrical wiring in the home. Basic X-10 powerline technology is almost 20 years old and was initially developed to integrate with low-cost lighting and appliance control devices. X-10 originally started out as unidirectional only; however, capability has recently been added for bidirectional communication if needed. Nevertheless, the vast majority of X-10 communication remains unidirectional.

X-10 controllers send signals over existing AC wiring to receiver modules. The X-10 modules are adapters that connect to outlets and control simple devices. X-10 powerline technology transmits binary data using an amplitude modulation (AM) technique. To differentiate the symbols, the carrier uses the zero-voltage crossing point of the 60 Hz AC sine wave on the cycle's positive or negative transition. The zero-crossing point usually has the least noise and interference from other devices on the powerline. Synchronized receivers accept the carrier at each zero-crossing point. To reduce errors, X-10 requires two zero crossings to transmit either a zero or a one. Therefore, every bit requires a full 60 hertz cycle and thus the X-10 transmission rate is limited to only 60 bps. A complete X-10 command consists of two packets with a 3-cycle gap between each packet. Each packet contains two identical messages of 11 bits (or 11 cycles) each. Therefore, a complete X-10 command consumes 47 cycles that yields a transmission time of about .8 seconds. Using X-10 it is possible to control lights and virtually any other electrical device from anywhere in the house with no additional wiring. The X-10 technology and resource forum designs, develops, manufactures, and markets products that are based on this standard. Today, scores of manufacturers make X-10-compatible products that, at $10 to $30, scarcely cost more than their incompatible counterparts; according to the X-10 group, more than 100 million such products have been sold. These home automation products are called "powerline carrier" (PLC) devices and are often installed by builders who want to offer home automation as an additional selling feature. The home automation line consists of "controllers" that automatically send signals over existing electric power wiring to receiver "modules," which in turn control lights, appliances, heating and air conditioning units, etc. With the X-10 standard, you can literally walk into a nearby electronics store and purchase all of the necessary equipment to automate your home with the X-10 standard. The main disadvantage for legacy X-10 technology is that it has very limited capability in terms of both speed and intelligence. It is a technology relegated to *control applications* only because of its low data rate and rudimentary functionality.

INTELLON CEBUS ....

Intellon Corporation is a leading supplier of communication solutions for networking with no new wires. Intellon provides low-cost, high-performance digital, mixed-signal, and radio frequency (RF) based systems on silicon to OEMs worldwide. Intellon's intellectual property, products, technologies, and services are key to a variety of open industry standards and fast-growing markets including telecommunications, networking, transportation, and consumer electronics. Intellon's powerline carrier and radio frequency technologies enable high-speed communication and extend the reach of the Internet to individual products without adding new wires.

Founded in 1989, Intellon is a privately held company based in Ocala, Florida, and operates as a fabless semiconductor company to develop, manufacture, and distribute integrated circuit-based products and modules that are supported by complete reference design information, development, and evaluation tools. The company produces products that conform to the Consumers Electronics Bus (CEBus) standard. The CEBus standard is an open standard that provides separate physical layer specification documents for communication on powerlines and other media. The Intellon technology is oriented toward providing control capabilities to home networks and consists of two fundamental components—a transceiver implementing spread spectrum technology, and a microcontroller to run the protocol. (The next chapter explains spread spectrum technologies in greater detail.) Data packets are transmitted by the transceiver at about 10 Kbps, employing spread spectrum technology. Each packet contains the necessary sender and receiver addresses. The CEBus protocol uses a peer-to-peer communications model so that any node on the network has access to the media at any time. To avoid data collisions, it uses a Carrier Sense Multiple Access/Collision Detection and Resolution (CSMA/CDCR) protocol. Basically, this Media Access Control (MAC) protocol requires a network node to wait until the line is *clear*, which means that no other packet is being transmitted before it can send a packet. A CEBus network is comprised of a control channel and potentially multiple data channels on each of the CEBus media. CEBus control channel communication is standardized across all media, with a consistent packet format and signaling rate, and is used exclusively to control devices and resources of the network, including data channel allocations. A control channel signaling rate of 10,000 unit symbols per second is used with a "one" bit taking one unit symbol time (UST) and a "zero" bit taking two UST, resulting in an effective control data rate of approximately 7,000 data bits per second. Data channels typically provide selectable bandwidths that can support high data rates and are used to send data such as audio, video, or computer files over the network. The characteristics of a data channel can vary greatly depending on the medium and connected device requirements. All data channel assignments and functions are managed by CEBus control messages sent via the control channel. CEBus includes a common application language (CAL) that allows devices to communicate commands and status requests between each other using a common command syntax and vocabulary. CAL defines various electronic device functional subunits called *contexts*. For example, the audio control of a TV, a stereo, a CD Player, or a VCR is a CAL context. Each context is further broken down into *objects*, which represent various control functions of the context; for example, volume, bass, treble, or mute functions. Finally, objects are defined by a set of *instance variables* that specify the operation of the function of the object, such as the default or current setting of the volume object. Further details of CAL and CEBus are available in Chapter 15.

By using the CAL specification, Intellon ensures their chips can communicate with other CAL-compliant devices. Intellon offers products ranging from chip sets to board solutions, depending on the level of integration the manufacturer wants to perform on their own. In addition to a wide variety of powerline-based products, Intellon also offers customers a range of RF based products. Just before the finalization of this guide, the HomePlug Powerline Alliance announced the selection of Intellon's Technology as the basis for its industry specification for powerline home networking. HomePlug Powerline Alliance, Inc. is a nonprofit organization established to provide a forum for the creation of specifications for home powerline networking products and services, and to accelerate the demand for these products and services through the sponsorship of market and user education programs. Founding HomePlug member companies include: 3Com, AMD, Cisco Systems, Compaq, Conexant, Enikia, Intel, Intellon, Motorola, Panasonic, S3's Diamond Multimedia, Tandy/RadioShack and Texas Instruments. For more information, see Intellon's Web site at http://www.intellon.com.

INARI POWERLINE NETWORKING TECHNOLOGY ....

Inari was founded in 1997 and is headquartered in Draper, Utah. Inari (formerly Intelogis) is a leading developer of powerline networking technologies. The company's core technology, which transmits high-speed digital signals over existing AC electrical wiring, was developed by its engineers while the company was part of Novell's Embedded Systems Technology (NEST) division. As a product company, Inari became well known for its PassPort Plug-in Network home networking product. Today

Inari is focussing its efforts on providing powerline chipsets to modem, gateway, and network interface card vendors as well as to OEM partners in the consumer electronics marketplace. The next section of this guide will describe the technical architecture of Inari's powerline networking technologies.

Inari Technical Architecture

Today, Internet access is a paramount concern for customers in the home and home-office market segment. Over 76.5 million homes in the United States have an Internet connection and that number is growing exponentially. As mentioned earlier, an even more interesting fact is that approximately 20 million homes have two or more computers competing for time on the Internet. These factors have driven the current demand for the ability to simultaneously share a single Internet connection within the home. Close on the heels of the Internet fascination will be the convergence of home entertainment and the home network. Technologies such as browsing the Internet from your TV or downloading your favorite songs off the Web are intriguing, yet they have not managed to fully capture the attention or appetite of the home consumer. While the computing industry might have not yet hit on the right product offering, most technology pundits agree that one of the next great crazes will deal with distribution of streaming video and audio data in the home. Experts also agree that once the challenges of streaming data have been overcome and become widely accepted by consumers in the home that the door will open for the home automation market. For home automation to succeed, networking technology needs to not only be inexpensive, but it has to reach a level of simplicity that non-computer users can implement and use. Streaming data solutions that enable voice activated control of home appliances will go a long way to achieve the necessary levels of simplicity. All of the above factors point to the conclusion that decreasing networking technology costs and availability of requisite networking technologies will drive the home and small business network market segment through three general stages of evolution:

- Distribution of Internet data
- Distribution of streaming data (audio and voice)
- Home automation

To meet the new requirements of these evolving marketplaces, Inari has created a set of networking technology components that allow solution providers to build products that take advantage of the ubiquitous powerline network medium at currents speeds up to 2 Mbps and future speeds in excess of 10 Mbps. The following sections detail the major portions of Inari's powerline networking technology (PNT).

Digital Powerline—Physical Layer

As mentioned, two of the main drawbacks of most powerline technologies are high electronic component expense and low data throughput rates. Inari created the Digital Powerline (DPL) protocol to overcome these obstacles that have historically stood in the way of communicating via powerlines. Anyone who has a general understanding of the powerline medium and its underlying physical layer realizes that it exhibits a very dynamic behavior. As loads are added or removed from the system, or as devices power on or off, the system characteristics change. Two of the more important characteristics that the physical layer and Media Access Control (MAC) layer must be aware of are time-varying attenuation and noise. Inari's Digital Powerline was created to address these issues at the physical layer. DPL delivers a set of rules that define how information is transmitted between the physical components of the network. The specific physical components of DPL are transceivers and the powerline cabling itself. The circuitry required for Inari DPL modulation is scalable, meaning that the number of data channels implemented is determined by the applications' need for throughput, which projects directly into affordability. Far fewer and less expensive components are required to implement Inari's modulation scheme than those needed for spread spectrum modulation.

Furthermore, Inari's DPL delivers low bit-error rates in the range of 10^{-9}, thus making DPL well suited to provide robust high-speed network service to any home and to many commercial environments as well.

Powerline Exchange Protocol—MAC Layer

Many devices residing in a home or small office network require not only deterministic, periodic access with guaranteed time slots, but also minimal latency between token rotations. One of the most powerful features of Inari's Powerline Exchange (PLX) protocol is its ability to provide deterministic time slots for streaming applications and devices. PLX can be characterized as a hybrid protocol that utilizes *Datagram Sensing Multiple Access* with a *Centralized Token-Passing* scheme, or DSMA/CTP. PLX was built from the ground up to support control systems and data networking devices as well as deterministic audio and video streaming applications. It features numerous quality of service (QoS) hooks that can be exploited by application developers, including the following:

- Prioritization by device type
- Packet life expectancy variability
- Flexibility in bandwidth allocation (multiple time slots)
- Intelligent channel management capabilities

- Reuse of unused time slots
- Real-time channel status information
- System throttling (packet-pacing) mechanism
- Minimized worst-case latencies for highest priority devices
- Packet bursting within a token session

PLX also incorporates a robust encryption algorithm as well as a mechanism to seed remote devices with the 32-byte encryption array (Diffie-Hellman handshake). The following outlines some of the other key features of PLX:

- Simple datagram (preamble) detection with random back-off for multinode contention phases
- Active server for prioritized, centralized token-passing phase
- System throttling (packet pacing), smart packet/channel retries
- QoS hooks, including multichannel registration
- 32-bit static node addressing, with 16-bit cyclic redundancy checking
- Ad hoc networking, multirate support, and security
- Guaranteed 64 Kbps timeslots for isochronous communications
- Small packets to facilitate low-latency switched circuits
- Normally "quiet" medium, only active nodes communicate
- Constant aggregate throughput characteristics
- Thin network and transport layers to support embedded applications

Since multiple benched players may contend for the same time slot, a random back-off mechanism is employed, to eventually isolate a single node. This contention period is similar to Ethernet's random back-off period.

Inari Common Application Language—Application Layer

At the application layer Inari provides a complete client-server solution. On the client side, Inari has adapted a hybrid of CEBus' Common Application Layer (CAL) that can reside on the network nodes. Still, the PNT architecture allows OEMs to implement other client solutions to interface with their network node's application. Inari also provides a rich set of server-side technologies that OEMs can take advantage of as needed.

Inari Implementation

As mentioned, Inari PNT has adapted the CEBus Generic Common Application Language as one of its application layer protocols for networked nodes with one major exception: CEBus Generic CAL uses a peer-to-peer topology, and Inari CAL utilizes a client-server topology. Using a client-server topology allows more of the intelligence of each Inari node's application to be placed in a centralized application server, such as an existing computer or similar device, instead of residing within each individual client node. On the other hand, the peer-to-peer environment of CE-Bus' generic CAL requires each node, however simple it might be, to contain information regarding all other network nodes. In a peer-to-peer environment, each node must contain the requisite circuitry, processing power, memory, protocols, and software intelligence to perform much of the application tasks that are performed by a single application server node in the Inari client-server architecture. Furthermore, in a peer-to-peer environment, each node must also be aware of all remote nodes with which it needs to communicate, as well as know about the capabilities and attributes of each of those nodes.

With the Inari architecture, each client node is totally unaware of the existence and capabilities of other nodes. Instead, that information is stored in a central database on the Inari application server. Additionally, an object-oriented rules engine on the application server stores the rules for behavior of each node on the network. The application server, therefore, is a real-time repository of all objects and variables residing within the distributed nodes of an Inari system. Furthermore, the application server is responsible for inter-node communication by executing the rules of behavior between nodes as configured by the user of the system.

Inari's implementation of CAL allows the application server to perform tasks requiring greater intelligence, storage, and processing power. In so doing, the cost of each client node is greatly reduced. In other words, a light switch is allowed to be a light switch with a minimum amount of memory and logic. Consequently, a minimum cost of the system is reached because each network node only carries with it the minimal amount of functionality, circuitry, and intelligence it requires to perform its function whether that function is extremely simple or very complex.

Finally, Inari CAL uses all of generic CAL's defined contexts, objects, variables, and methods. This allows the attributes of all Inari PNT devices to be exposed in a common format, facilitating interoperability and remote manageability.

Server Applications

Inari provides a critical set of server components that developers can leverage when creating home network servers or residential gateways for their customers. These server ingredients combine to provide the OEM with all the major software components, above the operating system, required to implement a residential gateway. These server technology components include the following:

- **Proxy server**—The Inari proxy server routes and distributes Internet data, voice, and video, including VOIP, within the home, providing shared access to a single Internet connection.

- **E-mail server**—Inari PNT offers OEMs an e-mail server solution to facilitate in-home and in-office mail, as well as providing automatic, unattended delivery and retrieval of e-mail between the server and the customer's ISP.

- **Network administration services**—Inari's network administration services enables customers to manage and secure their home or small office powerline network.

- **Network installation services**—Creating a network on Windows-based computers is not a trivial task. Inari's network installation services automatically loads the necessary protocol stacks, binds the protocol to the device, and configures the TCP/IP address on all of the networked computers.

- **Service provider interface**—Inari's service provider interface enables inter-device communication between the network nodes and the Inari services that reside on the server (i.e., proxy server, e-mail server, and network administration). Currently, Inari provides an Inari CAL interface for Windows, Win32, and LINUX. Inari is in the process of developing an interface for UPnP and plans to develop other interfaces that may include OSGi (Sun and Oracle) or emMicro (emWare).

SUMMARY ....

With the exception of battery-operated devices, everything electrical in your home is already connected to the powerline network. This makes the powerline a natural choice for home networking. Powerline networking allows you to connect your in-home appliances to the rest of the world through any electrical outlet. X-10 and CEBus are two popular technologies that deliver data over lines that previously delivered only electricity. A company called Enikia is providing a range of products and competing technologies that allow home electronics devices such as set-top boxes to connect to a powerline home network via the nearest electrical outlet.

Inari PNT provides a set of network technology ingredients and components that enables OEMs that cater to the home/home office network market to easily take advantage of the ubiquitous nature of the powerline infrastructure.

7 High-Speed Serial Technologies

In this chapter...

The computer industry has been promising users the ability to easily connect electronics devices such as digital TVs, cameras, cable set-top boxes, and stereo equipment to each other and to PCs for many years. USB and IEEE 1394 are the two solutions that have been developed to meet commitments to their customer base. While the two serial buses seem similar, they are intended to fulfill different bandwidth and cost needs. The 1394 standard can move more data in a given amount of time, but is more expensive than USB due to its more complex protocol and signalling rate. Applications that are best suited for 1394 are disk drives, high-quality video streams, and other high-bandwidth applications—all higher-end consumer devices. USB is appropriate for mid- and low-bandwidth applications such as audio, scanners, printers, keyboards, and mouses. USB and 1394 are complementary technologies. 1394 is for devices where high performance is a priority and price is not, while USB is for devices where price is a priority and high performance is not. This chapter examines these technologies in more detail.

USB ....

USB stands for Universal Serial Bus. It is a bus standard that was originally specified in 1995. The major goal of USB is to define an external expansion bus that makes adding peripherals to a PC as easy as hooking up a telephone to a wall jack. Virtually all new PCs come with one or more USB ports. In fact, USB has become a key enabler of the Easy PC Initiative, an industry initiative led by Intel and Microsoft to make PCs easier to use. This effort sprung from the recognition that users need simpler, easier-to-use PCs that don't sacrifice connectivity or expandability. USB is one of the key technologies used to provide this. Today, version 1.1 of the USB standard is enjoying tremendous success in the marketplace, with most peripheral vendors around the globe developing products to this specification. At the time of going to press, a core team from Compaq, Hewlett-Packard, Intel, Lucent, Microsoft, NEC, and Philips were leading the development of version 2.0 of the USB specification. From a user's perspective, USB 2.0 is just like USB 1.1, but with much higher bandwidth. Analysis that has been done by the electrical team suggests that at least 240 Mbps is easily achievable on USB 2.0, with higher speeds currently under investigation. It will look the same and behave the same, but with a larger choice of more interesting, higher-performance devices available. Also, all of the USB peripherals the user has already purchased will work in a USB 2.0-capable system.

For a detailed description of USB 1.1 and USB 2.0, we suggest you download the specification documents from the following URL: http://www.usb.org/developers/docs.html.

Let's take a closer look at the features that USB can offer to people who are considering the implementation of an in-home network. USB fully supports plug-and-play technology. With plug-and-play, hardware devices such as digital speakers, joy-sticks, and video cameras can be automatically configured as soon as they are physi-cally attached to your in-home network. USB also supports hot swapping of devices on a home network, so there is no need to shut down and restart devices.

Gone are the days of opening up your computer and installing a new card and setting the onboard switches. USB replaces all the different kinds of serial and parallel connectors that you have on the back of your PC with one standardized plug and port combination. Home networking devices that have a USB port let you connect 127 different peripheral devices at one time. USB supports two high-speed data transfer protocols: isochronous and asynchronous. An isochronous connection from the USB port on a desktop PC to a re-mote device will support data transfers at a guaranteed, fixed rate of delivery. This mode of data transfer allows scanners, video devices, digital cameras, CD-ROM drives, and print-ers to communicate at 12 Mbps. The asynchronous protocol is slower and is used to com-municate with keyboards, joysticks, and mouse devices at 1.5 Mbps.

To eliminate the need for clunky power-supply boxes in a typical home network, USB distributes the power to all connected devices. Because USB connections allow the transfer of data to flow in both directions between PC and consumer electronics devices, it is possible for you to use your desktop PC to control home appliances in new and creative environments. For instance, you could use your PC to tune a set of USB-compliant stereo speakers to match the acoustics of the room where the speakers are located. To be able to make use of all these features on your home network, you need a USB-compliant PC and your electronic devices need to have a USB port. Most PCs on the market today, including many notebooks, are fully USB-ready. You can al-ready select from USB digital cameras, computer telephony products, digital speak-ers, digital gaming devices, and even a new USB peripheral that protects network security by scanning fingerprints.

The other major consideration to be aware of when implementing a USB-based home network is that you need an operating system that is designed to understand USB technologies. Windows 98 and Windows 2000 provide you with the most com-plete support for USB technologies. If you are unclear about your PC's support for USB, then download an evaluation utility from the following Web address: http://www.usb.org/usbready.exe.

This utility will examine your PC's hardware and software and inform you of your computer's USB capabilities. As a quick rule of thumb, if your PC was made during or before 1996, it probably doesn't support USB. If it was made during 1997, it probably supports USB. If it was made during or after 1998, it almost certainly sup-ports USB. If you plan on installing a home network based on USB technologies, then you need to run cables between devices. Most USB-enabled devices will use standard A-to-B cables of various lengths. There are, however, some USB devices that require cables that use nonstandard connectors and come with their own cable. When planning the physical layout of the network, you need to make sure that distances between devices are less than five meters. If you need to connect two or three computers and printers together, then you need to purchase a device called a USB hub. Your home networking appliances will then plug directly into the USB hub.

IEEE 1394 ....

The IEEE 1394 standard, also known as the FireWire Bus, is a new interface alternative for high-speed data transfer between digital set-top boxes and personal computers. The FireWire Bus standard, originally created by Apple Computer, was born out of the need for a low-cost, consumer-oriented connection between digital-video recorders and personal computers. It grew into a standard called the IEEE 1394 for low-cost, high-data-rate connections.

In 1994, an organization called the 1394 Trade Organization was formed to support and promote the adoption of the 1394 standard. Today, the 1394 Trade Organization is comprised of over 170 member companies from all over the world.

Many of the major consumer electronics companies are currently working to incorporate IEEE 1394-ready ports into the next generation of digital set-top boxes. In order to understand how an IEEE 1394 port operates, we need to examine the standard itself in more detail. IEEE 1394 is a very complex serial bus protocol that is capable of bidirectional data rates at 400 Mbps. There is, however, a roadmap in place to eventually bring the speed of an IEEE 1394 port up to 1.6 gigabits per second (Gbps). Table 7.1 gives you an idea of how the IEEE 1394 data transfer rate compares with other connections used in a standard PC.

Table 7.1   Data Transfer Rates for PC Interfaces

Interface Description	Data Rate
RS-232	115 Kbps
Parallel port	920 Kbps
IDE interface bus	133.6 Mbps
Fast SCSI	160 Mbps
USB	12 Mbps
IEEE 1394	400 Mbps

The cabling required to interconnect devices on an IEEE 1394-based home network is quite similar to that of Ethernet. So, unlike other home networking technologies, IEEE 1394 requires the installation of new wires. The IEEE 1394 cable medium allows up to 16 physical connections (cable hops), each up to 4.5 meters in length. This gives a home network using IEEE 1394 a total cable distance of 72 meters. Similar to Ethernet and other high-speed networking systems, IEEE 1394 adopts a layered approach to transmitting data across a physical medium. The physical layer provides the signals required by the IEEE 1394 bus within the set-top box. The link layer takes the raw data from the physical layer and formats it into recognizable 1394 packets. The transaction layer takes the packets from the link layer and presents them to the home networking-based application. Like all IEEE standards, IEEE 1394 is an open, royalty-free standard.

IEEE 1394 and Other Standards

IEEE 1394 multiplexes a variety of different types of digital signals, including video, audio, and device control commands, on two twisted-pair conductors. Multiplexing is used in virtually all analog and digital networking systems, but usually only a single type is involved. Ethernet, for example, multiplexes digital data over one (10Base2, "Thin" Ethernet) or two (10BaseT, 100BaseT) pairs of conductors. Transmitting real-time, high-quality audio and video data over Ethernet, however, requires special protocols presently implemented only in proprietary multimedia networking systems. IEEE 1394 is much more flexible in its accommodation of different data types and topologies, using a "fairness" arbitration approach to ensure that all nodes having information to transmit get a chance to use the bus. Standard Ethernet does not provide this important feature. As mentioned, USB is a very popular new connector and bus for computers. However, every USB message must be processed by a personal computer host. This "bottleneck," as well as the dependence on a PC being present in the USB system, makes USB an unlikely alternative to IEEE 1394. A 1394 bus does not require that a PC be present; it is optional. Bandwidth is another issue: IEEE 1394 operates at a much higher speed, with guaranteed delivery of audio and video samples. USB does not have the bandwidth necessary to transmit multiple video streams. For a more detailed description of the IEEE 1394 standard, we suggest that you download the complete specification from any of the Internet draft repository sites: http://www.1394ta.org. Companies like Sony have already begun to lay the groundwork for using the IEEE 1394 home networking standard for interconnecting a range of hardware products within the household.

COMPARISON WITH WIRELESS SYSTEMS.................

Although proven high-speed serial technologies like USB and IEEE 1394 can support broadband data applications, both of these technologies involve running wires between devices across the home premises. This retrofitting process poses various obstacles, including high costs, significant technological complexity, and an awkward installation procedure, which eliminates these technologies as viable mass-market solutions. Instead, these technologies will likely exist as subnetworks, interconnecting clusters of devices, which will then interface with a "no new wiring" home network backbone. The next chapter will describe wireless systems in greater detail.

SUMMARY ....

The USB is the solution for any computer user who is looking for a hassle-free way of interconnecting their PCs and A/V electronic devices at home. USB plays a key role in the fast-growing area of home networking. The presence of USB means that PCs and peripherals will work together with a high degree of reliability. The 1394 bus is a versatile, high-speed, and inexpensive method of interconnecting a variety of consumer electronics devices (e.g., home theater equipment) and personal computer peripherals (e.g., color printers). IEEE 1394 allows the direct connection of up to 63 devices in one subnet. Up to 1,023 subnets may be interconnected to allow more than 64,000 devices on one bus. The 1394 standard defines three signaling rates: 98.304, 196.608, and 393.216 Mbps. These rates are referred to in the 1394 1995 standard as S100, S200, and S400. At present, existing implementations of IEEE 1394 deliver S200 or S400 performance. The 420-page standards document can be purchased by contacting the IEEE.

8

Wireless Radio-Frequency–Based Home Networks

In this chapter...

Market research analysts are predicting that wireless network technologies will eventually become more widespread than the various wired solutions discussed in previous chapters. A large technology consulting company called Strategy Analytics has forecast that 19% of the households in the United States and 15% of European households are expected to have wireless home networks by the year 2005. Wireless communications present the ideal solution for the home network, but these solutions have a variety of technical and deployment obstacles. This chapter explores the consumer applications and basic principles associated with deploying a home network using current wireless technologies. Once you have a firm understanding of the principles, we will then present you with a detailed description of companies and industry groups that are seeking to tap into this vast consumer market opportunity.

NEEDS OF WIRELESS HOME NETWORKING APPLICATIONS...

Today's home networking applications[1] are driving the need for a high-performance, wireless network protocol with high usable speed (high network throughput) and isochronous, multimedia-capable services. Factors driving the need for high performance are:

- **Home networks incorporate multimedia**—Existing and emerging digital devices such as televisions, DVD players, digital video recorders, digital audio/MP3 players, DBS systems, flat-panel displays, digital set-top boxes, and PCs create the need to support multimedia content in the home (Figure 8.1). The home network will have to support all types of digital content, including local content (e.g., DVD, MP3) and broadcast content (e.g., video on demand, streaming media). This content is multimedia in nature, encompassing audio, voice, video, and data. Internet multimedia broadcasting is already prevalent. Other initiatives such as Internet phones, VoIP, MP3 online music, and broadcast media applications such as RealNetworks' RealGuide, Microsoft's Media Player, and Cisco's IP/TV, ensure that multimedia content will continue to grow in home networking.

  The ability to support multimedia is the "killer app" that will drive the mass adoption of home networks. Therefore, a home network must support the coexistence of batch data (print jobs, file transfers) and isochronous content (video, voice, audio). The consumer needs to choose products today that will provide the foundation for multimedia network services.

---

1. This section has been adapted from ShareWave's white paper on wireless home networking, "Whitecap™ Protocol: High-Performance, Wireless Home Networking," October, 1999.

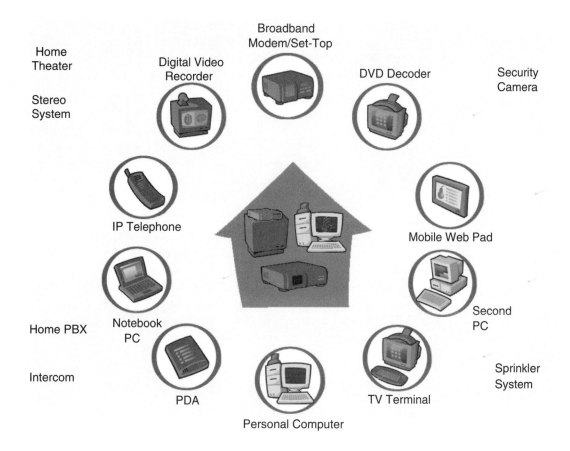

Figure 8.1
Home networking scenario. (Courtesy of ShareWave)

- **Consumers are adding more nodes to their home networks**—As mentioned earlier, the rapid growth of multi-PC homes indicates that the number of nodes in a PC network will continue to skyrocket as home networking appliances are introduced. It is estimated that by the year 2002, 33 million (or 55%) of the projected 60 million U.S. PC-owning households will have at least two PCs. Cahners In-Stat predicts that the average number of connected nodes per home network will increase from 2.9 in 1999 to 5.0 by 2003.[2] Simultaneously transmitting wireless appliances share the same bandwidth. Consequently, high network throughput

---

2. Cahners In-Stat, "Home Networking: Markets, Technologies, and Vendors," January, 1999.

and usable speed are necessary to accommodate more home network appliances. Choosing a wireless network with an access mechanism that supports multiple nodes without significantly degrading total throughput is essential to supporting a growing home wireless network.

- **The need to preserve high-speed broadband Internet access**—The desire for faster Internet access is driving the mass deployment of high-speed broadband access, such as xDSL and cable. Cahners In-Stat group predicts that by 2002, 45 million homes will have installed high-speed modems.[3] Cable and xDSL broadband are targeting and delivering bandwidth speeds in excess of 6 Mbps. Consumers need a high-performance, wireless network to preserve, and not bottleneck, high-speed broadband Internet access to devices.

- **Evolving personal computer applications**—File sizes of typical personal computer applications are growing rapidly with each generation of standard software applications. The file size of a word processing document with the same content has doubled over the last few years. Graphics and digital photography over e-mail are now commonplace. Files sizes greater than 20 MB are not uncommon for digital photos. A wireless network with high, usable throughput is mandatory to move files in a timely manner. For example, moving a 2 MB file over a 1 Mbps network with low effective throughput may take as long as three minutes. This need is further magnified as the network volume expands and more nodes are added.

BASIC PRINCIPLES...

In wireless technology, data is transmitted over the air. Wireless solutions are ideal platforms for extending the concept of home networking into the area of mobile devices around the home. Consequently wireless technology is portrayed as a new system that complements phone-line and powerline networking solutions. It is likely that wireless technology will not emerge as a home network backbone solution, but will instead serve to interconnect the class of devices that need mobile communications into a subnetwork. These mobility subnetworks will interface with other subnetworks and with the Internet by connecting to the home network backbone. Wireless home networks transmit and receive data over the air, minimizing the need for expensive wiring systems. With a wireless-based home network, you can access and share expensive entertainment devices without pulling new cables through walls and ceilings. At the core of wireless communication is a device called a transmitter and one called a receiver. The user interacts with the transmitter—for example, one of the children in-

---

3. Cahners In-Stat, "Videoconferencing and the PC Camera Market," March, 1999.

puts a URL into their PC. This input is then converted by the transmitter to electro-magnetic (EM) waves and sent to the receiver, which could be built into the set-top box. The receiver then processes these electromagnetic waves. For two-way communication, each user requires a transmitter and a receiver. Consequently, many of the homes networking device manufacturers build the transmitter and receiver into a single unit called a transceiver. The operation and functionality of a wireless and wired home network remain the same; however, there are distinctions in the technologies used to achieve the same objectives.

The two main technologies used in wireless home networks are:

- Infrared (IR)
- Radio frequency (RF)

IR

Most of us are familiar with everyday devices that use IR technology: remote controls for TVs, VCRs, and CD players. IR transmission is categorized as a line-of-sight wireless technology. This means that the workstations and digital appliances must be in a direct line to the transmitter in order to operate. An infrared-based network suits environments where all the digital appliances that require network connectivity are in the one room. There are, however, new IR technologies being developed that can work out of the line of sight, so expect to see these products in the very near future. IR home networks can be implemented reasonably quickly; however, people walking across the room or moisture in the air can weaken data signals. IR in-home technology is promoted by an international association of companies called IrDA (Infrared Data Association). Further details on this organization are available at: http://www.irda.org/.

RF

The other main category of wireless technology is radio frequency. RF technology is a more flexible technology, allowing consumers to link appliances that are distributed throughout the house. RF can be categorized as narrow band or spread spectrum. Narrow band technology includes microwave transmissions. Microwaves are high-frequency radio waves and can be transmitted to distances of up to 50 km. Microwave technology is not suitable for home networks but is, however, used to connect networks in separate buildings. Spread spectrum technology (SST) is one of the most widely used technologies in wireless home networks. SST was developed during World War II to provide greater security for military communications. As it entails spreading the signal over a number of frequencies, spread spectrum technology makes the signal harder to intercept. There are a couple of techniques used to deploy SST; a system called frequency-hopping spread spectrum (FHSS) is the most popular technique for operating wireless home networks. FHSS transmissions constantly hop over entire bands of frequencies in a particular sequence. To a remote receiver not synchronized with the hopping sequence, these signals appear as random noise. A receiver can only process electromagnetic waves by tuning to the relevant transmission frequency. The FHSS receiver hops from one frequency to another in tandem with the transmitter. At any given time there may be a number of transceivers hopping along the same band of frequencies. Each transceiver uses a different hopping sequence that is carefully chosen to minimize interference on the home network. Because wireless technology has roots in military applications, security has long been a design criterion for wireless devices. Security provisions are normally integrated with wireless home networking devices, making them more secure than most wireline-based in-home networks. Complex encryption techniques make it nearly impossible for hackers to gain access to traffic on your wireless network.

When implementing a wireless home network, you need to install specific hardware to complete the connections. Similar to phone-line, IEEE 1394, and powerline networking, you need to connect your network nodes in the house to the transmission medium. To do this, you install a wireless NIC. The NIC hardware comprises a card with onboard transceiver, a fixed or external antenna, and cable connections. To install the card, you remove the cover of the digital appliance and slide the card into one of the free slots. To complete the hardware installation, connect a fixed antenna to the rear of the NIC. Or else connect an antenna cable for mounting an external antenna. Usually the external antenna is placed as high up as possible on the wall or on the ceiling to improve coverage. The antenna resembles a TV aerial, in the sense that where you locate it is important in relation to signal transmission and reception. In addition to installing the wireless NIC, you must also complete a number of software installation steps. This entails configuring and loading device drivers. If the nodes on the network are PCs with Windows 98, then the software configuration will be performed automatically. The layout of digital appliances on a wireless digital network is normally dictated by the physical layout of the house.

A number of industry initiatives are underway to develop interoperable wireless in-home appliances. The following sections describe the most popular of these technologies.

IEEE 802.11 STANDARD ....

The development of any new technology is part theory and part practice. A key issue in telecommunications is the adoption of technical standards that govern the interoperability of equipment to provide a stable environment for deployment of products and services. This does not mean that all vendor equipment will work in the exact same way. A standard sets a norm or performance expectation on the function of the technology—not its implementation. The standard that governs the wireless LAN industry is the 802.11 family of standards that are part of the group that governs Ethernet data communications. This standard is evolving and adapting to meet the needs of industry as new technology is developed to allow new product design. IEEE 802.11 is comprised of two layers—physical and MAC layers.

802.11 Physical Layer

Like the IEEE 802.3 Ethernet and 802.5 token ring standards, the IEEE 802.11 specification addresses both the physical (PHY) and media access control (MAC) layers. At the PHY layer, IEEE 802.11 defines three physical characteristics for wireless local area networks: diffused infrared, direct sequence spread-spectrum (DSSS), and frequency-hopping spread-spectrum (FHSS).

While the infrared PHY operates at the baseband, the other two radio-based PHYs operate at the 2.4 GHz band. This latter frequency band is part of what is known as the ISM band, a global band primarily set aside for industrial, scientific, and medical use, but usable for operating wireless devices without the need for end-user licenses. For wireless devices to be interoperable, they have to conform to the same PHY standard. All three PHYs specify support for 1 Mbps and 2 Mbps data rates.

802.11 Media Access Control Layer

The 802.11 MAC layer, supported by an underlying PHY layer, is concerned primarily with rules for accessing the wireless medium. Some of the primary services provided by the MAC layer are as follows:

- **Data transfer**—Wireless clients use a Collision Sense Multiple Access with Collision Avoidance (CSMA/CA) algorithm as the media access scheme.
- **Association**—This service enables the establishment of wireless links between wireless clients.
- **Authentication**—Authentication is the process of proving a client identity.
- **Privacy**—By default, data is transferred "in the clear"; any 802.11-compliant device can potentially eavesdrop similar to PHY 802.11 traffic that is within range. Encryption techniques are employed to overcome this problem.
- **Power management**—IEEE 802.11 defines two power modes, an active mode, where a wireless client is powered to transmit and receive, and a

power save mode, where a client is not able to transmit or receive, but consumes less power. Actual power consumption is not defined and depends on the implementation.

Many of the wireless home networking technologies covered in the remaining part of this chapter are based on this family of standards.

In addition to promoting and developing 802.11, the IEEE organization has launched a new working group to develop standards for wireless personal area networks. A wireless personal area network, or WPAN, is best described as a low-cost networking scheme that enables computing devices such as PCs, laptop computers, printers, and personal digital assistants (PDAs) to wirelessly communicate with each other over short distances. It has a range of 10 meters and is capable of transmitting data around your home at speeds of 1 Mbps and above.

DECT . . . .

DECT (Digital Enhanced Cordless Telecommunications) is a flexible digital radio access standard for cordless communications in residential, corporate, and public environments. It is supported and promoted by the DECT forum. This forum has representatives in all the major geographical regions around the world. DECT provides for voice and multimedia traffic, and contains many forward-looking technical features that allow DECT-based cordless systems to play a central role in important new communications developments, such as Internet access and interworking with other fixed and wireless services like ISDN and Global System for Mobile Communications (GSM). The DECT standard makes use of several advanced digital radio techniques to achieve efficient use of the radio spectrum; it delivers high speech quality and security with low risk of radio interference and low power technology.

TDMA (Time Division Multiple Access) radio access, with its low radio interference characteristics, provides high system capacity for users of in-home networks. ADPCM (Adaptive Differential Pulse Code Modulation) speech encoding ensures a DECT cordless phone very high speech quality, comparable to wireline telephony. DCS/DCA (Dynamic Channel Selection/Allocation) is a unique DECT capability that guarantees the use of the best radio channels available. This happens when a cordless phone is in stand-by mode, and throughout a call. This capability ensures that DECT can coexist with other DECT applications and with other systems in the same frequency, with high-quality, robust, and secure communications for end users. Other features of the DECT standard include encryption for maximum call security and optimized radio transmission for maximum battery life.

Benefits for Users of Wireless Home Networks

- **Low cost**—Through the use of the same basic technology for everything from residential cordless phones (mass-market) up to complex multicell systems, DECT has an attractive and competitive cost position. DECT systems require no frequency planning during initial deployment or subsequent expansion. Once the radio infrastructure is in place, additional base stations and cordless terminals can easily and quickly be added.

- **High capacity**—The radio technology used in the DECT standard permits very high concentrations of users to be served.

- **Spectrum efficiency**—Through its advanced digital technology and unique capabilities like DCS/DCA, DECT very efficiently uses the available radio spectrum in the standard bands (1880 to 1900 MHz, 1900 to 1920 MHz, or 1910 to 1930 MHz). Various applications can share the spectrum, e.g., voice and data, or public and private applications.

- **Security**—The combination of digital radio technology and dynamic channel selection with additional encryption techniques and authentication and identification procedures, makes DECT radio transmissions extremely secure against unauthorized radio eavesdropping by third parties. The implemented encryption method enhances the security of DECT to a very satisfactory level.

- **High quality**—Speech quality in a DECT system is very high, thanks to the digital radio techniques applied.

- **High data transfer**—Data applications are becoming more and more important in home networks. Today, DECT products provide data links with up to 552 kbps. New modulation schemes will rapidly allow the rate to grow up to 2 Mbps.

HOMERF ....

Two major factors are presenting a real opportunity for data networking within the home. The first is the explosive growth and usage of the Internet. The Internet has clearly revolutionized the delivery of information and entertainment to the home. The second factor is the emergence of sub-$1000 powerful home PCs. With these low-cost devices, the barrier to getting on the Internet and discovering the utility of the PC is low enough to reach the vast majority of middle-income households. However, consumers soon find that the PC/Internet combination, though very compelling, lacks some key attributes in terms of mobility and convenience of location compared with many of their traditional information and entertainment options—newspapers, magazines, television, videos, FM radio, DVD/CD/stereo, etc. The powerful home PCs (and the printers and peripherals attached to them) often end up turned off 20 to 22 hours per day, tucked into a bedroom or den corner where access is possible only within a two to three foot "bubble." The major opportunity for networking in the home is thus to extend the reach of the PC and Internet throughout the home and yard, and connect the resources of the PC and Internet with legacy home applications such as telephony, audio entertainment, and home control systems. Another opportunity is the sharing of resources (such as an Internet gateway or high quality printer) among PCs in multi-PC homes. With these issues in mind, several major stakeholders in the PC industry formed the Home RF Working Group[4] in early 1997. The key goal of the group is to enable interoperable wireless voice and data networking within the home at consumer price points. The group began by pooling market research from the member companies to produce a *Market Requirements Document*. This document guided the technical proposals within the group. With tremendous cooperation from major stakeholders in the RF communications industry, and the nascent wireless local area network (WLAN) community, the Shared Wireless Access Protocol-Cordless Access (or "SWAP-CA") was created. In designing SWAP-CA, the HomeRF Technical Committee chose to reuse proven RF networking technology for data and voice communications and added simplifications where appropriate for home usage. With this approach, SWAP-CA inherited native support for Internet access via TCP/IP networking, and for voice telephony via the Public Switched Telephone Network (PSTN) and Voice over IP. Additionally, because of this design approach, the HomeRF Working Group made rapid progress in finalizing the specification and bringing it to market in a timely manner. Table 8.1 contains the results of the research carried out by the HomeRF marketing subcommittee on user expectations for a home networking wireless technology. These expectations were used as a guide by the HomeRF Technical Team, which then made design decisions to best fulfill the needs of the potential users.

Three subcommittees exist within the HomeRF Working Group. The HRFWG-Japan subcommittee was created to assist in defining SWAP and ensuring that it complies with local regulations. The group has also formed committees to plan future versions of SWAP that address wireless multimedia and a lower-cost alternative. In addition to ratifying the standard, 13 companies have also committed to building products based on SWAP. Products that adhere to the SWAP standard will carry voice and data traffic between various portable appliances within the home without using a wiring system. Additionally, these products will interoperate with the public telephone network and the Internet. The remaining parts of this section on HomeRF describe the vision, design, and implementation of the HomeRF standard.

---

4. The HomeRF section copyright © 2000 IEEE. Reprinted with permission. Adapted from "HomeRF: Wireless Networking for the Connected Home," by K. J. Negus, A. P. Stephens, and J. Lansford. *IEEE Personal Communications*, Volume 7, Issue 1, February 2000, pp. 20–27.

Table 8.1 Translation of Key Requirements from Market Survey to Design Decisions

Market (User) Expectations	Phase 1—Design Decisions
Reasonable data rates	1Mbps (standard), 2 Mbps (optional)
Support for multimedia traffic	Simultaneous support for 4 interactive voice sessions—multiple asynchronous data connections
Cover a single family dwelling	Range: ~150 feet
Usable battery life	Low power operation (nominal 100 mW) with explicit support for power management
Global interoperability	2.4 GHz unlicensed spectrum with world-wide availability
Tolerance to interference	Frequency hopping spread spectrum system
Protection against eavesdropping	Built-in encryption support (optional)
Connection to multiple devices	Up to 128
Legacy software should "just" work	Plug-and-play with tight integration with TCP/IP and PSTN
New applications that improve lifestyle	Family communications—advanced messaging system, etc.
	Entertainment/creativity—interactive games, etc.
	Home control—home security, baby monitoring, etc.
	Resource sharing—Internet, printers, file sharing, etc.
Affordable, sub-$100 range	Reuse available technology and reduce component cost however possible

Vision and Usage Scenarios

HomeRF sees SWAP-CA as one of several connectivity options in the home of the future. The relationship of SWAP-CA with other connection options is shown in Figure 8.2. In this scenario, the main home PC is linked to an Internet gateway that might be a 56K, xDSL, or cable modem. This link may be a simple cable, a wired network connection, or even a SWAP-CA network connection. This main home PC would likely have a variety of built-in or peripheral resources such as a printer, a scanner, a CD drive, a DVD drive, etc. For most home PCs today, and looking forward, it is likely that the USB would be the bus of choice for many peripherals that do not need to be mobile or remote from the PC. For video applications, which require connection to devices such as camcorders, the IEEE 1394 is the expected choice. For sharing resources among multiple PCs, options such as conventional 10/100 BaseT Ethernet, home phone line networks, and AC power line networks will exist. (This last option is particularly well suited for many home automation applications where very low data rates are acceptable). At this time, there are no viable RF alternatives at consumer price points that can be used as a wireless networking technology for home networks. The goal of the HomeRF Working Group is to fill this void. The SWAP-CA networking vision is apparent in Figure 8.2. The HomeRF technology supports both isochro-

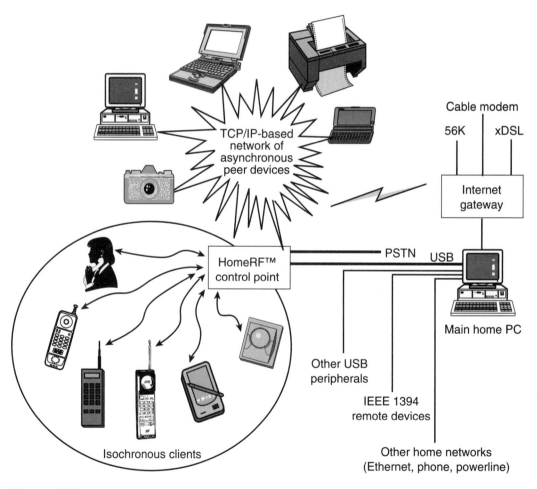

Figure 8.2
SWAP vision for home networking

nous clients that are slaves to the main Home PC and an asynchronous network of peer devices that is effectively a wireless Ethernet. In most cases, the system starts with a connection point, usually connected to the main home PC via USB. This connection point is not absolutely necessary for devices in the asynchronous network of Figure 8.2, but even in that case it offers some interesting power-saving options for ultra-portable devices as described in the MAC overview section. The isochronous clients, such as cordless telephones, wireless headsets, or remote I/O devices to the home PC (a consumer Personal Information Manager or PIM) are always bound to the connection point, which assigns them guaranteed bandwidth for bounded latency communication. The asynchronous peers can also communicate with the main home PC as with any other peer device. We now consider three major applications for the HomeRF technology.

Our first example is that of PC-enhanced cordless telephony. Today there are no standards-based digital cordless telephones for consumer use in the USA where interoperability of multiple vendors is enabled. HomeRF defines a new standard for interoperable digital cordless telephones both in the United States and globally. Furthermore, the SWAP specification includes a standard method for connecting the cordless telephone to the home PC software applications. Thus many new enhanced features are possible. For example, caller ID information could be sent to a PC application to look up the caller's name and then route the call to an individual handset (rather than a number) and display the caller's name on any given handset. For outbound calls, the PC could interpret a spoken destination name (e.g., "Call Mom") through voice recognition and then, based on date/time, determine the likely number for the person and route the call using the lowest cost approach (which might be IP telephony). The handset could be used to pick up voice mail for a specific user from the home PC call center.

With voice synthesis the handset could also be used to "listen" to e-mail. With more sophisticated application software, the handset could achieve PIM functionality by using voice or keypad I/O to store lists (e.g., "Add three quarts of milk to my shopping lists") or control home automation features (e.g., "Turn the temperature up three degrees"). All of these and undoubtedly much more creative features are possible because of the standard interoperable method of connecting to the Home PC. The cordless handsets themselves are slightly different but not substantially more complex or expensive than the existing "dumb" cordless handsets sold in multimillion unit volume today.

A second interesting example is a mobile viewer appliance. This could take many forms but fundamentally consists of a color LCD display (like that of a notebook computer) with some limited input device (such as a pen) and a SWAP-CA radio network connection. Such a device could be either an extension of the home PC (like an X-terminal) or simply a web-browsing extension of an Internet gateway. In either case the viewer communicates entirely through receiving and sending TCP/IP packets.

The third of many potential applications is resource sharing among multiple PCs in the same home. The resource to be shared could be a high quality printer, a back-up storage device, a file server, or an Internet connection. Another possibility for this is multiplayer gaming. Clearly these resource-sharing applications have received considerable attention from other home wiring-based alternatives to networking. It is important to note that the market for HomeRF is not strictly multi-PC homes. Any home with a modern home PC or an Internet gateway is a candidate for compelling mobile devices enabled by the SWAP-CA specification. Thus, the SWAP-CA protocol is a hybrid in several ways; it is client-server between the connection point and voice devices, but is peer-to-peer between data devices. The interactive voice transactions are circuit switched, but the asynchronous transactions are packet-switched. It is precisely this richness that gives SWAP-CA the capability to be broadly used in the home; it is not designed to support hundreds of users doing similar things in an enterprise, but rather the variety of applications that occur in a residential setting.

Before concluding this section, we briefly describe three usage scenarios that the SWAP-CA protocol was designed to enable. These were part of the marketing requirements document that the design team used as motivation for SWAP-CA. The primary focus in these scenarios is on the exchange of voice and data packets by portable devices within the home environment.

Scenario I: A Busy Family

- Two children, sitting in different rooms, play interactive games with each other on their wirelessly connected handheld PCs. They talk to each other using the PC's mike and speakers.

- A third child uses the Web for writing a school report from her room.

- Mom listens to her phone messages, recorded by the PC answering machine application, while making dinner in the kitchen.

- Dad completes an oil change in the garage. Using a handheld notepad, he enters the data into his car maintenance log, which he maintains on his desktop PC.

Scenario 2: A Montage of Voice Applications

- Mom uses her personal handset to record a message for the kids to listen to when they return from school.

- Dad asks for stock quotes from the Internet and gets an audio response through a TTS (text to speech) engine.

- Dad checks the temperature in the bedroom and turns the space heater on via a voice command.
- Uncle Ed listens to a soccer match on his wireless headset on the front porch. The match is being broadcast over the Web and transmitted by the PC to the headset.

Scenario 3: A Montage of Display Applications

- While in the kitchen, Mom pulls up a recipe from the PC and adds oregano to the shopping list.
- Dad updates the family financial portfolio.
- Junior plays Tetris.
- Daughter reads the latest online issue of *Teen* magazine while lying down on her bed.

In the scenarios described above, a common theme is tetherless multimedia connectivity between devices and to the Internet. Many companies are actively building SWAP-CA devices and software that will bring these envisioned scenarios to reality.

Network Architecture and Operation

In this section we describe the architecture of a SWAP-CA network and some of its key operational features.

The SWAP-CA network is designed to operate on the 2.4 GHz ISM band. The 2.4 GHz band is a nonlicensed frequency band that is available all over the world, ensuring that SWAP-CA devices would be operational globally. The protocol is unique in the way it combines with the ETSI Digital European Cordless Telephony (DECT) standard for carrying time-sensitive, real-time traffic.

Device Types

Four types of devices can operate in a SWAP-CA network:

1. A *connection point* (CP), which functions as the gateway between a SWAP-CA compatible device, the PSTN, and a personal computer (possibly connected to the Internet).
2. *Isochronous nodes* (I-nodes), which are voice-centric devices such as cordless phones and walkie-talkies.

3. *Asynchronous nodes* (A-nodes), which are data-centric devices such as handheld notepads and personal digital assistants.

4. Combined *asynchronous-isochronous nodes* (AI-nodes).

The connection point can either be a separate device, connected to the main (home) PC, typically via the USB connection, or can be an integral part of the PC. It can also have a direct connection to the PSTN. The CP is capable of performing data transfers to and from SWAP-compliant devices using both a contention-based and a contention-free protocol. When configured to do so, it can provide power management services to both A-nodes and I-nodes. Figure 8.3 shows an example of a typical SWAP-CA network consisting of two A-nodes, one I-node, and a connection point. .One of the A-nodes is a power-managed display pad whose communications traffic is managed by the PC so it can maximize battery life. Although not shown in this figure, the laptop A-node could also be power-managed. As this figure shows, SWAP-CA has

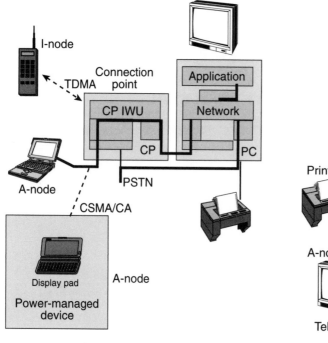

(a) Managed Network

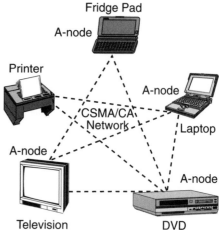

(b) Peer-to-Peer Ad Hoc Networking

Figure 8.3
SWAP network topology flexibility

a unique ability among networking protocols to mix intense, high-demand packet traffic with infrequent command and control traffic and high-quality real-time voice traffic. The personal computer is an integral part of the SWAP-CA system although peer-peer data networking is available even when the PC is inoperative. Every SWAP-CA device has a 48-bit IEEE MAC address, which is configured by the manufacturer prior to distribution.

Network Configuration

As shown in Figure 8.3, the HomeRF network is designed to operate in two basic modes: the network can be configured either as a *managed network* or as a *peer-to-peer ad hoc network*. In the managed network configuration, the network is explicitly under the control of a connection point, which is its gateway to other devices, the Internet, and the PSTN. Furthermore, it provides simultaneous support for both real-time audio traffic, such as interactive voice, and non-real time data traffic, such as traditional TCP connections. In the ad hoc network mode, the network provides traditional data networking support only and does not need a connection point for proper operation.

Multiple Overlapping Virtual Networks

Certain characteristics of radio frequency networks make them unique. One such characteristic is that radio frequency signals are not restricted to well-defined boundaries; consequently, a RF node can hear other RF nodes operating on the same frequency within its transmission range. It is likely that users of HomeRF equipment are interested in setting up their own independent networks with their own SWAP-CA nodes, but which happen to be within the range of other users' HomeRF equipment. Consequently, these networks may overlap

Scenarios like this can be fairly common in places such as an apartment complex where every apartment has a HomeRF network of its own, but since the apartments are close to each other, devices in one apartment are within range of devices in a neighboring apartment. Neighboring networks should in general not interfere and affect each other's performance. In SWAP-CA, a 24-bit *network identifier* (NWID) is used to separate the different overlapping virtual networks located in the same area of coverage. Devices having the same NWID are part of a logical network, and devices with a different NWID do not interact with one another. The network identifier is present as part of every data packet in the network. Depending on how a network device is configured, a node may either use the NWID assigned to it by the user, or alternatively, derive a NWID from a MAC address. For an existing network, new nodes can learn the NWID as they join the network. In general, different networks are not synchronized and use different frequency-hopping patterns.

Discovery and Creation of Networks

When a SWAP-CA node is turned on, it immediately enters into a *network discovery phase* in which it tries to determines if another node or connection point is present in its transmission range and if a network already exists that it can join. The node accomplishes its discovery phase by operating in a *passive scanning* mode. In passive scanning mode, the node listens on every channel within its operational frequency band for a specific amount of time, greater than a single *superframe*. "Listening" on a channel is accomplished by the physical layer, which forces the node to hop on a known scan pattern which is a good spread of the hopping patterns on all the channels of the network. During a scan, the node receives all network packets regardless of the NWID or destination address. These packets are analyzed by the node's MAC management module and a decision is made on whether or not to join the network. The scan can be terminated as soon as the first network is found, or when the management module so determines. When a network is found, the node sets its hopping pattern If the network identifier is known, SWAP-CA can join the known network by scanning all the channels for the NWID of interest and then locking-on to that channel. The scanning procedure is terminated as soon as the sought-after NWID is discovered. In case the node does not find a network with the particular NWID, it can either give up or start its own network. To start its own network, the node randomly selects an available hopping pattern, records the NWID as the network identifier, and starts transmitting synchronization signals. Not all nodes are allowed to create a network; specifically, a CP can create a managed network while an A-node can create a peer-to-peer ad hoc network. I-nodes do not create their own network. In a managed network, the CP is responsible for transmitting synchronization information, whereas in an ad hoc network all A-nodes participate in synchronization. Synchronization information contains the hopping pattern and the dwell time for the network and is transmitted by the CP as part of its beacon signal. A beacon signal is a broadcast packet transmitted by a node (a CP in a managed network) periodically. It contains information that the network devices need for proper operation within the network. When there are two or more devices in the network that are capable of CP functionality, the first one to join/create the network becomes the active CP while the remaining ones become passive CPs. When a passive CP does not hear 50 consecutive beacons from the active CP, it assumes that either the active CP has gone off-line or has moved out of range, and consequently creates its own network by transmitting synchronization information. If 100 or more simultaneous beacons are missed by the A-nodes in the network, they start the ad hoc network synchronization operation and create an ad hoc network. The entire process of scanning followed by either joining or forming a new network can take a few seconds.

Authentication and Privacy

As discussed, RF signals are not restricted to well-defined boundaries; consequently, unlike a wired network, an RF wireless network is difficult to secure. The transmission medium is open to anyone within range of the transmitter. Even when the physical layer of the network is based on spread-spectrum communication and different networks use different hopping patterns, the system is insecure as it is relatively easy for a malicious user to scan all channels and determine the hopping pattern and NWID of the target network. Thus, neighbors who receive RF signals from each other can conceivably "listen-in" on each other's conversations and intercept each other's data packets. This is clearly undesirable. Consequently, an encryption mechanism that provides security and privacy is clearly needed, and should be part of any wireless networking standard. Data privacy and authentication in a SWAP-CA network is accomplished by using a well-established shared-key encryption algorithm. Notably, all I-nodes follow the security model defined in the ETSI DECT specification. The authentication process in this model is split into a key generation process and the encryption process. The purpose for splitting this process is to support roaming of handsets between DECT base stations. HomeRF defines its authentication process in terms of the DECT security model. A node indicates that it supports encryption to the destination node as part of the capability exchange process. Data packets are encrypted only if the destination node can decrypt the message. The encryption algorithm takes a 56-bit key and a 32-bit initialization vector and uses these to convert unencrypted data (called *plaintext*) to encrypted data (called *ciphertext*). The initialization vector is a combination of the packet sequence number and a hash of the 48-bit MAC address of the source node. The sequence number keeps track of the number of packets the node has encrypted and prevents against replay attacks. A *magic number*, a byte containing all zeros, is appended to every packet before encryption. This allows the receiver to check, as it decrypts the packet, whether or not it has the right key. All A-nodes in the HomeRF network share a single common 56-bit key. The key may be entered though a *Management Information Base* (MIB), or computed dynamically. A MIB contains information that is used to manage the operation of a SWAP-CA node. This information can be used by higher-layer protocols to manage the node as well. A property of this algorithm is that the output ciphertext is of the same length as the input plaintext and the encryption algorithm is symmetric (i.e., decryption performs the same process as encryption). The core of the encryption algorithm is common to both asynchronous and isochronous data services. All multicast traffic is sent unencrypted.

Compression

An often-stated goal for wireless networking is to design a system that is bandwidth-efficient. One way to improve bandwidth utilization is to us compress the data before transmission. Data compression in a SWAP-CA network is optional and is left to the designer's discretion. It provides a trade-off between battery longevity and bandwidth. With data compression, nodes can transmit more data in a given amount of time than nodes that do not compress their data; however, compression consumes power and therefore contributes to battery drain for portable devices. Another issue to keep in mind is that data compression involves the reduction of redundancy in the data. Consequently, any corruption of the data is likely to have severe effects and be difficult to correct.

The recommended compression algorithm for a SWAP-CA network is a lossless compression algorithm that uses a combination of the LZ77 algorithm and Huffman coding, with efficiency that is comparable to the best currently available general-purpose compression methods. The data can be produced or consumed, for an arbitrarily long sequentially presented input data stream, and requires very few resources in terms of processing power and memory.

Compression is used only if the source node determines that the destination node is able to decompress the message. This can be determined during connection setup and capability exchange time.

Medium Access Control

The SWAP-CA medium access control protocol is optimized for the home environment. The protocol is derived from the ETSI DECT standard and from the popular wireless LAN standards such as IEEE 802.11. The MAC is designed to work over, and to take advantage of, the frequency-hopping radio subsystem. It includes a Time Division Multiple Access (TDMA) service for delivery of real-time isochronous data, and a Carrier Sense Multiple Access with Collision Avoidance (CSMA/CA) service for delivery of asynchronous data. The MAC's behavior depends on the devices that are in use in the network.

The highlights of the protocol are as follows:

- Simultaneous support for both voice and data traffic using a unique combination of TDMA and CSMA/CA access mechanisms.
- Support for four high-quality, 32-Kbps Adaptive Differential Pulse Code Modulation (ADPCM) voice connections.
- Data throughput of about 1.6 Mbps.
- Built-in power management capabilities for both isochronous and asynchronous nodes.
- Multiple levels of data security—none/basic/robust levels of encryption.
- Support for multiple networks in the same physical area with a 24-bit network identifier.

Figure 8.4 illustrates the protocol framing when the network is configured as a managed network. SWAP-CA defines a *superframe*, which is a periodic division of time. A superframe contains two contention-free periods (CFP1 and CFP2) and a contention period. The channel access mechanism used during the contention-free periods is TDMA and during the contention period is CSMA/CA. The duration of the superframe is fixed and a synchronization mechanism allows the nodes of the network to agree on the superframe timing. All nodes in the network hop together using the same hopping pattern and they hop to a different frequency at the start of every superframe. By hopping to a different frequency channel every superframe period, the dwell-time of the devices on a portion of the spectrum in which there may be high interference is reduced. This in turn reduces packet errors and packet loss, thus improving the overall throughput and reliability of the system. The start of a superframe is marked by a *Connection Point Beacon* (CPB) signal. The CPB is used for multiple purposes including: (1) maintaining network synchronization; (2) controlling the superframe; (3) managing the network during a contention-free period by indicating when each node should transmit and receive data—the CPB can include a list of active voice connections (and therefore slot assignments), retransmission slot assignments for the current connection status information, and paging information, and (4) providing power management services for isochronous and asynchronous nodes to maximize the battery life of portable devices. Slot assignment and synchronization information does not change on a per frame basis, so if a node misses a beacon it uses the information contained in the most recent valid beacon. All connection and paging status requests and information are repeated until they are acknowledged by the receiver.

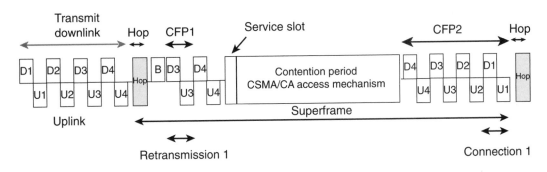

B - Beacon
Dn - Downlink slot
Un - Uplink slot
CFP1 - Contains two slots per connection for data that requires retransmission
CFP2 - Contains two slots per connection, one for downlink data and the other for uplink data

Figure 8.4
SWAP frame description

Voice Encoding and Transmission

HomeRF uses a 32 Kbps ADPCM codec, defined in CCITT Recommendation G.726, as a baseline voice encoding mechanism. I-nodes process 20 msec. segments of 14-bit linear PCM audio samples, sampled at 8 Khz. These samples are compressed and encoded to a sequence of 4-bit ADPCM code words before being packetized and queued for transmission in chronological order. Encoded voice packets are transmitted during the contention-free period. The contention-free periods are divided into a number of pairs of fixed-length slots, two per voice connection. The first slot in each pair is used to transmit voice data from the connection point to a node (downlink) and the second is used to transmit voice data from a node to the connection point (uplink). CFP2 at the end of the superframe is used for the initial transmission of the voice data, while CFP1 at the start of the superframe is used for the optional retransmission of any voice packet which was not received or was incorrectly received in the previous transmission. Each voice packet transmitted by an I-node includes in the packet header a piggyback acknowledgment of the last voice data message received by the node. That is, in the uplink packet, the voice node acknowledges the downlink packet sent by the connection point. This system allows the connection point to determine prior to a hop which voice data transmissions were lost, and determine whether or not retransmissions are required. Retransmissions are advertised in the beacon at the start of the next superframe; each voice data packet can only be retransmitted once. The time between the first voice packet transmission during CFP2 and its re-transmission in CFP1 is a function of the voice codec and is fixed at 20 ms. This provides an acceptable performance with respect to latency. The length of the transmission period is equal to a single voice data message, containing 20 ms segments of ADPCM data (640 bits), which is equivalent to an extended DECT B-field and 56 bits of control data, and equivalent to the DECT A-field plus some additional addressing information. With a 20 ms superframe, SWAP-CA can support up to four voice connections simultaneously with full re-transmission possibility. An important design goal for SWAP-CA was to provide robustness against interference. By choosing CFP2 for the initial packet transmission and the following CFP1 for retransmission, the system provides both frequency and time diversity. This is particularly important given the potentially noisy environment in which the protocol operates. At the end of CFP1 there is space reserved for a *service slot*. I-nodes use the service slot to request a connection from the connection point. Since there is only one service slot. it is possible for two or more modes to transmit at the same time and for their transmission to collide.

Each management message is explicitly acknowledged by the connection point in the CPB, and if there is no acknowledgment a node performs a random back-off across a number of transmission periods before re-sending the message.

Data Transmission

For data traffic a CSMA/CA access mechanism is used during the contention period of the superframe. With this scheme, the protocol provides efficient data bandwidth even with concurrent active voice calls. Peak effective user throughputs of up to 1 Mbps are possible under lightly loaded conditions in the 1.6 Mbps mode. Furthermore, data transfer between nodes can occur even when four voice calls are active simultaneously. The CSMA/CA protocol attempts to avoid collision by sensing transmissions on the radio medium and starting transmission when there is no such activity. The mechanism is similar to Ethernet (IEEE 802.3), enabling easy integration with an existing TCP/IP protocol stack within a host platform; the main difference with Ethernet is the slotted contention mechanism and the addition of MAC level acknowledgment of unicast packets.

Power Management Services

Battery energy is a limited resource that is not expected to increase in potential more than 30% in the near future. Consequently, for portable battery-operated devices, this resource needs to be used carefully and efficiently. A wireless network transceiver can typically use anywhere from 15 to 30% of the power from a typical portable computer, the display being the only part that consumes more power. Most wireless network interface cards that are on the market today consume close to 12 times the power of a standard 10 Mbps Ethernet card, and the battery longevity for wirelessly connected portable devices is reduced by as much as 60%, i.e., from three hours of operation down to 45 minutes. It is therefore mandatory for any wireless standard to support power management functions and be "power aware." One of the primary design goals that influenced the design of SWAP-CA was to provide power management services at the MAC layer.

Physical Layer and Components

The physical layer specification for SWAP-CA was largely adapted from the IEEE 802.11 FH and OpenAir standards with significant modifications to reduce cost while maintaining more than adequate performance for home usage scenarios. The SWAP-CA PHY provides the transmission and reception of data packets in the 2.4 GHz ISM band, using a 2-level Frequency Shift Key (2-FSK) modulation scheme, for 0.8 Mbps raw data rate performance, and an optional 4-FSK, for 1.6 Mbps raw data rate performance. Some key features of the SWAP-CA physical layer specifications are:

- Transmit power—up to +24 dBm (or nominally 100 mW-250mW)
- Low power transmit mode (optional)—between 0 and +4 dBm (for portable devices with limited peak current capability)
- Receiver sensitivity in 2-FSK (or 0.8 Mbps mode)—less than -80 dBm; in 4-FSK (or 1.6 Mbps) less than –70 dBm
- Hopping time—300 us (to allow conventional synthesizers to be used)
- Transceiver turnaround time—134 us (very easy to achieve with existing synthesizers)
- Adjacent and alternate channel filtering—no requirement

The combination of the transmit power and the receiver sensitivity represent a typical range that should easily exceed 50 m in most home environments. In the optional low-power mode, reliable indoor range is expected to be 10 to 20 m (which covers the bulk of the interior of most homes). Although the PHY layer design is quite similar to the IEEE 802.11 FH and OpenAir design, the SWAP-CA requirements impose substantially lower cost constraints for three reasons.

First, the required sensitivity limit is relaxed by about 10 dB. Second, the greatly relaxed channel filtering specification causes dramatically less intersymbol interference due to filter group delay variations in the passband. And third, the SWAP-CA packet headers for 4-FSK add a special training sequence to allow optimum slicing threshold values to be determined for the changing propagation environment. Thus for use within most homes, the 1.6 Mbps data rate is really available with SWAP-CA and adds virtually no cost to the 0.8 Mbps solution.

Software Architecture

Due to the availability on a wide scale of the Microsoft Windows operating system and its use as a de facto standard for home PCs, the HomeRF working group has sought to streamline operation of SWAP-CA devices on these systems. In this section, we briefly describe how SWAP-CA devices operate in the context of a main-line operating system. A SWAP-CA node connected to a PC exposes three distinct types of interfaces: asynchronous data, isochronous data, and management. Figure 8.5 illustrates the three types of interfaces. The interface exposed to legacy data-centric applications and voice applications is a standard part of the Windows operating system. Information about the device not covered in the standard programming interface is exposed by a private interface that may be provided by the hardware vendors to application writers as needed.

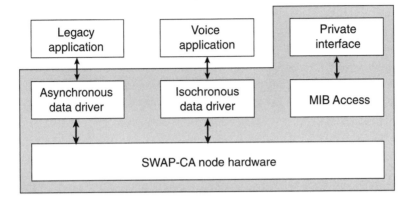

Figure 8.5
Interfaces exposed by a SWAP-CA device

Windows defines a *Network Device Interface Specification* (NDIS) for programming networking hardware. The NDIS software library, which is the implementation of this specification, performs many of the functions that are common to device drivers of networking hardware, including synchronization, device mapping, interrupt handling, event logging, etc. Furthermore, it provides a standard interface for higher-level protocols and applications, which can be independent of the underlying hardware. Manufacturers of network adapters write a *NDIS miniport* driver that provides functionality specific to their hardware. Miniports of a given media type can be used by higher-level protocols knowledgable about that media type with no further modifications. Figure 8.6 illustrates how the various software modules fit together. The shaded blocks are provided as a standard part of the operating system and the miniport device drivers are supplied by the hardware vendor. Miniport drivers that are written to conform to the NDIS specification are guaranteed to work with the Windows operating system.

NDIS exports two distinct interfaces—a *connectionless interface* (used by broadcast media such as Ethernet) and a *connection-oriented interface* (used by media that have explicit connections between endpoints, such as in Asynchronous Transfer Mode network connections). Hardware manufacturers who produce A-node SWAP-CA devices are required to write a connectionless miniport device NDIS driver only that declares itself as a member of the Ethernet media type. To higher-level protocols and applications, SWAP-CA A-nodes are then indistinguishable from normal Ethernet adapters, allowing Ethernet-knowledgable applications to immediately function with SWAP-CA devices. This inheritance of applications was an important design goal. Hardware manufacturers who produce I-node devices create a miniport driver that declares itself as a member of the Ethernet media type

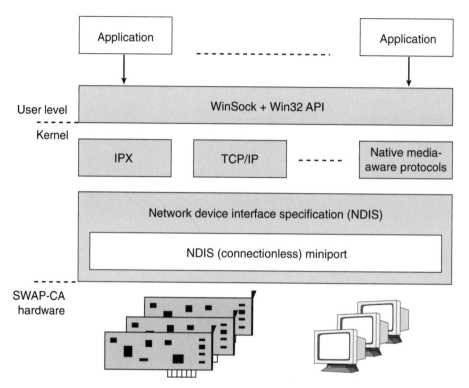

Figure 8.6
SWAP-CA A-node driver architecture

and exposes a connection-oriented interface, not the connectionless interface traditionally used. In addition to the basic miniport functions, I-node drivers provide call management functions such as those required for setting up and terminating voice calls. Call control of SWAP-CA I-node adapters is managed by the *Telephone Application Programming Interface* (TAPI). TAPI is a simple, generic set of objects, interfaces, and methods for establishing connections between devices; TAPI communicates with NDIS via a TAPI service provider also called a *TAPI proxy*. TAPI applications set up, control, and tear down calls on SWAP-CA devices via the TAPI proxy. The various software modules are illustrated in Figure 8.7; once again the shaded regions are part of the operating system.

Some applications may wish to stream voice conversations between SWAP-CA adapters and another adapter within the PC in real time. An example scenario is that of a SWAP-CA I-node (a cordless phone) user communicating with a SWAP-CA connection point, which is part of the PC. This connection is forwarded on to another

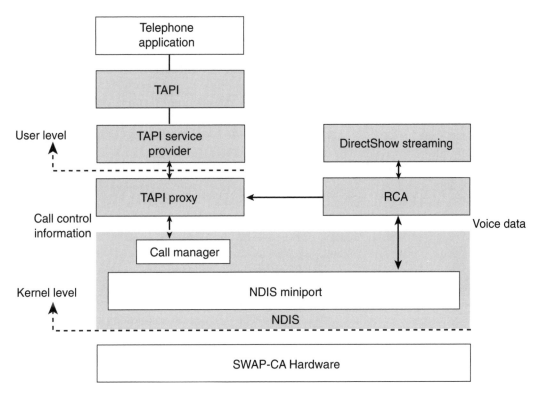

Figure 8.7
SWAP-CA for isochronous service driver architecture

adapter in the PC, possibly a modem attached to a phone line or a sound card attached to speakers and a microphone. To implement this application, the voice data is streamed between the SWAP-CA adapters via the *DirectShow Streaming* module. The DirectX architecture was designed to accommodate real-time traffic within a PC. A DirectShow filter is plumbed from the data source (in this case, the SWAP-CA adapter) to the data sink (the modem or sound card). Voice streams coming in via NDIS are redirected to the *Raw Channel Access* (RCA) filter, which in turn sends them into DirectShow. The RCA filter is part of the operating system, so connection-oriented miniports are automatically voice stream-enabled.

Positioning with Other Technologies

There are some wireless networking options that are either available today or will be available in the near future. Most have been designed for the enterprise market.

Table 8.2 lists some of these options with a comparative overview of the HomeRF attributes to "similar" technologies. Comparisons are generally typically controversial. These technologies are really more complementary than competitive. IEEE 802.11 and HIPERLAN are effectively wireless Ethernet technologies developed for the enterprise network. Both support multiple "cell" hand-offs and roaming for coverage of entire campuses and together permit users to trade off data rate with cost and power consumption. Note that while HIPERLAN is legal in Europe only, similar technologies are likely in the recently created Unlicensed National Information Infrastructure (U-NII bands) located at 5.15-5.35 GHz and 5.725-5.825 GHz in the United States. The HomeRF and HomePNA technologies are very synergistic for home electronics manufacturers because they share much networking infrastructure even though the physical media are quite different. In both cases, these are simplified "single-cell" networks where voice to the PSTN and data to the Internet can be combined simultaneously. Finally, for in-room (or in-car) point-to-point or point-to-multipoint connectivity, the proposed Bluetooth protocol and the industry-proven IrDA standards (over 60 million units shipped) are most appropriate. Between these two technologies, Bluetooth offers far greater physical convenience in its usage model as it is not line-of-sight and can pass through minor obstructions. The IrDA standards are very hard to beat by any radio technology in terms of their data rate, cost, or physical size (but Bluetooth is getting closer than any protocol before it has).

Note that in Table 8.2, the standby current refers to the average current draw for the transceiver portion of portable devices while retaining full network availability for the given technology.

Table 8.2 Comparison of SWAP-CA with Other Connectivity Options

Properties	HomeRF	Bluetooth	IEE 802.11 FH	HomePNA	IrDA	HIPERLAN
Operational spectrum	2.404–2.478 GHz	2.402–2.480 GHz	2.40–2.4835 GHz	Phone line	Infrared	51.15–5.3 GHz (& 17.1–17.3 GHz)
Physical layer	FHSS, 50 hops/sec, 2-FSK & 4-FSK	FHSS, 1600 hops/sec, GFSK	FHSS, 2-FSK, 4-FSK,...	?	Optical	Differential GMSK
Channel access	CSMA/CA + TDMA	Master-slave, polling	CSMA/CA with RTS/CTS	?	Polling	EY-NPMA
Peak raw data rate	0.8 & 1.6 Mbps	0.721 Mbps	1 & 2 Mbps	10 Mbps	16 Mbps (VFIR)	23.5 Mbps
Range	<150 feet	<30 feet	<150 feet	Phone jack	~3 feet	<90 feet
Standby & peak current	<1 mA & ~300 mA	<1 mA & ~60 mA	~10 mA & ~400 mA	?	<10 uA & ~300 mA	>2A
Data traffic	via TCP/IP	via PPP	via TCP/IP	via TCP/IP	via PPP	via TCP/IP
Voice traffic	via IP & PSTN	via IP & cellular	via IP	via IP & PSTN	via IP	via IP
Error robustness	CRC/ARQ Type 1	1/3 rate FEC, 2/3 rate FEC & ARQ Type 1	CRC ARQ Type II	?	?	BCH (31,26)
Mobility support	NA	NA	Yes	NA	NA	Not specified
Energy conservation	Directory based	Yes	Directory based	No	No	Directory based
Guaranteed latency	<20 msec for voice	?	None	?	?	<10 msec for voice
Speech coding	32 Kbps ADPCM	64 Kbps with CVSD/logPCM	NA	?	Not specified	32 Kbps ADPCM
Security	56-bit shared-key encryption	Stream cipher algorithm	64-bit shared-key encryption	?	?	?
Communications topology	Peer-to-peer, MS-to-BS	Master-slave	Peer-to-peer, MS-to-BS	?	Master-slave	Peer-to-peer, multi-hop, MS-to-BS
Price point (estimate)	Medium	Medium	Medium/High	Medium/Low	Low	High

HomeRF Products

Several companies are currently developing a range of end-user products that are based on the SWAP protocol. For instance, Proxim has recently announced that it will add SWAP 1.1 support into new members of its Symphony product family.

Proxim, Inc. is a leading supplier of 2.4 GHz wireless networking technology to both OEMs and end users worldwide. Details of other HomeRF-based products are shown in Table 8.3.

Table 8.3   Initial HomeRF Products

Company Name	Product Description
Cayman	ADSL gateway
Compaq	Consumer desktop and mobile wireless products
Diablo Research	Consulting for HomeRF chip integration
IBM	Personal computing devices and peripherals
Intel	PC card/USB adapter/bridge products
LSI Logic	HomeRF ASIC
MobileStar	Hot-spot service for business travellers
Motorola	Multiuser wireless cable modem

Furthermore, Siemens Communication Devices, a division of Siemens Information and Communication Products LLC, announced at CES 2000 that it will refine and deliver the voice communications element of the HomeRF networking specification.

With Siemens' addition of a voice component to home networks, consumers will enjoy greater convenience through wireless access to more voice, data, entertainment, and interactive services at affordable prices.

Future of HomeRF

The HomeRF organization is discussing a variety of future derivatives for the initial SWAP-CA specification. One possible derivative is simply to increase the data rate within the existing 2.4 GHz band while retaining full backward compatibility with the initial specification. The group is presently considering options in this regard that would scale SWAP-CA to 10 Mbps in the 2.4 GHz band.

In addition, HomeRF is also developing two major new market requirements documents. The first is SWAP-MM (for multimedia) which is looking at true video applications within the home enabled by wireless networking. This work will likely proceed to a formal technical proposal for the 5 GHz band. It is unclear at this point whether the SWAP-MM specification can ever be as near global as the 2.4 GHz SWAP-CA case. As with the SWAP-CA case, achieving consumer price points with a SWAP-MM solution will be critical. The other direction HomeRF is considering is an ultra-low-cost version called SWAP-lite that could be developed to be interoperable with future SWAP-CA devices while achieving much lower price and power consumption points. Keyboards, mouses, joysticks, remote controls, toys, etc. are the products that might use SWAP-lite. Clearly such a system overlaps in capability with infrared technology, which sets a tough measure to compete with in terms of price/ performance.

BLUETOOTH...

Bluetooth is another industry group developing a specification for low-cost, short-range radio links between mobile computers, cameras, and other portable in-home devices. Bluetooth technology is the result of cooperation between leaders in the telecommunications and computer industries. It is the code name for a technology specification for small form factor, low-cost, short-range radio links between mobile PCs, mobile phones, and other portable devices. It enables home networking users to connect a wide range of computing and telecommunications devices easily and simply, without the need to buy, carry, or connect cables. It delivers opportunities for rapid ad hoc connections, and the possibility of automatic, unconscious, connections between devices. It virtually eliminates the need to purchase additional or proprietary cabling to connect individual devices. Because Bluetooth can be used for a variety of purposes, it will also potentially replace multiple cable connections via a single radio link. Bluetooth is being promoted and has been adopted by a group of companies called the Bluetooth Special Interest Group (SIG). This includes promoter companies 3Com, Ericsson, IBM, Intel, Lucent, Microsoft, Motorola, Nokia, and Toshiba and 1,665 adopter companies (at the time of writing).

Technology Overview

The Bluetooth technology is an open specification for wireless communication of data and voice. It is based on a low-cost short-range radio link, built into a 9 x 9 mm microchip, facilitating protected ad hoc connections for stationary and mobile communication environments.

Bluetooth technology allows for the replacement of the many proprietary cables that connect one device to another with one universal short-range radio link. For instance, Bluetooth radio technology built into both the cellular telephone and the laptop would replace the cumbersome cables used today to connect a laptop to a cellular telephone. Printers, PDAs, desktops, table-sized handhelds, fax machines, keyboards, joysticks, and virtually any other digital device can be part of the Bluetooth system.

Bluetooth radio technology provides a universal bridge to existing data networks, a peripheral interface, and a mechanism to form small private ad hoc groupings of connected devices away from fixed network infrastructures. Designed to operate in a noisy radio frequency environment such as a home, the Bluetooth radio uses a fast acknowledgment and frequency hopping scheme to make the link robust. Bluetooth radio modules avoid interference from other signals by hopping to a new frequency after transmitting or receiving a packet. Compared with other systems operating in the same frequency band, the Bluetooth radio typically hops faster and uses shorter packets. This makes the Bluetooth radio more robust than other systems. Short packages and fast hopping also limit the impact of domestic and professional microwave ovens. Use of Forward Error Correction (FEC) limits the impact of random noise on long-distance links. The encoding is optimized for an uncoordinated environment. Bluetooth radios normally operate in the unlicensed ISM band at 2.4 GHz. From a security perspective, Bluetooth provides user protection and information privacy mechanisms at the lower layers of its protocol stack. Authentication is based on a challenge-response algorithm. Authentication is a key component of any home networking system, allowing you to develop a domain of trust between Bluetooth devices, such as allowing only your personal notebook to communicate through your cellular telephone.

Building Blocks of a Bluetooth Solution

The role of each component in a Bluetooth-based home network is briefly outlined in the following categories.

Piconets

The Bluetooth system supports both point-to-point and point-to-multipoint connections. A collection of devices that are connected to a home network via Bluetooth technology is called a *piconet*. A piconet starts with two connected devices, such as a digital set-top box and cellular phone, and may grow to eight connected devices. All Bluetooth devices are peer units and have identical implementations. However, when establishing a piconet, one unit will act as a master and the other(s) as slave(s) for the duration of the piconet connection. Several piconets can be established and linked together ad hoc, where each piconet is identified by a different frequency-hopping sequence. All users participating on the same piconet are synchronized to this hopping sequence.

Protocols

The Bluetooth protocol stack can be logically divided into four different layers according to their purpose in a wireless home networking environment.

1. **Bluetooth core protocols**—This group of protocols has been exclusively developed by the Bluetooth SIG group. The main purpose of these protocols is to enable RF communication links between Bluetooth devices.

2. **Cable replacement protocol**—The cable replacement protocol used by Bluetooth is called RFCOMM and is used to emulate RS-232 control and data transfer.

3. **Telephony control protocol**—This Bluetooth protocol defines the rules for making speech and data calls across a home network.

4. **Adopted protocols**—This layer consists of application-oriented protocols such as PPP, TCP/IP, HTTP, FTP, Wireless Application Protocol (WAP), and so on.

Software Framework

The software framework used by Bluetooth devices creates a positive experience for consumers. Interoperability between different devices is seen as an essential part of a successful home networking solution. The software that is integrated into Bluetooth devices allows them to discover each other and load appropriate in-home applications. To obtain this functionality, the Bluetooth software framework reuses existing specifications such as Human Interface Device (HID) and TCP/IP rather than invent sets of new specifications. Device compliance requires conformance to both the Bluetooth specification and existing protocols.

For a more detailed description of Bluetooth technical components, we suggest that you download the entire specification from the following Web address: http://www.bluetooth.com/developer/specification/specification.asp.

Practical Uses of Bluetooth Technologies within the Home

General PC Applications

The Bluetooth specification defines interfaces where the radio modules may be integrated into notebook personal computers or attached using PC-Card or USB port. Notebook PC usage models include:

- Remote networking using a Bluetooth cellular phone
- Speakerphone applications using a Bluetooth cellular phone
- Personal card exchange between Bluetooth notebooks, handhelds, and phones
- Calendar synchronization between Bluetooth notebooks, handhelds, and phones
- File transfers (file types include, but are not limited to, .xls, .ppt, .wav, .jpg, and .doc formats)

Bluetooth technology is platform-independent and not tied to any specific operating system. Implementations of the Bluetooth specification for several commercial operating systems are in development. For notebook computers, the implementation of the Bluetooth specification in Microsoft Windows 98 and Windows 2000 using Windows Driver Model (WDM) and NDIS drivers is being contemplated.

Telephone Applications

The Bluetooth specification defines interfaces where the radio modules may be integrated directly into cellular handsets or attached using an add-on device. Phone usage models include, but are not constrained to:

- Wireless hands-free operation using a Bluetooth headset
- Cable-free remote networking with a Bluetooth notebook or handheld computer
- Business card exchange with other Bluetooth phones, notebook, or handheld computers
- Automatic address book synchronization with trusted Bluetooth notebooks or handheld computers

The Bluetooth compliance document will require digital cellular phones to support some subset of the Bluetooth specification. The Bluetooth contingents within the telephony promoter companies are working with their fellow employees involved in the WAP Forum to investigate how the two technologies can benefit from each other.

Other Applications

Usage models and implementation examples centered on other contemplated Bluetooth devices include:

- Headsets
- Handheld and wearable devices
- Human Interface Device (HID) compliant peripherals
- Data and voice access points
- Digital set-top boxes
- Integrated digital televisions

The wireless headset will support untethered audio for phones and provide phone-quality audio for notebook computers operating in sound-sensitive environments.

SHAREWAVE ....

ShareWave, Inc., provides highly integrated semiconductors and networking software for high-performance, multimedia, broadband gateways and wireless in-home networks. ShareWave's core product lines include wireless network controllers, wireless bridge controllers, residential gateway controllers, and associated networking services and protocols. ShareWave sells these products to leaders of the broadband, consumer electronics, computing, and networking industries. Founded in 1996 by a group of former Intel and venture capital executives, ShareWave is privately held with its headquarters in El Dorado Hills, California. ShareWave's goal is to provide consumers with the freedom of unrestricted access to the digital content they want, where and when they want it. A home network enabled by ShareWave technology provides the high performance required to support fast, secure, and robust wireless distribution of all digital content types—data, voice, audio, and video—to user-chosen locations throughout the house. ShareWave has announced customer partnership agreements with NETGEAR (a wholly owned subsidiary of Nortel Networks), Cisco, and Kyushu Matsushita Electric, who will all incorporate ShareWave technology into consumer home networking solutions.

Technology and Product Overview

ShareWave is focussed on easily extending access to broadband platforms (such as xDSL modems, cable modems, and cable set-tops) beyond their initial termination point in the home, while also enabling the deployment of low-cost client applications. Share-Wave's technology is encapsulated in a set of ingredient products that are used by its OEM customers to develop home networking end products cited below. ShareWave's ingredient products are characterized by high performance, QoS-enabled delivery of multimedia content, ease of use, and superior price/performance. ShareWave's target consumer solutions, and respective product enablers, are described below.

- **Wireless broadband bridges**—ShareWave's Wireless Bridge Controller (SWB 2510) is used in bridging and routing products that attach externally to broadband modems to provide fast (11 Mbps and above) wireless connections to computers and other client access devices. This solution enables an easy extension of the broadband connection from where it initially enters the home to user-chosen locations throughout the home. Using industry standard connectivity options (e.g., Ethernet), wireless bridges enable the use and management of broadband content and services from anywhere in the home.

- **Residential gateways**—Broadband modems and set-tops will begin to add LAN routing to WAN access termination, becoming an early generation of the residential gateway. ShareWave's Residential Gateway Controller is a highly integrated, multi-interface chip that addresses the cost, performance, and interconnectivity requirements of emerging residential gateway platforms. It seamlessly enables the broadband connection to be shared across multiple physical layers, such as wireless, Ethernet, and phoneline, and across multiple connection technologies, such as USB and IEEE 1394. The SWG2710's highly integrated functions, interfaces, and programmability enable an optimized system architecture for current and future residential gateway products.

- **PC wireless connectivity**—ShareWave's wireless network controllers provide connectivity for desktop computers and laptops/mobile devices. These controllers enable low-cost PCI, USB, and PCMCIA cards that allow the client computer to be wirelessly connected to the broadband modems noted above. They also address traditional PC-to-PC networking products targeted at multi-PC households.

- **Audio/video clients**—ShareWave's series of high-performance semiconductors also enable new classes of consumer devices that allow ubiquitous consumption of multimedia content. Examples include wireless MP3 players, mobile web pads, personal video recorders, and digital audio and video jukeboxes.

A key element of ShareWave's technology portfolio is the Whitecap network protocol. It represents the "language" spoken by the high-performance, multimedia broadband in-home network. Whitecap's key features include dynamic TDMA, quality of service, and selectable error correction (FEC). Whitecap efficiently manages a network of heterogeneous devices and digital content: cable and xDSL modems, residential gateways, PCs, TVs, mobile pads, set-top boxes, digital audio and video jukeboxes, and other information appliances and servers. Whitecap can enable networks to handle bursty data communication among PCs and PC-like devices while simultaneously streaming full motion video to TVs and other entertainment devices and packet-based voice to Internet cordless phones. The next section of this guide will examine Whitecap in more detail.

Whitecap Technical Overview

The Whitecap protocol was designed to enable home networks that address the consumer's need for performance, reliability, scalability, interoperability, security, upgradability, and ease of use. The Whitecap protocol was designed from the ground up to accommodate and transmit all multimedia content including control data, voice, audio, and video in a noisy home environment (Figure 8.8).

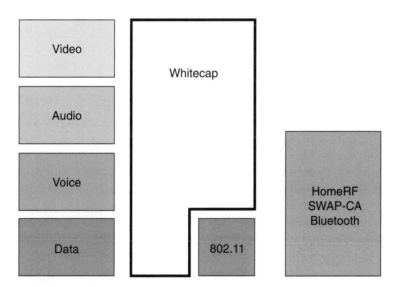

Figure 8.8
Whitecap protocol layers

The Whitecap protocol is designed to work with leading-edge, wireless digital radio technology to deliver the highest network utilization. The network architecture, services, and packet structure in the Whitecap protocol have been streamlined to minimize overhead, enabling greater efficiency for multimedia transmission. The Whitecap protocol is designed to easily support various types of network devices, including either desktop or mobile PCs, as well as non-PC devices such as wireless bridges, residential gateways, Internet phones, and TV terminals.

Whitecap's key features enable high-performance, wireless multimedia transmission that meets the needs of today's home environment. These features include dynamic TDMA, quality of service (QoS), multicast addressing with shadow clients, privacy and security, co-location, multichannel and channel selection, remote automatic firmware updating, master device redundancy, and selectable error correction, as described in the sections that follow.

Dynamic TDMA

The Whitecap protocol is a connection-oriented network protocol that uses a dynamic time division multiple access (TDMA) mechanism. Network bandwidth is slotted and shared among the multiple streams of network traffic.

The Whitecap network assigns a master device that is responsible for transmitting periodic beacons to synchronize clients. The master also allocates bandwidth and polices traffic when devices transmit on the network. Each node that needs to transmit is assigned a particular slot within a network frame. Dynamic TDMA adjusts slots based on the bandwidth needs of each node on the network.

Dynamic TDMA provides several benefits, including:

- **High network performance and efficiency (high usable network throughput)**—Dynamic TDMA allows the Whitecap protocol to assign network nodes only the bandwidth they need. This minimizes wasted bandwidth and preserves overall bandwidth for other network nodes and applications. More usable throughput means higher performance for all home network applications (e.g., higher video quality, faster file transfer times).

- **Eliminates unexpected delays and provides synchronization for multimedia content**—Delays and unpredictable latency are unacceptable when transmitting isochronous content (video, audio, and voice). Dynamic TDMA avoids unpredictable and long delays by eliminating collisions and the capture effect caused by carrier sense multiple access (CSMA) mechanisms. In CSMA access, shared bandwidth is not governed and network nodes are allowed to transmit at the same time. When network nodes realize they are transmitting simultaneously with other nodes, all nodes must back off and attempt to transmit later. This will result in unexpected and potentially long delays in multinode networks. Networks may also experience the "capture effect" where one node transmitting a long sequence of data can monopolize the entire bandwidth while other nodes must wait—particularly problematic for time-sensitive multimedia content.

Whitecap protocol's dynamic TDMA architecture enables predictable latencies and provides the synchronization crucial for transmitting isochronous multimedia content (i.e., voice, audio, and video). The dynamic TDMA architecture provides the foundation and ability to support sophisticated QoS features to enable high-quality video, voice, and audio transmission simultaneously with batch data.

- **Supports home network growth and expandability (adding more nodes)**—As more and more nodes are added in a CSMA network, collisions become more frequent and the total usable throughput of the network degrades exponentially. Dynamic TDMA better supports additional nodes by eliminating collisions. Consequently, as network nodes are added, additional bandwidth is simply reallocated and the overall available throughput is gracefully maintained.

Quality of Service (QoS)

Guaranteed Bandwidth Reservation

The Whitecap protocol can reserve bandwidth for multimedia isochronous content that has extremely stringent bandwidth and latency requirements (e.g., MPEG video).

Priority Service

The Whitecap protocol provides a best-effort priority service. Priority services are applied to transmit traffic at each network node. High-priority traffic is differentiated from low-priority batch data (e.g., print jobs, file transfers) by decoding packet fields such as IP precedence bits and payload. Differentiated packets are separated and buffered into three queues of high, medium, and low priority. After differentiating network traffic, time-sensitive, high-priority traffic is transmitted first. Priority service is applied as packets are transmitted out of the three queues in a weighted fair queuing (WFQ) arbitration mechanism into the remaining bandwidth of each node's corresponding slot. WFQ arbitration transmits a higher ratio of higher-priority packets than lower-priority packets during the given slot time.

The benefits of QoS include:

- **Higher multimedia quality**—Guaranteed bandwidth allows the support of high-bandwidth isochronous content such as MPEG-2 video. Priority services enhance the performance of multimedia applications by providing more bandwidth and better latency to multimedia content such as Internet video and audio.

- **Simultaneous multimedia (video, voice, audio) and batch data (print jobs, file sharing) transmission**—The ability to support *simultaneous* multimedia and batch data transmission without compromising multimedia quality is mandatory in a home network. Multimedia quality must be maintained when the home user is simultaneously printing a file to a remote printer or transferring a file from PC to PC.

  Whitecap protocol's guaranteed bandwidth reservation QoS preserves high-quality isochronous data transmission even in high-batch data traffic environments. By prioritizing network traffic and delivering time-sensitive traffic first, priority services allow low rate data (email, print jobs) to coexist with multimedia content without any degradation in the user experience.

- **Preserves QoS of high-speed broadband Internet**—Internet applications, services, and multimedia content distribution such as video on demand, VoIP, and streaming audio need end-to-end quality of service to operate properly. Internet QoS initiatives including Resource Reservation Setup Protocol (RSVP), the audiovisual data transmission standard H.323, Real-time Transport Protocol (RTP), and priority services implemented in head-end routers, provide high-quality distribution of content to the house. The network distributing content within the home must preserve QoS to utilize Internet content throughout the home in its intended form.

Multicast Addressing with Shadow Clients

Shadow clients in a Whitecap network allow the support of more multiple media streams. Viewing the same multimedia content at different locations is a common requirement for the home. Popular multicast protocols such as IP multicast and IGMP are being deployed by the Internet to deliver multiple media (audio, video, voice) streams to the home. Shadow clients reduce the required bandwidth to support sharing media streams by allowing traffic to be sent only once vs. individually to each client receiving the media stream. Shadow clients enable multicasting of multimedia content and data. A shadow client is a client that has been given permission from the master to decode and receive traffic destined for another client on the home network.

Privacy and Security

Privacy and security will become increasingly important as more and more wireless networks are deployed in the home. Unlike wired networks, wireless networks cannot be secured or contained physically. E-commerce over the Internet, copyrighted multimedia content (e.g., CDs, DVDs), and personal or financial information in the home require a high need for privacy. The Whitecap protocol employs several security mechanisms that prevent unauthorized access to data. Whitecap protocol privacy and security exists in three different layers of the network stack (Figure 8.9).

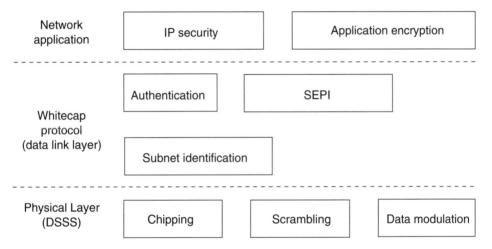

Figure 8.9
Privacy and security layers

Physical Layer

Direct sequence spread spectrum (DSSS) radio transmission offers isolation at the physical layer. The implementation of DSSS is difficult to intercept and decode. Radios must also be tuned to the correct frequencies to receive data. The original data stream is essentially encoded through chipping and scrambling.

Data Link Layer

To avoid unauthorized access, the Whitecap protocol follows a strict authentication procedure before a connection is granted. Each Whitecap protocol network is identified by a unique 16-bit subnet ID. The subnet ID is a field in the Whitecap protocol header and is unique to a specific network. Packets with the incorrect subnet ID authentication are dropped and denied access to all devices on the network. The Whitecap protocol subnet ID provides reliable security by exercising security on a packet-by-packet basis. The Whitecap protocol data link layer provides an optional interface, ShareWave Encryption Protocol Interface (SEPI), to implement encryption schemes. SEPI allows traffic of different encryption types to exist on the same network by tracking encryption schemes on a stream-by-stream basis. Possible schemes for authentication/encryption include RC2, RC4, DES, and IDEA. This gives Whitecap protocol implementers the option to select an encryption scheme that is best for a given application.

Network Layer

The Whitecap protocol does not inhibit encryption or security mechanisms employed by higher-level network applications or protocols. For instance, encryption applied by the IP protocol (e.g., SSL) to IP data is preserved by the Whitecap protocol and decrypted by the IP protocol at the receiving end. Internet or Web transaction encrypted data will be transmitted through the Whitecap protocol and decrypted by the Web browser at the receiving end.

Multichannel Channel Selection

The Whitecap protocol allows operation across several independent, nonoverlapping channels. Each channel is capable of transmitting the full network bandwidth. Whitecap protocol channel selection can identify and switch network operation to the channel with the lowest packet error rate. Benefits of channel selection include network reliability and higher performance.

Network Reliability

Channel selection improves the interference immunity of the network. The Whitecap protocol can avoid interference (e.g., from cordless phones, microwaves) by monitoring channel conditions and selecting the channel with the least interference.

Higher Performance

Usable data throughput of the Whitecap protocol network is increased. Channel selection allows the Whitecap protocol to find the frequency channel that has the highest data throughput and the least interference. High usable throughput increases multimedia quality and speeds up batch data applications such as file sharing, print jobs, and Internet surfing.

Co-location

Co-location enables the deployment of Whitecap protocol networks in closely located homes and apartment complexes. Ideally, the distribution of wireless subnets should be nonoverlapping to avoid interference with each other. Realistically, closely located homes and dense apartment complexes may make overlapping subnets commonplace to wireless home networks. Co-location and channel selection features allow overlapping networks to operate without degrading performance.

Overlapping subnets first utilize channel selection to find and change network operation to an available open channel, allowing both overlapping networks to transmit at full bandwidth. In the scenario where there are more overlapping subnets than available channels, the Whitecap protocol co-location feature is enabled. The operation of nonoverlapping networks in the same channel is achieved by sharing the available channel bandwidth through appropriate negotiations between overlapping subnet masters.

Remote Automatic Firmware Updating

Remote automatic firmware updating allows users to install product enhancements and upgrades. Upgrades ensure scalability of the Whitecap protocol with new home networking applications and services. Packet types and the command protocol used to update network nodes are clearly defined in the Whitecap protocol so that updates are seamless to the end user. The update process is initiated when the master or client receives a new version of firmware. The master then identifies and updates all network nodes that do not have the latest firmware revision. The ability to update network protocols over the Internet benefits end users by significantly reducing device obsolescence.

Master Device Redundancy

The master device redundancy feature protects against the possibility of a master device failure bringing the whole network down. This feature eliminates a single point of failure and improves network reliability. Master device redundancy also allows users to power down master nodes in a Whitecap protocol network without disabling the entire network. Ease of use is improved because the user does not have to treat the master node differently from the clients.

Selectable Error Correction

Different network applications and content drive different requirements of delivery quality and error correction. For instance, every packet of a bank statement is mission-critical data and needs to be retransmitted until the data is received correctly. On the other hand, CD-quality audio would sound terrible if packets were retransmitted, causing unexpected delays. Video also cannot tolerate delays, but missing packets may cause poor image and viewing quality. The Whitecap protocol's selectable error correction offers several classes of delivery qualities to apply according to the type of media stream to deliver the highest possible performance and quality.

Auto Repeat reQuest (ARQ)

The Whitecap protocol supports selectable retransmissions or lossless streams with Auto Repeat reQuest (ARQ). ARQ does not guarantee latency of delivery; therefore, it is best applied to bulk and mission-critical data. The number of retransmissions is stream-dependent, as these parameters can be changed from a default value during stream initiation. ARQ is selectable to accommodate isochronous data and to interoperate with lossy upper network protocols such as UDP.

CRC and Forward Error Correction

Lossy streams are not retransmitted, but high-quality delivery is achieved through Forward Error Correction coding (FEC). FEC recovers data "on the fly" while other correction mechanisms, such as CRC, filter and drop corrupt data, requiring retransmission. Consequently, FEC actually increases the available usable throughput. CRC is reserved for data streams that require guaranteed reliability for every bit in the packet. FEC can be used by either lossy or lossless data; however, FEC is essential for video which is not retransmitted because even just a few dropped frames can cause poor image quality.

PROXIM...

Proxim, Inc., is a leading vendor in the worldwide wireless LAN industry. Headquartered in Sunnyvale, California, Proxim has more than 15 years of experience in the wireless LAN market. Today Proxim is the world's leading supplier of spread-spectrum wireless LAN products to OEMs and wireless solutions providers. Proxim is a founding member of the Wireless LAN Interoperability Forum (WLI Forum), established to deliver and test interoperable wireless LAN products and services (www.wlif.com). Proxim is also a core member of HomeRF, which is committed to providing a broad range of interoperable cordless consumer devices. In 1994, Proxim was first to market with its industry-leading RangeLAN2 2.4 GHz frequency-hopping wireless LAN product family, which has attracted more than 100 OEMs and wireless solutions providers worldwide. In 1998, the company introduced its high-performance RangeLAN802 product line, which operates at 2 Mbps and is fully compliant with the IEEE 802.11 standard. In 1999, Proxim has established itself as a leader in the emerging home networking market with its award-winning Symphony suite of cordless networking products for home and small office environments.

Symphony Technologies

Symphony emulates an Ethernet network. However, instead of using wire to connect the computers, Symphony products use radio technology. The technology is similar to that of a cordless telephone.

Proxim's Symphony Cordless Networking Suite operates in the 2.4 GHz frequency band and uses frequency-hopping spread-spectrum radio frequency technology, which is both highly secure and exceptionally immune to interference. It delivers data rates of 1.6 Mbps in a single-cell environment with an indoor coverage radius of up to 150 feet, or enough area to cover nearly any single family home or small office. Up to 10 Symphony-enabled computers can communicate simultaneously.

Symphony includes device driver software for the Windows 95, Windows 98 and Windows NT 4.0 operating systems. For a more detailed description of Proxim home networking technologies, we suggest that you visit: http://www.proxim.com/symphony/learn/index.shtml.

SUMMARY ....

A wireless home network is an intriguing alternative to phone-line and powerline wiring systems. Wireless home networks provide all the functionality of wireline networks without the physical constraints of the wire itself. They generally revolve around either IR or radio transmissions within your home. Radio transmissions comprise two distinct technologies—narrowband and spread-spectrum radio. Most wireless home networking projects are based on spread-spectrum technologies. To date, the high cost and impracticality of adding new wires have inhibited the widespread adoption of home networking technologies. Wired technologies also do not allow users to roam about with portable devices. In addition, multiple, incompatible communication standards have limited acceptance of wireless networks in the home. A group called HomeRF was formed in 1998 to address these issues and develop a standard that allows the connection of A/V devices and PCs without laying any cables. Since its formation, the group has developed a specification for wireless communications in the home called SWAP-CA. The group believes that this open specification will:

- Allow consumer electronic devices and PCs to talk to each other without being concerned with the existing wiring system in the home.
- Enable interoperability between many different consumer electronic devices available from a large number of manufacturers.
- Provide the flexibility and mobility of a wireless solution. This flexibility is important to the success of creating a compelling and complete home network solution.

Companies including Cayman Systems, Compaq, IBM, MobileStar Network, Motorola, and Proxim have announced plans to launch HomeRF-based products. The DECT standard is designed to be one of the core building blocks for the communications services of the future. Bluetooth technology is another popular solution for people who want to deploy wireless in-home networks. Bluetooth technology facilitates real-time voice and data transmission between devices on a home network. It eliminates the need for numerous, often proprietary, cable attachments for the connection of practically any kind of communication device.

Connections are instant and they are maintained even when devices are not within the line of sight. The range of each radio is approximately 10 meters, but it can be extended to around 100 meters with an optional amplifier. Today's home networking applications are driving the need for a high-performance, wireless network protocol with high usable speed (throughput) and isochronous, multimedia-capable services. ShareWave has designed the Whitecap protocol from the ground up to address consumers' needs for high performance, ease of use, reliability, and scalability. Whitecap is ideally suited to efficiently and seamlessly extending the broadband experience, delivered to the home by cable and xDSL modems and residential gateways, to any location in the home. Proxim is another established player in the emerging home networking market.

9

Residential Gateways

In this chapter...

In today's rapidly changing communications industry, the boundaries between PC networks, Internet-based systems, and broadcast television have begun to blur. The evolution of new residential data broadcasting services has created the need for a special interface or gateway device that can be used to pass digital content between the Internet and a home network. These gateways provide the fat pipeline that is required to carry information between the Internet and appliances in your home. Home gateways sit between the access network and the in-home network and allow multiple appliances in your house to share a single connection to the Internet. With the deployment of high-speed Internet connections and the push by service providers to offer integrated voice, data, and video services over the same high-speed pipe to different nodes throughout the home, the residential gateway is expected to become a key integrated services enabler. Technology drivers of the emerging residential gateway market are:

- The rapid emergence of viable, standards-based home networking technology such as those based on HomePNA and HomeRF
- New entertainment options, including digital TV and Web-based interactive TV
- Non-PC-based Internet appliances

A recent study by Cahners In-Stat Group expects the residential gateway market to go from one that is nearly nonexistent today to a $2.4 billion market by 2003. In an aggressive market scenario, the market could reach as high as $8.8 billion by 2003. Many of the home networking devices that are currently being used by consumers to access broadband networks will incorporate residential gateway functionality in the near future. In addition to these devices, a number of dedicated residential gateways such as home servers are expected to emerge. In this chapter we will focus our energies on the various types of devices that are competing for a share of the residential gateway marketplace—cable modems, digital set-top boxes, digital video recorders, DSL modems, and home servers.

CABLE MODEMS ....

For cable operators, home networking is an opportunity to increase the use of broadband data and video services. Historically, cable companies were in the business of offering traditional TV services to their customer base. These companies are moving into the telecommunications sector to offer a variety of services, including high-speed Internet access, free e-mail accounts, hosting of e-commerce sites, and delivering advanced IP-based applications. If you want your home network to interface with these services, you need to buy or rent a home gateway device called a cable modem. The number of North American cable modem subscribers surged to 1.8 million in 1999 and is expected to double by the end of 2000, according to Cahners In-Stat Group. The high-tech market research firm also forecasts that there will be more than 9.5 million broadband cable data subscribers worldwide by the end of 2002. In-Stat's research also found:

- More than 110 million homes in North America are passed by a broadband coaxial cable line and more than 77 million of those homes currently subscribe to cable TV services.

- Cable broadband service revenues will increase from $1 billion to almost $4 billion by the end of 2002.

From a technical perspective, a cable modem is a digital modem that uses a coaxial cable connection. Cable modems operate over two-way hybrid fiber and coaxial lines. Some cable operators that have not upgraded their networks to provide full bidirectional services use their hybrid fiber coaxial (HFC) network for high-speed downstream data transfer and use the local telephone network for return path data. A standard cable modem will have two connections; one port is connected to the TV outlet on the wall and the other to the subscriber's PC. The cable modem will then communicate over the cable network to a device called a CMTS (Cable Modem Termination System). The speed of the cable modem depends on traffic levels and the overall network architecture. Theoretically speaking, cable modems are capable of receiving and processing multimedia content at 30 Mbps, literally hundreds of times faster than a normal telephone connection to the Internet. However, in reality subscribers can expect to download information at between 0.5 and 1.5 Mbps because the bandwidth is shared by a number of home networks throughout the neighborhood. In regard to frequency ranges, operators define a portion of the frequency spectrum to carry the data. In general, the downstream path (head-end to home network) will lie between 50 MHz and 750 MHz. The frequency range can vary from network to network and from country to country. The frequency range 5 to 42 MHz is used when transmitting information from the in-home network to the head-end. Cable modems are primarily used for receiving and transmitting TCP/IP traffic including multimedia content and Web access data. A major benefit of a cable modem home gateway is the fact that the connection is always open, so you never have to go through the slow procedure of establishing a dial-up connection. In some cases, this can take up to a minute, which is very frustrating.

When using a cable modem as a home gateway, a couple of installation issues need to be considered. First and foremost, it is well documented that the in-home coaxial wiring system is the major source of electromagnetic interference. To reduce noise levels, it may be necessary to install a new piece of coaxial cable. Also of concern to home network users is the presence of various terminals such as TV sets,

VCRs, and radios. Because these devices can generate interference, which could affect the performance of a home gateway, it may be necessary to identify ways of isolating the cable modem from other electrical devices in the house. Today, the provisioning of a cable modem service in the home may require a technician to install the new hardware and configure the TCP/IP protocol stack. The service provider will also need to configure the servers that run the applications (Web hosting, chat, e-mail, etc.). This whole process is expensive and very time consuming. Consequently, the strategy for most service providers is to develop cable modem technology to allow users to provision the service themselves. Once a cable modem is connected to the HFC network, users would be presented with a registration Web site where they can select or confirm specific service plans. The elimination of the need for a cable technician is unlikely to happen in the short term. However, as people become more familiar with home networking technologies and manufacturers begin selling computers with internal cable modems, the need to send a technician to a home will decrease. The security of cable modems is also an issue for users of home networks. An intruder could, in theory, tap into the coaxial cable in a HFC network and capture packets of data that have been transmitted by devices on the network. So a cable modem used to transmit confidential information needs to make life difficult for the "cable hackers" by using encryption technologies.

There are many cable modem brands. The most common are from Com21, Motorola, Bay Networks, RCA, Cisco, Toshiba, 3Com, and Terayon. For more information on cable modem manufacturers, visit http://www.catv.org.

How a Cable Modem Works

Cable modems are different from standard modems that perform a "handshake"—an agreement on how to transmit data—with a compatible modem outside of the provider's network. Cable modems need to handshake with modems located at the cable operator site. Complex signalling, use of frequencies, and authentication need to be agreed on between the two modems. Modems located at the operator's site provide the following functionality:

- Equalization to compensate for signal distortion
- Address filtering so that the modem only accepts messages intended for the correct recipient
- Transmitting and receiving functions
- Automatic power adjustments to compensate for power fluctuations
- Adjustments in amplitude (signal strength or wave height) due to temperature changes

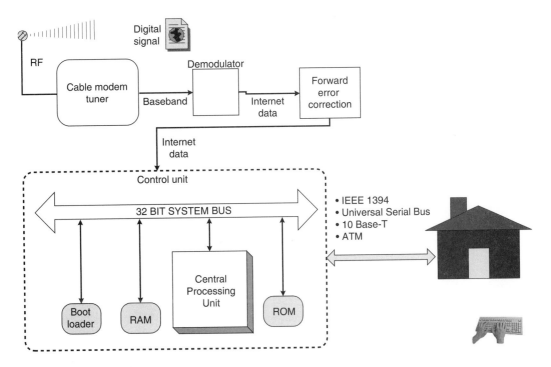

Figure 9.1
Architecture of a typical cable modem

- Modulation of the signal (i.e., analog to digital conversions and vice versa)
- Compensation for delays caused by variable distances

From Figure 9.1, we can see that the tuner in the cable modem receives a digital signal from the network and isolates a particular channel that contains the Internet data. It then converts the signal from RF levels back to baseband.

The baseband output signal from the tuner is then forwarded to a demodulator. The function of the demodulator is to sample the signal and convert it to a digital bit-stream. The bit-stream contains video, audio, and IP data. Once the bitstream has been recovered, it is forwarded to the forward error correction unit and checked for problems. The signal is then passed to the control unit.

The control unit comprises the following subsystems:

- Boot loader to ensure that software updates are completed in a secure manner.

- Read-only memory to store firmware and Media Access Control addresses.
- RAM used as a temporary storage area for data flowing between the processor and the various hardware components.
- A processor to manage all devices in the control unit and execute program instructions. Note that the cable modem uses a 32-bit bus to carry information between the various control unit components.

From the control unit, data is passed on to your home network using one of the following high-speed data port interfaces:

- Universal Serial Bus
- ATM
- IEEE 1394
- 10 Base-T

In regard to sending data from devices on your in-home network to the Internet, the signal is again processed by the control unit. It then needs to be error-checked and processed in compliance with international standards.

The data then needs to be converted into a quadrature phase-shift keying (QPSK) format using a modulator. Once the signal has been modulated, it is passed to the transmitter component and interfaced with the HFC network using the diplex. The diplex unit has the main task of separating upstream and downstream informational flows.

Bridging and Routing

In addition to simply passing data between your home network and the operator's HFC network, a cable modem gateway device needs to also be capable of bridging and routing information.

In the case where a cable modem behaves as a bridge between an in-home system and the outside broadband world, it must ensure that local traffic is not transmitted on to the broadband network. To support bridging functionality, the cable modem needs to learn the MAC addresses of all the devices that are connected to its high-speed data port interface. Once the modem knows the MAC addresses of all the devices, traffic can be filtered according to location. For instance, if a file is sent from your desktop computer to a printer, the cable modem will prevent this file from been broadcast to the broadband network. Security conscious users may want to configure their modems to behave like routers. The primary functions of a gateway router are as follows:

- Relaying Dynamic Host Configuration Protocol (DHCP) messages between both networks, if the DHCP server on the broadband network is assigning addresses to hosts on a LAN.

- Making decisions of where to direct TCP/IP traffic.

- Restricting access from all other users connected to the cable operator's broadband network.

Standards

If consumers purchase cable modems from retailers, they need to be certain that the modem is compatible with their provider's modem. To this end, the cable industry has set standards for cable modems.

If you live in North America, most of the cable modems will be compliant with a standard called Data Over Cable Service Interface Specification (DOCSIS). If you live in Europe, Asia, or Australia, you will more than likely be purchasing a gateway device that is compliant with a specification called EuroModem.

Let's take a closer look at technical features of both of these standards.

DOCSIS • In the United States, a consortium called MCNS (Multimedia Cable Network System) has developed a set of technical documents for bidirectional communications over a cable network called DOCSIS (Data Over Cable Service Interface Specification). This group comprises the four leading cable television operators: Comcast Cable Communications Inc.; AT&T; Cox Communications Tele-Communications, Inc.; and Time Warner Cable. These companies have partnered with Rogers Cablesystems Limited, Continental Cablevision, and Cable Television Laboratories, Inc. to implement the project. A number of large networking companies have built products based on the DOCSIS standard that are commercially deployed around the world. The main focus of the DOCSIS standard is on offering Internet services to PC users. Today, most new cable modem deployments throughout the world are DOCSIS-compliant networks.

EuroModem • The EuroModem specification was developed to allow cable operators to deliver Internet access and timing-critical services, such as voice telephony and video conferencing services, to their subscribers. The EuroModem specification describes a cable modem solution that fits very well into European cable networks.

Members of an organization called EuroCableLabs have developed the EuroModem specification. The cable operators who are involved in the consortium are from various European countries. The consortium has defined two different types of modems: Class A modems are capable of transmitting data at very high speeds in a downstream direction (maximum of 50.8 Mbps) and 3 Mbps in the upstream direction. They are capable of accessing the Internet at high speeds and support a number of security technologies. Class B is the second type of modem being considered by the group. It extends the functionality of class A devices through the support of time-critical services such as video conferencing and telephony. For a more detailed description of the EuroModem home gateway, we suggest that you consult the EuroCableLabs Internet draft repository site: http://ifn03.ifn.ing.tu-bs.de/ecl/EuroModem.html.

Cable Modem Service Providers

There are several popular cable modem providers, but the big three are:

- Excite@Home
- Chello
- Road Runner

Excite@Home

Excite@Home is a fast Internet service for home networks. With Excite@Home, users can access the Internet at speeds up to 100 times faster than a 28.8 Kbps telephone modem. Excite@Home leverages the high-bandwidth capabilities of cable TV lines, as well as a hierarchical, distributed network architecture with proprietary caching and replication technologies to overcome many of the bottlenecks that plague typical Internet connections today. Excite@Home has affiliate partnerships with 16 leading cable companies in the United States and Canada, including AT&T Broadband and Internet Services, Bresnan Communications, Cablevision Systems, Century Communications, Charter Communications, Cogeco Cable, Comcast, Cox Communications, Garden State Cable, Insight Communications, InterMedia Partners, Jones Intercable, Midcontinent Cable, Prime Cable, Rogers Cablesystems, Shaw Communications, Suburban, and Videon CableSystems—access to over 60 million households. The massive demand for the Excite@Home service has not been limited to the North American market. The company's international division has been creating and marketing Excite@Home services around the globe. At the time of writing, Excite@Home had become the largest broadband provider in the world with the announcement that they had topped a million customers.

Chello

Chello is Europe's first and leading broadband Internet service provider and is commercially active in six countries. It has the largest reach in Europe, delivering next-generation, always-on interactive services and broadband content to consumers via a state-of-the-art network—without huge phone bills. It also provides a turnkey service to international cable network operators. Chello is an operating company of United Pan-Europe Communications (UPC), headquartered in Amsterdam. Chello has developed its own IP backbone, called Aorta, with nodes in Amsterdam, Brussels, California, Chile, Frankfurt, London, Miami, New York, Oslo, Paris, Stockholm, and Vienna, and satellite links to Australia and New Zealand. To maintain its position as Europe's fastest-growing and largest broadband network, Chello has established strategic alliances with the following companies: Inktomi, Terayon, Sun Microsystems, Microsoft, Cisco Systems, GTS Carrier Services, and Nortel Networks. At the time of going to press, Chello had announced that 106,500 subscribers had signed up for their high-speed data offerings.

Road Runner

Road Runner is currently Excite@Home's biggest rival. Road Runner is a high-speed online service delivered to the PC over the cable television infrastructure. By employing the latest advances in Web technology and leveraging the speed made possible by cable's HFC network, Road Runner integrates multimedia programming with communication tools and personalized services such as e-mail, chat listings, and personal home pages—all within a broadband environment. Road Runner is a joint venture among affiliates of Time Warner, MediaOne, Microsoft, Compaq, and Advance/Newhouse. The Road Runner IP infrastructure is an end-to-end client-server-enabling network. It transports multimedia applications to the PC based on TCP/IP and related technologies. The foundation of this infrastructure lies in the existing cable television network, upgraded with fiber optics. The networking model assigns significant operating and technical responsibilities to the technical staff. The company owns, operates, and maintains the regional network and all of the IP infrastructure beyond the distribution hub, while the cable operator maintains and operates the HFC plant and the cable modem. This structure creates a hierarchy that separates functions and keeps protocols isolated, providing a manageable architecture that will facilitate the integration of ever-evolving new technologies into Road-Runner-based systems.

ADVANCED DIGITAL SET-TOP BOXES ....

For cable, terrestrial, and satellite companies, home networking is another opportunity to increase the use and revenue streams of broadband interactive data and video services. The deployment of digital TV and interactive services is already under way in various locations around the globe. Central to this migration from analog to digital broadcasting is a small device called a set-top box. These set-top boxes will retail for about $250 and provide consumers with a much better video quality compared with today's existing analog systems. Other capabilities of these devices include:

- Advanced programming information for 7 days
- Embedded modems that will enable a television to be used as a display for Internet access
- Compression so that 6 to 12 compressed digital TV signals can be carried in the same amount of frequency as one TV signal without digital compression
- An Ethernet plug on the back of the set-top box so that computers or home routers can be connected to the set-top box
- Video on demand, so users can order premium movies from their set-top boxes

The Federal Communications Commission (FCC) has mandated that set-top boxes be available for retail sale by July of 2000. Let's take a closer look at this gateway device.

Basic Concepts

When you think of a set-top box, picture a TV set and a black box connected to the set with lots of wires. The true picture of a digital set-top is one of a complex electronics device comprised of many hardware and software components.

It is usually connected to your TV and the cable connection on the wall. Your local cable, terrestrial, or satellite operator normally installs these devices. This may change next year when set-top boxes enter retail stores across the globe. Set-top boxes can also be described as types of computers that translate digital signals into a format that can be viewed on a television screen.

The main features of a set-top box may be classified as follows:

- Decodes the incoming digital signal
- Verifies access rights and security levels
- Displays cinema-quality pictures on your TV
- Outputs digital surround sound
- Processes and renders Internet and interactive TV services

Under the Hood

At the moment, every network operator has unique set-top box requirements; therefore, manufacturers are forced to have a distinct design for each operator. The architecture we describe in this chapter is for a fairly advanced set-top box and is not specific to any network operator or set-top box manufacturer.

The physical components may be roughly divided into the following categories:

- System board
- Tuner(s)
- Modulator and demodulator
- Demultiplexer and decryptor
- Decoders
- Graphics processor
- CPU and memory
- Storage devices
- Physical interfaces
- Physical characteristics

If we look more closely at the anatomy of a digital set-top in Figure 9.2, you will notice that the hardware architecture is very similar to a standard desktop multimedia computer. This figure shows an expanded and simplified view of a set-top box gateway device.

System Board

If you were to open up a digital set-top box and look inside, you would see a large printed circuit board—the system board. The system board is made of a fiber glass sheet that has miniature electronic circuitry embedded in it.

Tuners

The tuner module is available for accessing QAM-, OFDM-, and QPSK-based networks. Tuners can be divided into two broad categories:

- **Broadcast in-band (IB) tuner**—Once the signal arrives from the physical transmission media, the IB tuner isolates a physical TV channel from a multiplex of channels and converts it to baseband.

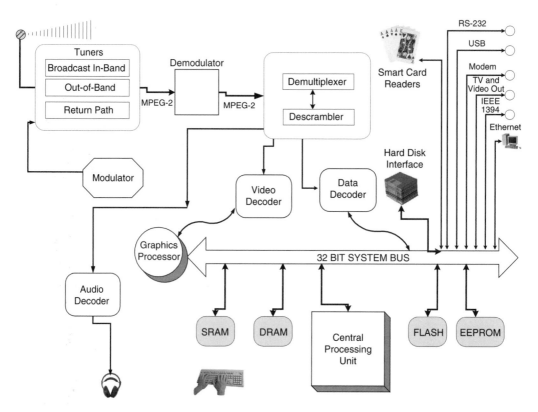

Figure 9.2
Architecture of a digital set-top box

- **Out of band (OOB) tuner**—This type of tuner facilitates the transfer of data between an in-home system and broadband network servers. Implementations of the OOB tuner tend to operate within the 100 to 350 MHz frequency band.

Modulator and Demodulator

The baseband output signal from the tuner is forwarded to a demodulator. The function of the demodulator is to sample the incoming signal and convert it to a digital bitstream. The bitstream contains video, audio, and possibly some data. Once the bitstream has been recovered, it is checked for errors and forwarded to the demultiplexer. The modulator reverses the actions of a demodulator and is used by the set-top box to deliver a signal to the return path tuner.

Demultiplexer and Decryptor

A standard MPEG-2 data stream will consist of a number of uniquely identified data packets. MPEG-2 uses an identifier called a Packet ID (PID) that identifies a packet as containing a particular format of data—audio, video, or interactive services. European and Japanese TV operators have agreed on 32 unique PIDs for identifying various data formats. The demultiplexer is an application-specific integrated circuit (ASIC) chipset that examines every PID and selects, decrypts, and forwards particular packets to a specific decoder. For example, all packets with the data PID will be forwarded to the data decoder.

The decryption unit is based on a complex algorithm that prevents unauthorized users from viewing programs or accessing Internet-based services. The exact details of the decryption process are operator-specific and are shrouded in secrecy.

Decoders

A digital set-top box will normally contain three separate decoders for converting the digital bitstream into a format that can be heard and viewed by the subscriber. A video decoder will transform the video packets into a sequence of pictures, which are displayed on the TV monitor. Video decoder chips are capable of formatting pictures for TV monitors with different screen resolutions and support for still pictures. The compressed audio bitstream is sent to an audio decoder for decompression. Once the MPEG-2 bitstream is decompressed, it is presented to a set of speakers on the network. Current digital set-tops are capable of supporting the following audio modes:

- Mono and dual channel
- Stereo
- Joint stereo

The last type of decoder is used to forward the data to a high-speed interface port that is connected to the in-home network.

Graphics Processor

The main purpose of a graphics processor is to render a range of Internet file formats and proprietary interactive TV file formats.

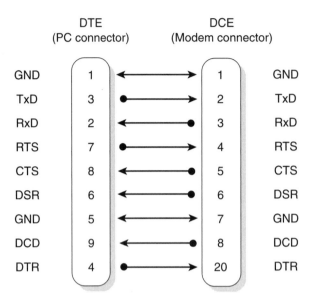

Figure 9.3
Standard 9-pin RS232 connectivity

RS232 Serial Interface

Set-top boxes normally come equipped with the RS232 standard serial interface. The interface uses a D connector with nine pins and allows connectivity to serial printers, computers, and standard telephone modems. Figure 9.3 illustrates the pin-outs of a connection between a set-top box and a telephone modem.

Central Processing Unit

The CPU (Central Processing Unit) is the brains of the set-top and is housed in a single chip called a processor. In terms of functionality and processing, the CPU is the most important element of a digital set-top box. Functions typically provided by a processor include:

- Initialization of the various set-top hardware components
- Processing a range of Internet and interactive TV applications
- Monitoring and managing hardware interrupts
- Fetching data and instructions from memory
- Running various programs

Memory Configuration

Just as a computer needs memory to function, a set-top also requires memory to store and manipulate instructions that are issued by the subscriber. Memory comes in chip format and is comprised of millions of integrated circuits (ICs). These chips are connected to the system board inside the set-top box. Most elements within the set-top box will require memory to perform various tasks. The graphics engine, video decoder, and descrambler all require a certain amount of memory to fulfill their specific functions within the set-top box. Set-top memory can be divided into RAM and ROM.

RAM—Random Access Memory • Most functions performed by the set-top box will require access to RAM, which is used as a temporary storage area for data flowing between the processor and the various hardware components. If we open a set-top box and look inside, we see that RAM is located on Single Inline Memory Modules (SIMMs), which are connected to the system board. SIMMs are best described as small circuit boards that hold a group of memory chips. They are very easy to install and are ideal for users of home networks who need to improve the performance of their set-tops.

There are two basic types of RAM in a set-top box:

- Dynamic RAM (DRAM)
- Static RAM (SRAM)

Both memory types hold information; however, they differ in the technologies used to store the data. DRAM will continue to refresh its memory thousands of times a second, whereas SRAM does not refresh its data bits, making it faster but also more expensive. The contents of both types of memory are lost once the consumer powers down the set-top.

ROM—Read-Only Memory • Once data has been written onto a ROM chip, you cannot remove it. ROM is nonvolatile, which means it does not lose its contents when the set-top is powered off. Most set-tops contain EEPROMs and flash ROM, which are variations of the basic ROM technology.

- **EEPROM (Electrically Erasable Programmable Read-Only memory**—EEPROM is a special type of memory used in set-top boxes to store controls and boot-up information. The data is permanently stored on the chip even when you power the set-top box off.

  To remove this control information, you need to expose the EEPROM chip to ultra violet light and electrical charges. A set-top box will contain a small amount of EEPROM (usually, Kbytes) and has slower access rates than RAM.

- **FLASH memory**—A flash memory chip is very similar in functionality to an EEPROM. The only difference between the two is that a flash memory chip can be erased and reprogrammed in blocks of data bytes instead of one byte at a time. This feature allows operators to update the set-tops operating system and resident software applications over the network without physically visiting the subscriber's home.

Storage Devices

The ability to locally store and retrieve information is expected to become the most important commodity to users of home networking technologies. While the storage space on the first generation of set-tops was limited to flash memory, today we are beginning to see designers adding interfaces to the motherboard that will allow consumers to integrate high-capacity hard drives into their set-top boxes. Hard disks can be integrated within the set-top or else connected as an external device through the USB or IEEE 1394 data interfaces. By adding high-capacity drives to set-top boxes, home network users will be able to download and store digital movies.

Modems

Computers "talk" to each other using modems. In the context of a home networking environment, modems are added to set-top boxes to facilitate the implementation of two-way interactive services. Now, almost all new set-tops come with a built-in modem. Once activated, the modem can use the return path for a number of things, including:

- Sending requests to Web servers on the Internet
- Enabling set-top users to upload files and send e-mail
- Facilitating two-way interactive TV services, such as video on demand

The modem options available to set-top users are:

- Standard telephone modem for terrestrial, satellite, and MMDS environments.
- Cable modems for a standard cable network. New cable modem chips are under development that will fit directly into cable TV set-top boxes. Having cable modems that fit into set-top boxes will enable consumers to purchase and install one device instead of two separate devices for Web access and cable TV.

Home Networking Interfaces

As consumer electronic technologies and home PCs continue to converge, consumers and set-top box suppliers are anxious to take advantage of a number of high-speed data transfer technologies. Many of the new set-top box designs are incorporating interfaces which will allow set-tops to communicate in real time with devices such as camcorders, DVDs, CD players, mixing consoles, and music keyboards. Manufacturers are capable of adding the following interface options to a digital set-top box:

- IEEE 1284 Parallel Port
- USB
- IEEE 1394 or FireWire Bus Interface Standard
- Ethernet

Common Interface

The common interface (CI) is added to some of the set-top boxes that are manufactured for the European market. The CI is a European interface that has been defined to accept Personal Computer Memory Card International Association (PCMCIA) modules. This PCMCIA card has a number of uses including:

- Extending the set-top memory capabilities
- Networking different CA systems within the home
- Adding hard disk space to the set-top box
- Adding new tuners to the set-top box

TV and VCR Interfaces

Set-top boxes communicate with A/V devices on a home network through two output ports called Scart connectors. The interfaces use female-type connectors with 21 pins. The pin assignments are vendor-specific.

Smart Card Readers

A standard set-top box will contain two slots. The first slot is used for a smart card that authorizes subscriber access to various digital services and the second slot may be used for e-commerce purposes.

Software for Set-top Gateway Devices

A set-top box needs a suite of software programs to work. There are many software systems that have been developed specifically for these powerful home gateways, including:

- PowerTV
- OpenTV
- Liberate Technologies
- PlanetWeb
- Microsoft TV
- Java
- Multimedia Home Platform (MHP)

Detailed descriptions of these software systems are available in my book *The Essential Guide to Digital Set-top Boxes and Interactive TV* (Prentice Hall PTR, 2000).

PERSONAL VIDEO RECORDERS ....

The digital television industry has been abuzz the past couple of months about a new category of product called personal video recorders—PVRs, for short. PVRs are similar to traditional VCRs in many ways—they record, play, and pause TV shows and movies. There are, however, a number of fundamental differences.

Instead of using traditional videotapes, PVRs use a large hard disk along with sophisticated video compression and decompression hardware to record television streams. The PVR software is optimized to allow recording and playback at the same time. This lets the user pause live television, do instant-replay, and quick-jump from place to place. If you are using a VCR tape, you must fast-forward and rewind to move from place to place. These new PVRs are more like DVD players and allow you to quickly move to any location on the recording media. Coupled with an easy-to-use electronic program guide and a high-speed online service, these devices can pause live television, recommend shows based on your tastes, and record your favorite shows automatically. For instance, a viewer could pause a movie, take a break, come back, and resume viewing, even though the movie in reality has continued past that point.

Under the Hood

For all intents and purposes, a PVR is a stripped-down PC with a large hard disk that reserves storage space for downloading program listings every day. You use a remote control to select what you want to record, and the PVR captures and stores these programs on a hard disk for future viewing.

The easiest way to understand how these gateway devices work is to remove the cover and examine the functionality of their main components, described in the following list.

- **Hard drive**—At the time of writing this guide, the average size of a hard drive in a PVR was 10 Gbytes and was suitable for recording approximately 20 hours of standard quality broadcasts. There was also an option to increase storage capacity by purchasing additional disks to increase the recordable storage time. The presence of a hard disk allows you to pause or replay a broadcast in progress while the recording continues. All of the drives are qualified to meet the thermal, acoustical, and mechanical requirements of a consumer electronics product.

- **RAM chips**—Similar to a PC or set-top box, the RAM chipsets serve as the operational memory for the PVR.

- **MPEG-2 decoder and encoder**—Similar to a digital set-top box, these chips are used to compress and decompress video signals.

- **Modem**—Used to download TV schedules and system upgrades every night.

- **CPU**—Runs the real-time operating system.

- **Boot ROM**—Similar to set-top and cable modem network devices, the boot ROM contains the software that allows the PVR to start up as soon as it is powered on.

- **NTSC decoder and encoder**—Because these gateway devices have been designed for the North American market, the PVRs currently available use these chips to process NTSC (National Television Standards Committee) signals. The decoder is used to digitize analog television signals and the encoder reverses this action (i.e., it restores the decoder's compressed digital output stream into an analog TV signal).

- **Input/output jacks**—Used for interconnecting the PVR to a TV or satellite receiver.

- **Tuner**—These gateway devices contain only one tuner; consequently, you can't watch one broadcast channel while recording another. A way around this restriction is to install a splitter and connect to your VCR.

- **Processing chips**—The types and models of the processing chips are PVR-specific. However, most PVRs will contain a video processor for manipulating and processing multimedia content.

PVR Providers

TiVo and Replay Networks were the first companies to release the first generation of products into this marketplace, which, according to consulting firm Forrester Research forecasts, will reach 14 million customers in 5 years and a number equal to the current number of VCR owners in 10 years.

ReplayTV

Replay Networks, Inc., based in Mountain View, California, is a leader in personal television technologies. ReplayTV is a VCR-sized box that sits on or near a television and automatically records and stores favorite television shows, sporting events, and other TV programs, making them available for viewing on the user's schedule (see Figure 9.4). ReplayTV lets users watch their favorite programs when they want—truly TV-on-demand.

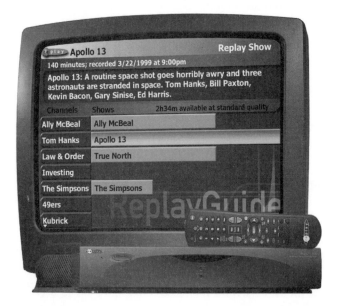

Figure 9.4
ReplayTV guide

ReplayTV is different from a VCR in many ways, the biggest difference being that ReplayTV does not use videotape. ReplayTV's digital storage technology provides many advantages over the limited tape format. For instance, with ReplayTV, there's no need to scramble to find a blank tape before recording, and users never have to fast-forward or rewind the tape to locate a safe record space. Since ReplayTV's storage is random-access, it can record and play two different sections of a show at the same time. So now viewers can start watching the beginning of a recorded show while it is still being broadcast. This also allows for pause, rewind, and fast-forward of live TV shows. ReplayTV is smart enough to search its built-in channel guide and record shows based on the user's search criteria. When it does this, it creates a Replay Channel. For instance, someone could tell ReplayTV to get Demi Moore movies, and ReplayTV would create a Demi Moore Replay Channel and record a new Demi Moore movie every time one is broadcast. The user would simply select the Demi Moore Replay Channel from the channel guide and begin watching the movie.

That's an example of an actress-based Replay Channel, but ReplayTV can also create theme-based Replay Channels, like your own cooking channel, or home improvement channel, or show-based Replay Channels like the Frasier channel or the Ally McBeal channel. Replay Channels automatically manage space using sophisticated software that prevents running out of storage space. Every ReplayTV has a built-in telephone jack that allows it to be connected to a telephone line. Every night the ReplayTV dials into a secure server and downloads the latest channel guide information. ReplayTV even resets the clock so users never have to worry about the perennial flashing 12:00. From a technical perspective, ReplayTV uses the MPEG-2 compression system, which allows a range of video quality settings. The ReplayTV compression rates are user adjustable from the default setting of 2 Mbps to 6 Mbps. All storage times are calculated based on the default setting of 2 Mbps. At 2 Mbps the picture quality is better than VHS tape. At 4 Mbps the quality is better than SVHS tape. Above 4 Mbps the quality approaches the level of DVD. The default rate can be easily changed by controlling the ReplayTV onscreen menus.

For more information on this residential gateway device and service, visit the Replay Networks home page at http://www.replaytv.com.

TiVo

TiVo is another new personal TV service that lets you watch what you want, when you want. TiVo's unit is sold under the Philips brand name and supports the following technologies:

- **Compression**—Supports MPEG-2 for high-quality digital television.

- **Advanced processor**—High-performance Power PC running Linux.

- **Storage**—14 or 30 hours depending on configuration. The drive in the 14-hour receiver is 13.6 GB and in the 30-hour receiver is 27.2 GB.

- **Inputs**—Cable-ready tuner, S-video, and composite video support all U.S. standards.

- **Outputs**—RF, S-video and two composite video outputs.

- **Remote control**—30-button remote, programmable for TV/AV control.

- **Channel control**—Channel and power control of cable and satellite boxes with serial or IR connection.

- **Telephone**—RJ-11 connection to telephone line.

- Compatible with all cable, satellite (DBS), and terrestrial broadcast TV systems in the United States.

- Latest encryption technology protects viewer privacy.

Because the receiver uses the MPEG-2 compression system that allows a range of video quality settings, the video settings are user-adjustable, with four choices—best, high, medium, and basic (see Table 9.1). The default is best. At the highest setting, the quality approaches the level of DVD (but can only be as good as the original source—i.e., no picture loss). At the lowest setting, the picture quality is closer to VHS tape.

The receiver is able to record 14 hours at basic quality and less than that at higher quality settings. The TiVo service also ensures that there are no recording conflicts by warning you ahead of time if one program is too long or coincides with another. The results will vary, depending on the type of signal received and the quality of that signal. The times shown in Table 9.1 assume that all programs on the receiver are recorded at the same quality setting. Since a different level can be set for each program, the actual number of programs on the receiver may vary. The personal video recorder works with virtually all cable boxes, direct broadcast satellite receivers, and antennae. The PVR interfaces with satellite receivers and cable boxes through the use of either

Table 9.1   *TiVo PVR Quality Levels*

Quality	14-Hour Receiver	30-Hour Receiver	Suggested Use
Basic	14 hours	30 hours	Animation, "talking heads"
Medium	8	18	Daytime talk shows
High	6	14	Dramas, movies
Best	4	9	Sports, action

an IR blaster or a serial connection (whichever is available). All the necessary IR blasting and serial cables are included with the receiver. For more information visit http://www.tivo.com.

DSL MODEMS ....

DSL modems are very suitable gateway devices for boosting the Internet bandwidth available to appliances running on an in-home network. DSL modems support data transmission over standard telephone lines as much as 50 times faster than the analog modems used by most homes and small businesses.

A Digital Subscriber Line (DSL) circuit consists of two DSL modems connected by a copper twisted-pair telephone line. To maintain backward compatibility with the standard telephone system and to avoid disruption of service due to equipment failure, the voice part of the frequency spectrum is separated from the digital modem circuitry by means of a passive filter called a POTS splitter. This means that if the DSL modem fails, the POTS service is still available. Under this configuration, users are able to simultaneously make voice calls and transmit Internet data over the same broadband DSL pipe. When a DSL transmission is received at the central office, a more advanced POTS splitter is used to send the voice traffic to the public telephone network and data to the Internet.

DSL modems can be based on one of two different modulation schemes: DMT (Discrete Modulation Tone) and CAP (Carrierless Amplitude Phase).

DMT

The official standard for DMT is International Telecommunications Union G.992.1. DMT divides the spectrum from 4 kHz to 1 MHz into 256 components called subchannels. Each subchannel's noise level is analyzed, and information is sent along a subchannel according to its noise level. So if a given subchannel has a lot of noise, few or no bits are transmitted on it. DMT uses a discrete Fourier transform to split the frequency band into subchannels.

CAP

CAP is not a standard that is defined by any of the major international bodies; however, it was the first to market. CAP doesn't divide the frequency band into subchannels. Instead, it uses the whole band at once, relying on the amplitude modulation and phase shifts of signals to transmit at the high bit rates of xDSL. CAP is based on the quadrature amplitude/phase modulation (QAM) technique used by high-speed digital set-top boxes and cable modems.

CAP-based xDSL is easier to implement than solutions built on DMT, and so CAP equipment was used in early field trials of xDSL. But CAP has disadvantages—for a start, it's more susceptible to noise than DMT. Also, CAP is a proprietary technology, whereas DMT is defined in a standard. Consequently modems that use the DMT modulation scheme have been chosen as the standard line modulation for DSL in the future. Many manufacturers still build CAP-based modems; however, most vendors are building their current products based on the DMT standard. So if you are selecting a DSL modem, you need to make sure that it supports DMT; otherwise you can experience problems connecting to your local service provider. From a consumer's perspective, using a DSL modem as a gateway device to the outside world has become significantly easier over the past couple of years. In 1998, large PC manufacturers such as Dell and Compaq began shipping computers with high-speed DSL modems.

HOME SERVERS...

Instead of using a modem or a set-top box to receive and process broadband applications, some companies are promoting the use of powerful home servers to take responsibility for these services. The server is used to connect an in-home network to the high-speed Internet connection. It handles the automatic configuration of devices that are plugged in to a home network. Most of the servers currently available on the marketplace are either based on PowerPC or Intel processors. The gateway interfaces with a high-speed modem through a standard Ethernet port and to the home network through its port that is specific to the in-home transmission medium (i.e., phone wires, powerline, wireless, or one of the serial technologies). Also included with most home servers is a suite of software programs to support the following capabilities: IP address sharing, automatic IP configuration, Web presence, and home information database. The home networking software suite normally includes the following components:

- **Network Address Translation (NAT)**—NAT enables all the devices on a home network to share a single IP address provided by an ISP. The NAT program makes all the necessary address translations. In addition, NAT provides inbound access security so that access to appliances within a home can be controlled.

- **DHCP server**—DHCP is short for Dynamic Host Configuration Protocol. It is a standard method for computers to automatically configure all network settings. DHCP is covered in Chapter 10.

- **Micro-Web server**—This server program provides a point of presence on the Web for such things as remote management and administration.

Some of these home servers can be dedicated to specific tasks. For instance, music servers are used to download and store music over the Internet and then stream the music to multiple speakers throughout the home. The deployment of these types of home servers effectively eliminates the need to purchase CDs at retail music stores.

A mix of companies—including 3Com, Motorola, S3's Diamond Multimedia, PC makers like Dell Computer, and start-ups like 2Wire—are working on gateway products. 3Com, for example, plans to build a range of home server devices that specialize in Internet telephony and streaming audio and video.

SUMMARY ....

The explosion in demand for high-speed Internet access combined with the push by service providers to offer integrated voice, data, and entertainment services has fuelled the development of a new range of products called residential gateways. These new gateways allow individuals to control in-home appliances from a single console. A residential gateway is best described as an intelligent hardware device that connects home-based Web devices and appliances to the Internet. This chapter has examined the various types of residential gateways and how they allow service providers to deliver integrated services such as data, video, and voice to the home. The cable industry, for instance, is currently spending billions of dollars in rebuilding its cable network to support secure and reliable two-way broadband connectivity. At the same time, there is an explosion of demand from consumers using their home PCs to access the Internet at high speeds. The cable industry is in a unique position to offer these high-speed data services rapidly. People who want to connect their PCs and consumer electronic devices to these "fat pipes" need to purchase a device called a cable modem. Most cable modems currently available are compliant with a particular specification. The presence of open, well-accepted standards leads to competitive pricing from multiple cable modem suppliers. Also on offer from the TV industry is a residential gateway device called a digital set-top box. Set-tops are used to connect in-home networks to a high-speed Internet pipeline. Many set-top box manufacturers have announced a new set-top reference platform called a PVR. These new devices have two tuners and enable simultaneous recording and viewing of live TV broadcasts. Analysts say these systems are going to change the way people watch television. By 2004, 14 million television viewers will be using PVRs to control their programming, estimates Forrester Research analyst Josh Bernoff. ReplayTV and TiVo are the best-known devices; others are due out soon, including Dishplayer, which will incorporate a WebTV net-browsing service. DSL technologies, which allow existing phone lines to be used simultaneously for high-speed Web and voice traffic, are the main competitors to cable modems. For phone companies, DSL modems represent a competitive revenue-generating alternative to cable modems and digital set-top boxes. With the rapid increase in demand for high-speed data services, DSL modems offer telecommunications providers with a technology that increases the bandwidth of the local loop without making huge investments in new fiber technologies. To make use of DSL technologies, the consumer would buy a modem in a local retail store and connect it directly into one of the phone jacks at home. In 1999, hardware companies began shipping a new generation of residential gateways called home servers that connect PCs, audio-video equipment, and household appliances to the Internet.

10 Home Networking Services

In this chapter...

With the development of broadband local loop technologies, a new concept has emerged for service providers to begin deploying entirely digital networks. The main driver for these new generation networks is the ability to offer the consumer "converged voice and data" services. Basically, this means that a broadband service provider could now offer local and long distance telephony *and* high-speed Internet access to consumers as a bundled service. To be able to fully interoperate with these new service offerings, home networks have some basic requirements. This chapter examines some of the core services that are required to support the smooth operation of an in-home network.

ASSIGNING IP ADDRESSES ....

In a TCP/IP-based home network, domestic appliances and PCs use IP addresses to identify each other. Within the next five years, each light switch, TV, appliance, and so on will have its own IP address for access and control from anywhere in the world. An IP address is a series of four numbers separated by dots that identify the exact physical location of a digital appliance, similar to a home address that identifies a place of residence. An IP address is a 32-bit binary number. This binary number is divided into 4 groups of 8 bits ("octets"), each of which is represented by a decimal number in the range 0 to 255. The octets are separated by decimal points. An example of an IP address is 190.100.5.54. The options for assigning IP addresses for hosts on a home network are:

1. Manually assigned by the consumer
2. Assigned by a local DHCP server
3. Assigned by a DHCP server located on the broadband network

The first option of manually configuring TCP/IP addresses for every appliance on an in-home network can be a painful process and is extremely time consuming. The second option for assigning IP addresses to devices on a home network involves the establishment of a local DHCP server. DHCP is a TCP/IP standard that automatically assigns each A/V device and PC on a home network a unique network number. Each time a host device on the network starts, it requests IP information from a DHCP server, including the following:

- An IP address
- A subnet mask
- Optional values, such as a gateway or a Domain Name System (DNS) server address

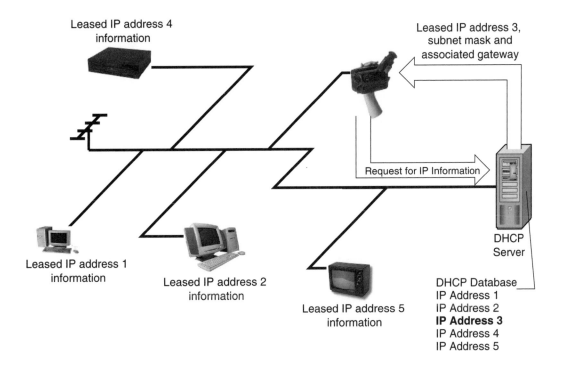

Figure 10.1
A DHCP server providing an IP address to a digital camcorder

When the DHCP server receives a request from a entertainment device, it selects IP addressing information from a pool of addresses that are defined in its database. Once it has selected the IP information, if offers these values to the requesting device on the network. If the device accepts the offer, the DHCP server will then lease the IP information to the device for a specified period of time. The process of automatically assigning an IP address to a digital camcorder is graphically illustrated in Figure 10.1.

The use of this system simplifies the administration of a home network because the software keeps track of IP addresses. Automatically configuring TCP/IP also reduces the possibility of assigning duplicate IP addresses and of mistyping other configuration information. This means that new appliances can be added to a home network without the hassle and time of manually assigning new addresses. This all sounds great; however, setting up a DHCP server requires a certain amount of IT knowledge and costs money. Consequently, option three is the most popular system for allocating IP addresses to computers and domestic appliances that are connected to home networks. In this architecture, the DHCP server is physically located on the premises of the service provider that is supplying the broadband connection to the Internet. So if every device on every home network in the world will eventually need an IP address, does that mean we will be out of addresses? Absolutely correct. When the Internet's IP address structure was originally developed in the early 1980s, it was intended to meet the needs of current and future users. The creators of this structure could not have foreseen the scale and speed of growth of the Internet, not to mention the proliferation of in-home networks. To keep up with the demand for IP addresses, an organization called Internet Engineering Task Force launched IPV6 (Internet Protocol Version 6). IPV6 greatly increases the available address space. In fact the number of addresses possible under IPV6 will be four billion times four billion.

USER LOGONS TO A BROADBAND NETWORK ....

In a home networking environment, the connection to the Internet is always on. There are some providers such as telecommunication companies that provide a logon mechanism for authenticating the user. The process of authenticating a user on a home network involves the establishment of a session. The concept of sessions is already widely accepted and deployed in the telecommunications business. All Internet dial-up services rely on a protocol called the point-to-point protocol (PPP) to create a session. PPP is the Internet standard for transmission of IP packets over serial lines.

In the broadband arena, DSL and cable technology providers extend this communications model with a variation of PPP called point-to-point tunneling protocol (PPTP). Microsoft and several vendor companies, known collectively as the PPTP forum, have jointly developed this protocol. With PPTP, home networking users create a logon session every time they access the broadband network. The process of logging on to a broadband network is illustrated in Figure 10.2 and works as follows:

1. Once a digital appliance on the home network is powered up, the DHCP server on the broadband network allocates a private IP address to the device. Thus, without going through the complicated logon procedure, the device on the home network has limited access to specific resources.

2. When you want to use this device to reach content on the Internet, a type of virtual networking link is established between the home network and the PPTP servers on the broadband network.

3. Next, the home network initiates a second virtual connection based on the PPP protocol. This connection will then prompt you for authentication details (i.e., username and password).

4. Once the service provider is happy with the logon credentials, a public IP address is assigned to the home networking session for the duration of the browsing session.

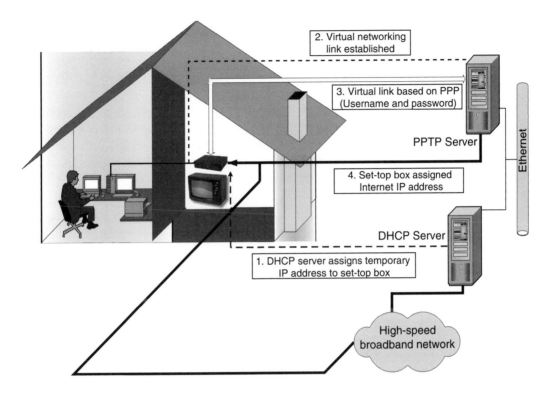

Figure 10.2
Home network logon process

The advantage of this solution for connecting to a broadband network is that it allows service providers to control access to different types of services. Today most service providers do not enforce the logon mechanism process for browsing (as described above); however, they are deploying this mechanism for accessing value-added applications such as online shopping.

QUALITY OF SERVICE ···

As new entertainment-based applications are deployed over home networks, Quality of Service (QoS) features will be needed to arbitrate between traffic flows that are competing for different resources on the network. QoS allows home networking applications to prioritize individual services. An example is videoconferencing, which uses QoS to guarantee enough bandwidth to deliver high-quality video. Any application that is deployed in an in-home network must provide the following guarantees.

- **Minimum latency**—Latency is best described as the amount of time it takes for a packet of multimedia data to get from the sending appliance to the receiving appliance on the in-home network. The latency delay can have a serious impact on the quality of the multimedia stream of data that is flowing around a house.

- **Minimum jitter impact**—Whereas the exact sequence of regular network traffic that arrives at the receiving host isn't always important, multimedia-based information must always be delivered to the receiving device in sequence. Jitter in the transmission signal causes dropped packets and decreases the overall performance of an in-home network.

- **Coexistence parameters**—This value is used to measure the impact of broadcasting unpredictable bursts of multimedia data across a home network. This type of traffic behavior can cause gaps in the multimedia data stream.

- **Bandwidth**—Rich multimedia applications such as home video distribution systems require large amounts of bandwidth. QoS needs to guarantee that these types of applications do not overpower all other network traffic on a home network.

So what type of technologies are able to support services such as QoS? ATM provides QoS guarantees that other transport protocols such as TCP/IP are unable to deliver. Ethernet is able to give you speeds of 100 Mbps, but only ATM can give the QoS services required for real-time communications within a home. Many of the home networking technologies that we discussed in previous chapters also provide QoS mechanisms. Implementing and managing a QoS-aware network is a complex task for most people. Fortunately, companies like Microsoft are integrating QoS components into the next release of operating systems, which should make life easier for all of us.

SHARING A BROADBAND INTERNET CONNECTION ....

Convergence between home networks and the Internet is providing a revolution in home entertainment. Through this phenomenon, physical walls within a home are slowly being opened up with virtual windows that bring entertainment into any and all rooms within the house.

Today, most members of a family would like to have access to the Internet without the constraints associated with installing and running separate telephone lines. Home networks can deliver significant savings and greater family entertainment value by allowing all family members to share a common high-speed Internet connection.

To address the issue of sharing an Internet connection, a number of vendors have developed tools that allow multiple devices in the home to share a single broadband Internet connection. Rather than giving you a brief description of each of these tools, we decided to present a detailed overview of a software program developed by Microsoft called Microsoft Internet Connection Sharing (MICS). The MICS service runs on a home server that is connected to a broadband Internet connection. The MICS tool consists of three separate components.

- **Network Address Table (NAT)**—The NAT allows multiple digital appliances on a home network to share the IP address that was allocated to the home server by the DHCP server on the broadband network.
- **DHCP address allocator**—The address allocator is a DHCP mechanism used to dynamically assign a private IP address to each appliance and PC on a home network. For instance, if the home server receives the address 10.16.0.1 from the broadband DHCP server, the ICS service will then assign an IP address to each device on the home network by using a subnet mask (i.e., 255.255.220.0). The allocator can be disabled if you decide to use static addresses.
- **DNS service**—The DNS service allows PCs and A/V devices on the home network to query a DNS server on the broadband network. A service provider normally uses a DNS server to store domain names and IP addresses that have been allocated to devices on an in-home network. The home server running the MICS program will simply forward the requests to the external server.

BROADBAND SECURITY AND HOME FIREWALL SERVICES ....

Today more and more people are beginning to take advantage of the always-on feature of broadband technologies. This makes a lot of sense; however, users need to be aware of the risks associated with connecting in-home appliances to the outside world. First and foremost, they are exposing their private network to a variety of security risks. Breaches on a home network could result in any of the following:

- Introduction of viruses
- Loss or damage of files stored on DVD players, set-top boxes, and desktop PCs
- Breach of personal privacy
- Financial loss

- Pirating and distribution of sensitive information to unauthorized recipients

Consequently, owners of home networks connecting to the Internet should always treat it as a potentially hostile environment. There are a number of steps that may be taken to minimize the security risk of connecting a private in-home network to the public Internet. The implementation of a home firewall is a key step in warding off hacker attacks on a home network. In the world of corporate IT, firewalls are the most popular method of protecting local area networks from outside intruders. A firewall is a hardware or software system that is used to protect sensitive data from being accessed by unauthorized people. A firewall in the context of a home networking environment is normally located at the interface between the local devices and the high-speed broadband connection. All data, video, and voice traffic between these two networks is examined by the in-home firewall. Other features of a typical home firewall system include:

- Automatically closing your broadband connection on the detection of attempts to hack into one of your digital appliances.
- Allowing different members of your family to set their own levels of security
- Recording all broadband Internet access events

An in-home firewall normally consists of a variety of hardware and software components. The exact combination of components chosen to build a firewall depends on the level of security required. A typical home firewall comprises a standard desktop PC running a personal firewall system. The personal firewall consumer product examines each data packet that passes through the firewall and filters it according to a set of authorization rules. The software program checks the header of each packet and examines the services and addresses contained within each packet. This information is compared with a set of criteria, which have been defined by the user. If the packet of data is acceptable, it is forwarded to its destination point; otherwise, it is discarded.

The home networking security market has matured in the past few years, with software companies offering consumers a variety of sophisticated security products. The next sections give profiles of some popular firewall products currently available.

Some Home Firewall Products

ConSeal Private Desktop

Easy to install and easy to use, ConSeal Private Desktop runs seamlessly with all desktop applications and has all the power and robustness required to fully protect home connections to the Internet. A Canadian-based company called Signal9 has developed this in-home firewall product. For more details on this product, visit the following Web address: http://www.signal9.com/index.html.

SyShield

SyShield is an easy-to-use, cost-effective, and transparent security software solution for appliances and computers that are connected to a home network. A California-based company called Sybergen Networks has developed this in-home firewall product. For more details on this product, visit the following Web address: http://www.sybergen.com/.

Norton Internet Security 2000

Norton Internet Security 2000 stops all sorts of viruses, malicious Java applets, ActiveX controls, and even hackers—before they can access valuable data on a home network. Symantec is one of the largest anti-virus software makers in the world. For details on its range of home networking firewall products, visit the following Web address: http://www.symantec.com.

SofaWare HomeSecure

HomeSecure is a firewall embedded inside the residential gateway (e.g., cable modem, DSL modem), based on Check Point's Stateful Inspection technology. SofaWare Technologies was established in 1999 by Check Point Software Technologies, a worldwide leader in securing the Internet. SofaWare focuses on providing solutions for the home broadband Internet access market, leveraging Check Point's expertise and technologies to address the needs of consumers and service providers.

Guard Dog

Guard Dog, developed by McAfee, does the following:

- Checks incoming mail, files, and downloads
- Builds a firewall around your PC
- Protects against hostile cookies, applets, and ActiveX controls
- Is easily updated

McAfee is a leading consumer Application Service Provider (ASP), offering users on-line services to secure, manage, repair, update, and upgrade their PCs over the Internet. For more details on this product, visit the following Web address: http://www.mcafee.com.

Virtual Private Networks

Another popular method of securing home networks from the dangers of the Internet is to establish a virtual private network (VPN). A VPN is a network that connects private in-home systems using a public network, such as the Internet. The purpose of a VPN is to allow home appliances to communicate safely with each other using the Internet while ensuring that the network traffic is safe from attack. Frost and Sullivan predict that revenue from IP-based VPN services will exceed $18 billion by 2004 in the United States alone. A VPN can use a combination of several internetworking technologies, including tunneling and network security. Tunneling is a VPN technology that preserves network security by allowing VPN-enabled home devices to share address and routing information without exposing that information to the public network. The protocols that are most relevant to home-networking-based VPNs include:

- Point-to-point tunneling protocol (PPTP)
- Layer-two forwarding (L2F)
- Layer-two tunneling protocol (L2TP)

PPP is a method of connecting a residential gateway to the Internet. PPTP is a technology used to provide security in VPNs, ensuring that messages can be safely transmitted from one VPN in-home node, or end system, to another. The layer-two forwarding protocol, abbreviated to L2F, is a tunneling protocol used in VPNs. Developed by Cisco Systems, L2F is similar to the PPTP protocol. Like other VPN protocols, L2F allows organizations to use the Internet to transport data safely. Because of the similarities between PPTP and L2F, Microsoft and Cisco agreed to combine their protocols into a single, standard protocol. This is known as layer-two tunneling protocol (L2TP). L2TP is designed to combine the best features of PPTP and L2F. Home-based VPNs are mostly used for telecommuting purposes.

SUMMARY ....

The first section of this chapter explained in real terms the various options that are currently available for assigning IP addresses to in-home digital appliances. Another important feature of a home network is the mechanism used to connect with a broadband network. Most logon procedures are based on the concept of using the PPP protocol to establish a virtual session. All home networks need to have enough QoS features to allow the prioritization of applications. If, for example, a customer wants fewer delays on video and voice communications, the customer has the option of selecting a QoS, such as a constant bit rate, on which fewer delays are present. In homes where multiple devices want access to the broadband access network, a commonly deployed architecture consists of a gateway server running a special software process. The main benefit of this approach is that it reduces the number of public IP addresses in your home. Because broadband users' computers have constant connection to the Web, analysts fear cable and DSL lines will become an attractive target for hackers or crackers. Consequently, many users of home networks are beginning to invest in security solutions such as firewalls and VPN technologies to keep their home networks safe from attack.

11 HAVi

In this chapter...

Consumer electronic devices, such as digital set-top boxes and DVD players, are sophisticated and expensive digital processing systems. By connecting these devices to home networks, it is possible to share processing and storage resources between members of a family. Central to the fabric of all home networks is a software system called middleware. This software system allows connected devices to exchange both control information and streaming multimedia content. "Middleware" is a relatively new term in the home networking business. If we compare it to an IT environment, it equates to the presentation layer of the OSI (Open Systems Interconnect) seven-layer model. OSI is a networking framework that defines a set of protocols for implementing communications between two devices. Middleware is used to isolate application programs from the details of the underlying hardware and network components and provide a set of system interfaces to their functions. In the world of home networking, we encounter many types of hardware devices from different manufacturers. To provide interoperability between these diverse systems, a number of home networking middleware applications have evolved. This chapter takes a closer look at one of these systems—HAVi.

ABOUT HAVI ....

HAVi is an abbreviation for Home Audio/Video Interoperability. It is a project that was started by eight promoter companies—Grundig, Hitachi, Panasonic, Philips, Sharp, Sony, Thomson, and Toshiba. Eighteen other participant companies have joined—Digital Harmony Technologies, Loewe Kenwood, LG Electronics, Mitsubishi Electric, Pioneer, Samsung Electronics, Sanyo, Seiko, Epson, Sun Microsystems, Tao Group, QNX Software Systems, Vivid Logic, 3A International, Infineon Technologies AG, Teralogic, Wind River Systems, and Yaskawa Information Systems. HAVi adopted the IEEE 1394 bus standard as the underlying network technology for the HAVi protocols as well as for the transport of the real-time A/V streams.

The HAVi architecture specifies a set of APIs that allow consumer electronic manufacturers and software engineering companies to develop applications for IEEE 1394-based home networks. One of the main reasons HAVi selected IEEE 1394 over other transmission protocols is because of its support for *isochronous* communications. The term isochronous ("iso" meaning "equal" or "identical" and "chronous" meaning "time") refers to the ability of 1394 to guarantee delivery of data packets at fixed intervals. This feature underpins its usefulness in an A/V-centric home network because it ensures that audio and video streams can be guaranteed to meet the real-time constrains, such as television at 30 frames per second. HAVi comprises software elements that facilitate the interoperability between different brands of entertainment devices within your home. Interoperability is an industry term that refers to the ability of an application running on an in-home appliance to detect and use the functionality of other appliances that are connected to the same network.

The HAVi standard specifies the home networking protocols that are required to achieve this interoperability. The HAVi architecture is an open, lightweight, and platform-independent specification that allows developers to write home networking applications. It specifically focuses on the transfer of digital A/V content between in-home digital appliances, as well as the processing (rendering, recording, and playback) of this content by HAVi-enabled devices. It does not, however, address home networking functions such as controlling the lights or monitoring the climate within the house. The HAVi middleware system is independent of any particular operating system or CPU and can be implemented on a range of hardware platforms including digital products such as cable modems, set-top boxes, integrated TVs, Internet TVs, or intelligent storage devices for A/V content. Today, in the world of analog consumer electronic appliances, there exists a number of proprietary solutions for interoperability between devices from one brand or vendor. In the upcoming world of digital technologies, HAVi extends this networking model by allowing communication between consumer electronic devices from multiple brands. Some examples of this new interoperability are:

- A VCR can use the clock of the TV (e.g., as received via its satellite, terrestrial, or cable receiver) to set the time on its own clock.

- A TV can program the VCR based on the Electronic Program Guide the TV receives. This is done completely by the TV: the user does not have to program the VCR separately.

- When a HAVi device is plugged in to or unplugged from the HAVi network, other HAVi devices will detect this and can adapt their functionality. For instance, when the VCR is unplugged, the TV can inform the user that the programmed recordings are no longer possible and it can try to find another VCR in the HAVi network and use that one.

- HAVi devices can use the display of other HAVi devices to present a user interface. For instance, the VCR could be programmed in the dining room from a TV in the bedroom.

The underlying structure for a home network based on HAVi technologies is a peer-to-peer network, where all devices can talk to and interact with all others. HAVi has been designed, however, to allow the incremental addition of new devices, which will most likely result in a number of interconnected clusters of devices. Typically, there will be several clusters in the home, with one per floor or per room. Over time these clusters will be connected with technologies such as *1394 long* or wireless 1394. As the name indicates, 1394 long supports distances of up to 100 meters.

COMPONENTS AND MANAGEMENT ....

The HAVi architecture is based on the IEEE 1394 standard, so you need to install specialized cables to interconnect in-home appliances. HAVi classifies appliances into the following categories:

- **Full A/V devices (FAV)**—A FAV device contains a complete set of software elements comprising the HAVi architecture. This type of appliance generally has a rich set of hardware resources and is capable of supporting a complex software environment. A complete description of the myriad of software elements that are supported by FAVs is included in the next section of this chapter.

- **Intermediate A/V devices (IAV)**—These types of electronic appliances are generally lower in cost than FAV appliances and have more limited resources. They do not provide a runtime environment for Java bytecode and so cannot act as controllers for devices within the home network.

- **Base A/V devices (BAV)**—A BAV does not host the HAVi middleware software. Rather it hosts a Java-based control module that can be uploaded to any FAV device in the home network. This mechanism allows device vendors to continually innovate and improve their devices without forcing other vendors to track new features. When the new BAV device is plugged into the home network, the FAV that will control it simply uploads and runs the control module and needs not care about the actual internal details. In other words, BAV devices, via the upload model, are future-proof.

- **Legacy A/V devices (LAV)**—The transition of stand-alone consumer electronic devices to networked devices is going to be slow and gradual. HAVi acknowledges this fact and supports all legacy consumer electronic devices—that is, appliances that were built before the advent of the HAVi networking standard. These appliances use proprietary protocols and standards for their control. These devices can work on an in-house network, but they require a FAV or an IAV to act as a gateway. In the context of a HAVi network, a gateway is used to translate HAVi commands to and from the legacy command control.

Rather than trying to remember all these acronyms, HAVi appliances can also be categorized according to the degree to which they support the 1394 standard:

- Non-1394-based appliances
- Appliances that use 1394 but do not support the HAVi architecture
- Appliances that use 1394 and support HAVi

Currently, most of the appliances we have in our houses fall into the first category.

Now that we have described the physical components of a basic HAVi network, let's examine the system that is used to control or manage these appliances. The model used by HAVi to manage an in-home network makes a distinction between *controllers* and *controlled appliances*.

- A controller is an application that acts as a host for controlled appliances. In terms of a HAVi environment, a host has the required hardware resources to store data and home networking software applications.

- As the name suggests, a controller manages a controlled appliance.

For instance, an intelligent television in a family room might be the controller for a number of appliances around the house. The television could contain a particular software program that builds a user interface for controlled appliances. When family members want to interact with one of the controlled appliances, such as a mobile phone, the controller (the television in this case) will build and present the family member with a customized user interface.

SOFTWARE ANATOMY...

Home networking services in the HAVi architecture are modeled as objects. An object is a self-contained entity that consists of both data and procedures to manipulate this data. Each object has a unique name and identifier. HAVi objects are commonly called software elements because they are accessible to programmers through a well-defined interface. All objects make themselves known to other objects via a system-wide naming service known as a *registry*. The registry is a distributed database that stores information about the HAVi objects. Objects often use the registry to find other objects on the network. All objects communicate with each other using a message-passing model. The intercommunication between HAVi objects commences with the assignment of software element identifiers (SEIDs). All SEIDs are unique; however, they may change as a result of a reconfiguration of the devices on the network. Objects use this identification number in conjunction with a general-purpose messaging mechanism to request services from other objects. The messaging mechanism consists of a suite of network and transport layer protocols that provide HAVi software elements with communication facilities. The actual implementation of this messaging system differs from vendor to vendor; however, the format of these messages and the protocols used for their delivery remains common across all HAVi-based home networks. To improve our understanding of the HAVi software architecture, let's examine the software elements of a typical FAV device (see Figure 11.1).

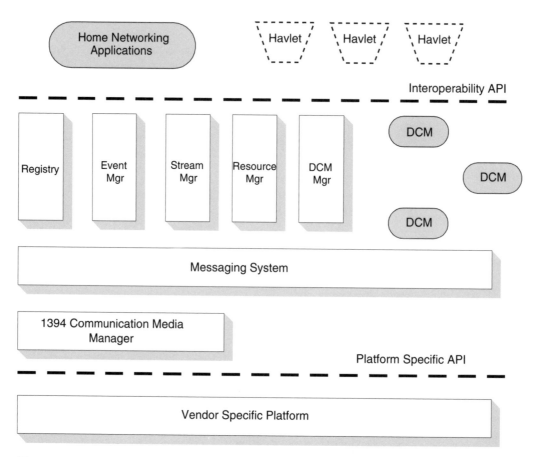

Figure 11.1
HAVi software architecture

1394 Communication Media Manager (CMM)

The CMM is a network-dependent entity that is embedded in all FAV and IAV devices connected to the HAVi network. It interfaces with the underlying communication media to provide services to other HAVi components or application programs residing on the same device as the CMM. Each physical communication medium has its own CMM to serve the above purpose. This section concentrates only on the CMM for the 1394 bus. Two types of services are provided by CMM. One is to provide a transport mechanism to send requests to and receive indications from remote in-home appliances. The other is to abstract the network activities and present information to the HAVi system. The 1394 bus is a dynamically configurable network. When devices are plugged into or removed from the network, a "bus reset" occurs. After each bus reset, a device may have a completely different physical ID than it had before. If a HAVi component or an application has been communicating with a device in the network, it may want to continue the communication after a bus reset, though the device may have a different physical ID. The Global Unique ID (GUID) is used by CMM and other HAVi entities to uniquely identify a device regardless of frequent bus resets.

A GUID is a 64-bit number that is composed of 24 bits of IEEE 1394 vendor ID and 40 bits of chip ID. While a device's physical ID may change constantly, its GUID is permanent.

One of the advanced features the 1394 bus provides to the HAVi system is its support for dynamic device actions such as hot plugging and unplugging. To fully support this up to the user level, HAVi system components or applications need to be aware of these network changes. CMM works with the Event Manager (discussed below) to detect and announce such dynamic changes in network configuration. Since any topology change within the 1394 bus will cause a bus reset to occur, the CMM can detect topology changes and post an event to the Event Manager about these changes along with associated information. The Event Manager will then distribute a related event (called *a network reset*) to all interested HAVi entities or applications.

Messaging System

The messaging system provides HAVi software elements with communication facilities. It is independent of the network and transport layers. A messaging system is embedded in all FAV and IAV devices. The messaging system of a device is in charge of allocating identifiers (SEIDs) for the software elements of that device. These identifiers are first used by the software elements to register. They are then used by the software elements to communicate with each other within the home network.

Registry

The registry is a system service whose purpose is to manage a directory of software elements available within the home network. It provides an API to register and search for software elements. The registry service is present on all IAVs and FAVs. Within one device, any local software element can describe itself through the registry. If a software element wants to be contacted, it must register with the registry. The registry maintains, for each registered object, its identifier (SEID) and its attributes. The registry also provides a query interface that software elements can use to search for a target software element according to a set of criteria.

Event Manager

The event manager provides an event delivery service. An event normally happens when either a software element or the home-network itself changes state. For instance, the connection or disconnection of a digital appliance implies a change of state of the network and is likely (but not necessarily) to trigger an appropriate event. The delivery of an event is done either locally within a single device or globally to all devices in the network. To support this service, the event manager functions as an agent to help ensure the event posted by a software element will reach all software elements that care about the event. If a software element wishes to be notified when a particular event is posted, it must register such intention with its local event manager. Each event manager maintains an internal table containing the list of events registered by software elements. When a software element posts an event, it does so via a service provided by the event manager. The event manager checks its internal table and notifies those software elements that have registered this event. Software elements that do not register the event will not receive a notification. If the event was posted globally, the local event manager also relays the event to all remote event managers in the network. Each remote event manager performs the same lookup and notifies the registered local software elements. An event manager notifies software elements by using the HAVi messaging system; in particular, it sends a notification message to the software element that is to be notified. An event has an optional buffer that can be used to pass information related to the event. For instance, consider an input device with multiple buttons, a button-pressed event could be generated when the user presses a button. The software element that is notified of this event may also be interested in knowing which button was pressed. The event poster can optionally put additional information in a buffer and let the event manager pass this information to other software elements. A software element would get the optional information as part of the notification process and it is the software element's task to interpret the information. The event manager process is also present on all IAVs and FAVs connected to the HAVi-based home network.

Stream Manager

When a home network is up and running, HAVi uses different types of *streams* to transfer data between appliances. To manage the continuous flow of multimedia streams across a network, HAVi employs a software element called a *stream manager*. The main responsibility of a stream manager is to allocate network resources (such as network bandwidth and channel numbers) to home networking streams. The stream manager provides an easy-to-use API for configuring end-to-end isochronous connections. The streaming of content across a HAVi home network is based on the IEC 61883 plug control model. Under this model, any appliance on a home network that is capable of transmitting or receiving isochronous data implements virtual *plugs* for its inputs and outputs. A plug is best described as a software object that represents hardware I/O ports contained within a home networking device. A *connection* is made between an output plug on one appliance and one or more input plugs on other in-house appliances. *Plug control registers* (PCR) on each appliance specify the isochronous channel, device-specific I/O port numbers, and other parameters necessary for managing virtual connections across the bus. The stream manager is responsible for managing the plug control model. It should be noted that the stream manager can also support plugs associated with purely software elements. This enables an application to build a graph of connections, from source to sink, which pass through hardware and software processes—or filters. In this way, an A/V stream can be manipulated by various filters before eventually being consumed. An example might be a MPEG stream that is sourced from a VHS player, transcoded to digital video format, passed through a software filter that acts as a simple edit suite, and recorded (or consumed) in digital format on a hard drive that is connected to the home network. The following points summarize the features of the stream manager software element:

- The stream manager provides services only to applications that are running on the same appliance as the stream manager itself.

- A stream manager is required on FAV appliances. Implementation on a IAV appliance is required only if applications on the IAV need stream manager services.

- The stream manager is capable of constructing a map of all connections within the home network established by HAVi applications. The stream manager is also capable of reporting on usage of 1394 isochronous bandwidth by non-HAVi applications.

- Every stream of multimedia data that is managed by the stream manager has an associated stream type. This parameter identifies the representation of data, bandwidth allocation, and other attributes of the actual stream. A stream type identifier is formed from a 24-bit IEEE 1394 vendor ID and a 16-bit type number.

- After a home network reset, the stream manager invokes a set of procedures for restoring connections on your network.

- The stream manager establishes and maintains connections (internal and external). An internal connection transfers data within an in-home appliance. An external connection, on the other hand, transfers data between appliances and may involve the 1394 network or other forms of physical cabling.

Device Control and Functional Component Modules

In a HAVi network, a DCM (Device Control Module) exists for each appliance known in that network. The DCM provides home networking applications with an interface to the physical appliance. A DCM is a HAVi object in the sense that its details are stored in the registry and can communicate with other HAVi objects via the HAVi messaging system. Associated with a DCM are zero or more FCMs (Functional Component Modules). FCMs are software elements that represent the different functional components contained within a networked device. The number of FCMs within a DCM is flexible and may vary over time. HAVi applications do not communicate with a functional component directly but only through the FCM. HAVi has defined the following FCMs: tuner, VCR, clock, camera, A/V disc, amplifier, display, A/V display, modem, web proxy, and converter. The HAVi specification has also defined a number of interfaces for FCMs to help programmers develop home networking applications. FCMs and DCMs are identified to applications through a number called a HAVi unique identifier (HUID). Each DCM and FCM stores its HUID in the registry.

A DCM can be asked for the list of FCMs it currently contains. This flexibility allows a DCM to represent the functionality of an external device as FCMs. (An external device is one connected via an external plug to the device represented by the DCM itself.) External devices will normally contain a configuration parameter that describes itself to the HAVi DCM. For instance, it's an MP3 player manufactured by Sony and its model number is xxxxxx.

A DCM and its FCMs are obtained from the *DCM code unit* for the device. A DCM code unit is a piece of programming code that is related to a particular HAVi appliance. DCM code units can be written in Java bytecode or native code. The DCM management system is responsible for installing and uninstalling DCM code units.

For different types of HAVi devices, DCM play a different role:

- An IAV device may host one DCM representing itself and may host one or more DCMs representing LAVs (or BAVs operating in LAV mode).

- An FAV device may host one DCM representing itself and may host one or more DCMs representing LAV devices and/or BAV devices.

- A LAV device does not have any notion of DCMs. When attached to a HAVi network where one or more FAV or IAV devices know how to handle the LAV, one of them has to provide the DCM code unit to make the LAV available to other HAVi components.

- A BAV device does not host any DCMs, but provides a DCM code unit in Java bytecode. When attached to a HAVi network with one or more FAVs, one of them uploads and installs the DCM code unit to make the

BAV device available to other HAVi components. Installation of the DCM code unit results in the installation of the DCM and all FCMs related to the device.

- When a BAV device is attached to a HAVi network with no FAV devices but with an IAV device that knows how to handle that BAV, an IAV device can provide a DCM code unit itself to make the BAV device available to other HAVi components.

Besides an API for controlling the in-home appliance, a DCM may also contain a device-specific application called a "havlet." Through this application, a manufacturer can provide consumers with a way to control any special feature of the electronic device in a way that is decided by the manufacturer. Because developing DCMs and FCMs requires knowledge of the underlying hardware and firmware architecture of the in-home device, they are normally developed by the device makers themselves.

Resource Manager

Within a HAVi environment, the management of resources is split between the stream manager and the resource manager. As described earlier, the stream manager handles the management of connections and bandwidth requirements. The resource manager deals with the reservation and release of hardware resources on your network. The hardware resources of in-home appliances can be reserved by an application for exclusive use, but can also be shared by more than one application. The resource manager is responsible for "scheduled actions." It allows applications to identify actions that are to take place at some specific time (such as a VCR recording) and then triggers these actions at the appropriate times. There is a resource manager on each FAV and IAV device that hosts or can host at least one DCM. All resource managers cooperate on a HAVi-based network to ensure that resource deadlocks are prevented.

In-Home Software Applications

In general, a HAVi application is one that creates software elements that use other software elements to provide specific services. A HAVi application may be developed in native code and embedded (resident) on an FAV or IAV. The applications that are run across an in-home network are conceptually similar to DCMs. They typically have proprietary functionality and can be created by third-party application developers. These applications use the APIs defined by HAVi, and supported by the HAVi software elements and HAVi DCM/FCMs to interact with and control home network devices.

HAVi in-home applications can be upgraded using two different techniques:

1. The standard method in HAVi is to download the application from a URL or cable service provider and run it on the Java virtual machine (JVM) inside an FAV device.

2. Nonstandard (proprietary) methods by which the application can be introduced into the HAVi device are via PCMCIA Flash-ROM card, MO disk, floppy disk, and so on.

Havlets

In addition to the above software elements specified by the HAVi architecture, devices on an in-home network may also contain a number of havlets that are specific to a home-networking environment. A havlet is typically a proprietary application that offers a user interface for controlling appliances. For the actual control of the appliance, the havlet makes use of a DCM. A havlet is an object in the sense that it is registered in the registry and can communicate with other HAVi objects via the messaging system described earlier. Havlets only run on FAV-enabled appliances.

HAVi User Interfaces

The primary goal of the HAVi user interface for home networks is to provide the user with a comfortable operating environment. The HAVi Architecture allows users to control appliances through familiar means, such as via the front panel or via the buttons of a remote controller. In addition, the HAVi architecture allows manufacturers to specify graphical user interfaces (GUIs) which can be rendered on a range of displays varying from text-only to high-level graphical displays. The GUI need not appear on the device itself, it may be displayed on another device and the display device may potentially be from another manufacturer. To support this powerful feature, the HAVi architecture provides two mechanisms—the first, the *Level 1 UI*, is intended for IAVs and is called *Data Driven Interaction* (DDI); the second, the *Level 2 UI*, consists of APIs that are based on the Java programming language. DDI is essentially the encoding of user interface elements. The DDI elements can be loaded and displayed by a DDI controller. This controller is used by the home network to generate messages in response to user input—for example, the pressing of a key on a remote control.

HAVI AND JAVA ....

HAVi has specified the Java programming language for the development of DCMs and applications for in-home appliances. To understand the benefits of using Java applications on a home network, it is necessary that we take a quick look at the programming language itself. The Java language is extremely powerful and incorporates many of the benefits of the C and C++ languages. Java is highly object-oriented—everything in the language is an object, apart from the simple data types. Unlike C++, which is an object-oriented derivative of the C programming language, Java was designed from the ground up using object-oriented technologies. Virtually everything in Java is an object, which makes the Java computing model easy to extend. To complement the various objects, the language also contains a variety of data types, which have been categorized into numeric, character, or Boolean data types. When we speak about data types, we are talking about the classification of a particular type of information. The Java environment comes with a rich collection of classes that deal with standard computing functions such as I/O, networking, and graphics. Programs written in the Java programming language are platform-independent. When a program is first written, the source code is compiled into a language that is very similar to machine instructions called *bytecode*. The main difference between bytecode and machine code is that bytecode is not specific to any particular processor. The use of bytecode allows software engineers to write once and execute the program on a variety of different platforms, including network computers, thermostats, mobile phones, VCRs, toasters, and digital set-top boxes.

Once the program has been translated into bytecode, it can be transferred across the HAVi-based home network and executed by a Java virtual machine. Bytecode files are easily recognized by their .class file extensions. Java is a secure language because the virtual machine verifies the bytecode before executing the program. In addition to verifying the integrity of bytecode, the Java program is unable to access system resources such as hard disk drives. Not all categories of HAVi appliances are able to run havlets, DCMs, and applications that are written in Java bytecode. All FAVs support the uploading and execution of Java bytecode because it supports a Java virtual machine on which these entities can run. Consequently, Java applications can be executed on any FAV from any vendor or brand and anyone can write Java applications for FAVs, not just the vendor of the FAV. The ability to install Java applications on any FAV offers the following benefits:

- **Future-proof**—When consumers buy a new device whose full functionality was unknown at the time of purchasing, they can install new Java applications once they become available.

- **Platform independence**—Because Java is platform-independent and the APIs are standardized by HAVi, Java applications will run on any FAV, independent of the vendor or brand.

- **Programmer's support**—Java is supported by a large community of developers and is being adopted by a growing number of standards bodies like Digital Video Broadcasting (DVB) and Advanced Television Systems

Committee (ATSC). This provides for a large base of potential application developers for HAVi.

- **Link with the Internet and broadcast systems**—Java is the key language for internet-based applications. Standards bodies like DVB, ATSC, and Digital Audio Visual Council (DAVIC) are defining Java APIs to enable interactive applications to be downloaded to digital set-top boxes. The Java APIs as defined by HAVi, when implemented on such a set-top box or an Internet TV, will allow these applications to use all the HAVi appliances in the home.

HAVI SECURITY

All software elements on a HAVi-based home network can in principle send messages and events to each other without any restriction. However, to prevent applications from sending, whether accidentally or deliberately, messages or events to system components that were intended to be used only by other system components, a protection mechanism is needed. HAVi specifies, for each defined HAVi message and event, the kinds of software element that are allowed to use it. The protection mechanism simply implies that a system component will check whether the message sender is allowed to send this message (or event). Protection of a device (and the home network) from hostile or flawed applications is the responsibility of the vendor of the device. Such protection is particularly crucial for FAV devices since HAVi specifies an open programming environment for FAVs and applications may be introduced to FAVs (e.g., via Web download, broadcast download, or installation from hard media).

The basic security mechanism used to protect HAVi home networks from external threats is a digital authentication certificate. This digital certificate is attached to all downloadable DCMs; the provider of the DCM can only obtain the certificate if the provider asserts that the DCM is HAVi compliant.

HAVi uses a two-level protection scheme. When a software element is created it is assigned an access level which is one of *trusted* or *untrusted*. When one software element sends a request to another element, the receiver decides whether or not to honor the request by examining the access level of the requestor (and optionally other information associated with the request).

TYPICAL HOME NETWORK CONFIGURATIONS

The HAVi architecture defines the way devices are abstracted within the home network and establishes a framework for device control. It defines the ways that interoperability is assured, and it defines the ways that future devices and services can be integrated into the architecture. The HAVi network makes no restrictions, however, on what types of devices must be present in the home network. As a result, several configurations are possible—networks without FAV devices, networks with multiple FAV devices, networks with LAV and BAV devices only, etc. Depending on the types of devices on the home network, several configurations are possible. The following sections describe some of these possibilities.

LAV and BAV Only

The HAVi architecture does not provide any support for networks consisting of only BAV and LAV devices. However, with the addition of a HAVi controller (an IAV or FAV) to the network, these devices can be made available to home applications.

IAV or FAV as Controller

IAV and FAV devices act as controllers for the other device types and provide a platform for the system services comprising the HAVi Architecture. To achieve this, FAVs provide a runtime environment for Java bytecode DCMs, while IAVs may host embedded DCMs. From an interoperability perspective, the primary role of a controller is to manage DCMs and provide a runtime environment for DCMs. Applications use the APIs provided by the DCM to access the controlled device. This particular home configuration is illustrated in Figure 11.2.

IAV or FAV as a Display Unit

Generally, IAVs and FAVs will have an associated display device that is used for display of A/V content and GUIs. However, the architecture does not mandate this and an IAV or FAV device may be "headless" (without display capability). In this case, they will cooperate with other IAV or FAV devices with display capability. Such devices will typically support a DDI Controller or, in the case of an FAV, a Level 2 UI. Proprietary low-level graphic manipulation APIs can be used by the DDI Controller to access the display itself, but these interfaces are not exposed as part of the interoperability APIs.

Peer-to-Peer Architecture between FAVs and IAVs

In a home network, there may be more than one FAV or more than one IAV. In this case, each controller (IAV or FAV) cooperates with other controllers to ensure that services are provided to the consumer. This allows devices to share resources. An example is described in the previous configuration (IAV or FAV as a display unit) where a device without display capabilities uses a remote device to display DCM user interfaces.

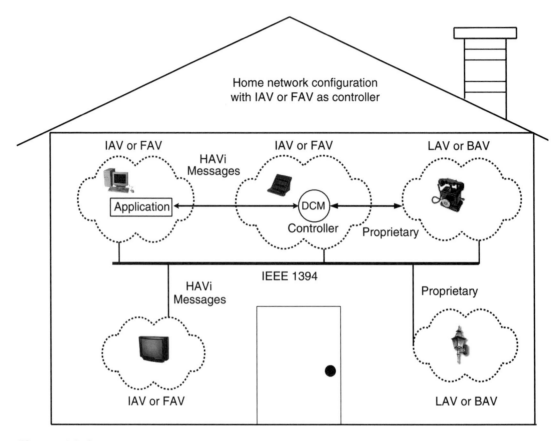

Figure 11.2
IAV or FAV controller-based configuration

SUMMARY ....

Middleware supports the seamless convergence of broadcast and home network applications. The fusion between both of these technologies facilitates the deployment of a range of new entertainment services within the home. HAVi is a protocol and set of APIs that defines a set of software services that enable 1394 devices to expose their A/V capabilities to peer devices on the network. For a middleware technology to be successful in the world of home networking, it must meet several requirements. These include:

- Timely transfer of high speed multimedia data streams
- Self configuration and management of connected devices

- Support for plug and play technologies
- Low cost cabling and network interfaces

The HAVi architecture meets all of these requirements. The architecture of a HAVi-based network is open, lightweight, and platform-independent. Table 11.1 summarizes the functions of the various architectural software elements that are present in a HAVi-based appliance.

A HAVi software element can provide a user with the ability to control another software element using mechanisms based on the DDI protocol and the Java programming language. HAVi specifies an open and standardized Java programming environ-

Table 11.1 HAVi Software Elements

Software Element	Description
Communications media manager (CMM)	Allows other elements to communicate over a home network based on 1394 bus technologies.
Messaging system	Main responsibility includes the passing of messages between different elements.
Event manager	An event is the change in state of an object or the home network. Once this happens, the event manager reports the details to "interested" software elements.
Registry	Acts as a directory service. It allows any object to locate another object on the home network.
Stream manager	Manages real-time transfer of multimedia content between components on a network.
DCMs and FCMs	A DCM represents a device; an FCM represents the functionality of a device. For instance, a DCM may represent a physical VCR; within a VCR, you'll find a tape transport, i.e., storage and a tuner. Therefore, two FCMs will be created and managed by the DCM.
Resource manager	Manages the sharing and allocation of resources on your network.
Havlet	A device-specific application that can be retrieved from a DCM.
Applications	Provide an interface to a specific service on your network.

ment for applications and DCMs on HAVi appliances. The use of Java guarantees that applications and DCMs will run on any HAVi appliance from any brand or manufacturer that offers this environment. The first and foremost goal of the HAVi architecture is to support interoperability between A/V devices. This includes existing and future equipment. Consequently, HAVi networks can have several different operational configurations. This chapter examined some of the most popular configurations for home based networks.

12 Digital Harmony

In this chapter...

Digital Harmony Technologies sells standards-compliant IEEE 1394 interface modules to manufacturers of A/V devices. Positioning its technology as a certified interoperability solution for IEEE 1394 home entertainment devices, Digital Harmony provides firmware that implements open standards running on certified integrated circuit processors. This chapter describes the main technological components that comprise the Digital Harmony solution. By embracing open industry standards, Digital Harmony is trying to be for IEEE 1394 what C-Cube was for MPEG, and what Novell was for Ethernet.

ABOUT DIGITAL HARMONY ....

Digital Harmony's business model and technology were created from the following observations:

- Open interoperability standards such as the Musical Instrument Digital Interface (MIDI) have been shown to stimulate existing markets, seed new businesses, and create price competition, all to the benefit of consumers.
- New digital technologies such as IEEE 1394 are complicated and difficult to implement in traditionally analog consumer devices.
- Consumers won't tolerate home entertainment devices that "crash" like computers have been known to do.
- It is unlikely that independent manufacturers can implement the myriad of IEEE 1394 open standards with exactly the same results.
- The surefire way to guarantee the consumer success of IEEE 1394 technology is to independently test and verify device operation within a system; testing is necessary to guarantee that devices work in harmony in a home network.

Digital Harmony is developing Digital Harmony certification centers to test IEEE 1394-enabled A/V devices for compliance with open standards. Those devices that pass the certification test bear the Digital Harmony logo, shown in Figure 12.1, near the connectors—a "seal of approval."

Figure 12.1
Digital Harmony logo

DIGITAL HARMONY PARTNERS ....

At the time of writing, the companies shown in Table 12.1 were using Digital Harmony technology in their A/V devices and participating in the certification program.

Table 12.1 *Digital Harmony Partners*

Company	Profile
Boston Acoustics	Leading manufacturer of high-performance audio systems for home theater, automotive, and computer markets.
California Audio Labs	Uses technology to provide outstanding audio performance. A Sensory Science company.
Cirrus Logic/Crystal Semiconductor	A premier supplier of precision linear circuits and advanced mixed-signal ICs. Cirrus Logic is designing the first Digital Harmony-compliant Node Controller integrated circuit.
DENON	One of Japan's leading manufacturers of high quality audio and video devices.
Go Video	A premier video recorder manufacturer. Now known as Sensory Science Corporation.
Harman International Industries	Owns companies in four markets: consumer electronics, automotive, professional, and computer audio.
Harman/Kardon	Uses signature audio technologies to ensure that their audio devices deliver realistic reproduction of music. A Harman International company.
Infinity	A leader in multichannel audio systems for home theater. A Harman International company.
JBL	Manufactures home theater and professional audio systems and speakers. Speaker systems with Digital Harmony interfaces will be available in 2000. A Harman International company.
Leviton-Telcom	The largest manufacturer of home wiring products in the world, now developing Digital Harmony 1394 wiring products for the home.
Loewe	Germany's premier manufacturer of audio/video devices, including the first 100 Hz digital television.

Table 12.1 Digital Harmony Partners (Continued)

Company	Profile
Madrigal Audio Labs	Audiophile brands include Mark Levinson and Proceed. A Harman International company.
Mark Levinson	Manufacturer of high-performance audio and video devices and systems. A brand of Madrigal Audio Labs.
Meridian Audio	Manufactures all-digital audio/video systems. In 1998, the DVD Forum selected Meridian Lossless Packing (MLP) as the audio compression format standard for the upcoming DVD Audio format.
Monster Cable	A manufacturer of audio/video cables. EnTech, a division of Monster, manufactures audio/video devices.
Onkyo	A premier Japanese manufacturer of audio amplifiers, A/V receivers, CD players, MD decks, tuners, and speakers.
Panja	Integrates and automates control for home and business devices and systems, including delivery of Internet information and services.
PAVO	The first certified Digital Harmony third-party developer, able to provide full turnkey product design support for Digital Harmony manufacturing partners. Developer of the popular MIDItools family of devices.
Phast	Acronym for Practical Home Automation Systems Technology, providing integrated solutions for home automation. A subsidiary of Panja.
Proceed	Manufacturer of high performance audio/video devices and systems. A brand of Madrigal Audio Labs.
Stellar One	A developer of terminals that enable network owners to deploy Internet, video, and other information services over "broadband" networks.
Sensory Science Corporation	Formerly Go Video, specializing in innovative audio/video devices, including California Audio Labs audio/video devices.
White Jay International	Designs entertainment and environment Systems Management Software (SMS) for residential, commercial, marine, and aerospace venues.

A DIGITAL HARMONY ENTERTAINMENT SYSTEM ....

A typical home entertainment system comprised of Digital Harmony-certified A/V devices is shown in Figure 12.2.

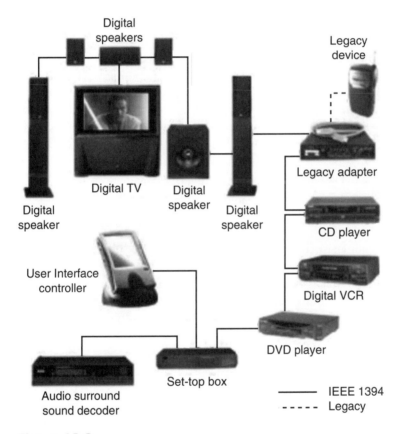

Figure 12.2
A typical Digital Harmony home entertainment system

Digital Harmony systems have the following characteristics useful to consumers:

- Digital Harmony system firmware complies with relevant nonproprietary (i.e., open) international standards.

- Digital Harmony systems are easy to connect and set up. Each device is connected to another device using a certified IEEE 1394 cable. The connectors are "keyed" so that the cable cannot be connected improperly. There is only one connector type—no more "inputs" and "outputs," no more separate audio, video, and control connectors.

- Digital Harmony systems are easy to use via a bidirectional universal remote control that allows the consumer to set up, use, diagnose problems, and upgrade their home entertainment system. The system automatically recognizes new devices and their capabilities, and adds them to the user interface.

- Digital Harmony systems are comprised of multiple devices. Each system can have up to 63 IEEE 1394 A/V devices. In addition, larger systems of more than 64,000 devices can be created using industry-standard "bridge" devices that connect multiple busses together. This feature allows cruise ships, hotels, and apartment buildings to operate as a single Digital Harmony entertainment system.

- Digital Harmony systems are comprised of devices made by multiple brands. Consumers can choose Digital Harmony-certified devices from many different manufacturers based on features, price, and other personal preferences.

- Digital Harmony systems can be comprised of devices found in multiple rooms. Using longer-distance 1394 cables (e.g., Category 5 and optical fiber) and the associated transceivers (to translate standard 1394 copper cable signals into the other cable formats) in the walls of a structure, consumers can have one system with devices physically located in multiple rooms.

- Digital Harmony systems can take advantage of non-1394 A/V devices. Consumers do not need to replace equipment in use today. Digital Harmony legacy adapters exist that allow consumers to connect such devices to their system.

- Digital Harmony systems can take advantage of pre-Digital Harmony 1394 devices—primarily DV camcorders and computers—in use today.

- Digital Harmony-certified devices are backward compatible. A Digital Harmony Composer purchased in 2003 will be able to intelligently control an A/V device purchased in 2000.

- Digital Harmony system firmware can be upgraded by the consumer, as new standards are released in the future.

DIGITAL HARMONY TECHNOLOGY OVERVIEW...

Digital Harmony Protocol Suite

Digital Harmony-certified devices comply with the Digital Harmony protocol suite, a suite of open, international protocols and specifications that, when implemented, enable digital home entertainment devices to operate together in a 1394 network.

"Home entertainment devices" is loosely defined to be the audio and video devices that a normal person would have in the living room. This includes stereo equipment, speakers, televisions, DVD players, CATV set-top boxes, VCRs, etc. It does not include non-entertainment devices that might be found in the home—e.g., printers, scanners, HVAC, kitchen appliances, security systems. (These nonentertainment devices can, however, be connected to a Digital Harmony system via bridge devices.)

At the heart of this protocol suite is the IEEE 1394 standard (also referred to as "i.LINK" and "FireWire") that defines basic transport protocols, enabling devices to exchange data quickly and reliably. The IEEE 1394 standard, however, does not dictate the meaning of the data transferred between devices. Therefore, the Digital Harmony protocol suite specifies additional protocols for formatting audio and video streams, controlling and monitoring parameters on devices, saving/restoring the state of the system (i.e., "presets"), setting up and configuring the system, and performing diagnostics.

When implemented, the Digital Harmony protocol suite delivers the following complete family of system functions:

- Transporting of IEEE 1394 packets
- Formatting of audio and video data streams
- Management of audio/video stream synchronization
- Enforcement of media copyrights (copy protection)
- Control and monitoring of device and system parameters
- Saving and restoring the state of the system
- Upgrading of system firmware
- Configuration of the system
- Conducting system and device diagnostics

The Digital Harmony protocol suite specifies the IEC 61883-1 through -6 international standards for streaming audio and video, as well as the A/V control family of protocols developed by the 1394 Trade Association. It also provides a mechanism for transporting infrared and serial control protocols (e.g., MIDI, RS232) through the system, enabling legacy adapters to connect non-1394 devices to the system. Other protocols currently supported include IEEE 1394-1995, IEEE 1394a, digital transmission content protection (copy protection), content management and protection, and more.

In the future, the Digital Harmony protocol suite will be extended to include forthcoming standards such as HAVi (Digital Harmony is a participant in the HAVi Organization), UPnP, XCA (copy protection), etc. In addition, planned extensions to the Digital Harmony protocol suite will include relevant protocols for other applications such as A/V production (Digital Harmony Studio), digital cinema (Digital Harmony Cinema), and automotive (Digital Harmony Auto).

While the protocol suite itself is open (i.e., nonproprietary), only Digital Harmony licensees can use the Digital Harmony firmware, related patents, hardware interfaces, or logo.

Digital Harmony Device Architecture

A Digital Harmony-certified device has four major components: stream management, device control, system management, and the application. Stream management covers all details for generating isochronous streams, transmitting them to other nodes, receiving them, and synchronizing them properly (one of the greatest challenges for the 1394 bus, since it is by design a nonsynchronous bus). Device control covers all details for modeling a device and controlling its parameters. System management covers configuration of the bus environment and the device. Finally, the application performs the device's particular function, such as playing a DVD or decoding an MPEG transport stream.

Digital Harmony Device Classifications

The Digital Harmony Protocol Suite defines three device types: Digital Harmony target, Digital Harmony controller, and Digital Harmony composer.

Digital Harmony Target ▪ A target is a device with the following properties:

- Allows devices to read its configuration ROM and identify its capabilities
- Sends/receives isochronous streams to/from other nodes (optional)
- Accepts device control commands
- Executes self-diagnostic tests and reports to composer
- Stores and recalls system presets
- Accepts firmware updates

There are two special target devices. A Digital Harmony legacy adapter is used to connect legacy (non-1394) A/V devices to the Digital Harmony system. It has a Digital Harmony interface, as well as legacy audio input/output connectors, and/or legacy video input/output connectors (e.g., S-Video, component, composite, RF), and/or legacy control protocol connectors (e.g., RS232, MIDI, infrared).

Digital Harmony Controller • A controller shares the functions of a target, and adds the ability to identify targets and provide a user interface for them. Digital Harmony does not define the nature of the user interfaces; this is left to the device manufacturer to determine, based on product definition.

The controller is often the only device that a user interacts with, aside from inserting media into players. The controller's user interface can be programmed to provide an endless variety of system presets such as:

- **"Listen to music" preset**—For example, causes the surround sound decoder to accept audio from the DVD player, the video decoder/monitor to turn off, and the audio amplifier to adjust volume and equalization for the user's preferred music settings.
- **"Watch TV" preset**—For example, causes the surround sound decoder to accept audio from the set-top box, the video decoder/monitor to accept video from the set-top box, and the audio amplifier to adjust volume and equalization for optimal television settings.

In addition to managing system presets, the controller provides user interface controls for adjusting audio volume, turning devices on and off, navigating the electronic program guide on the set-top box, etc. One controller can control a Digital Harmony system, but there can be multiple controllers present.

Digital Harmony Composer • A composer shares the basic functions of a controller, and adds the necessary functionality to set up and configure (i.e., "compose") the audio/video system. This functionality includes:

- A mechanism for discovering all devices in the system
- A means for the user to set up media connections between devices
- A means to execute system diagnostics and report them to the user

The composer is typically implemented as application software running on a custom hardware controller, a digital television, a set-top box, or personal digital assistant (see Figure 12.3).

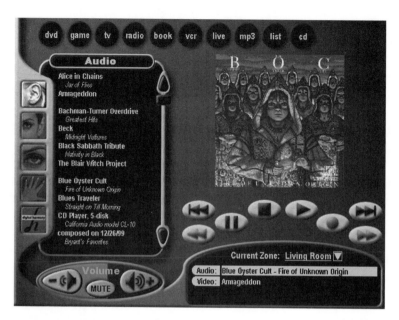

Figure 12.3
Prototype of a Digital Harmony composer

Digital Harmony Firmware

Digital Harmony firmware implements the Digital Harmony Protocol Suite. Licensed to product manufacturers, the firmware enables companies to quickly add an inexpensive, standards-compliant 1394 interface to products. The code is based on reduced instruction set computer (RISC) based devices, containing implementations of Digital Harmony's patents and trade secrets, a real-time operating system (RTOS), and other code. Part of the firmware library is application-specific C source code, available to Licensees for use in their host processor.

As the protocol suite is upgraded (corresponding to the release of new, accepted standards such as HAVi and UPnP), system firmware can be upgraded automatically by the user via 1394 using a patent-pending feature of Digital Harmony.

Digital Harmony Node Controller
Integrated Circuits

Digital Harmony is designing various integrated circuit modules that are licensed to semiconductor manufacturers. Licensees will use these designs to build one- or two-chip solutions for consumer electronics manufacturers, optimized as a processing engine (node controller) for executing the Digital Harmony Firmware. Digital Harmony does not manufacture integrated circuits; it licenses IC modules to its semiconductor design and fabrication partners.

Together, Digital Harmony firmware and Digital Harmony-compliant node controllers are used by manufacturers to build certified A/V devices—all that remains is for the manufacturer to add a specific A/V application (e.g., MP3 player, speaker, television, etc.).

DIGITAL HARMONY NON-1394 TECHNOLOGIES..

Digital Harmony's intellectual property portfolio contains four complementary non-1394 technologies that are valuable to manufacturers and home network installers: Bi-DAT, WireFree, PAWS, and REALM.

BiDAT Transceivers • Digital Harmony's BiDAT (U.S. and foreign patents pending) transceivers allow data and audio to share existing speaker wires or line-level interconnect cables. This allows simple devices (such as a speaker) to communicate with an intelligent device (such as a decoder/amplifier) without incurring the expense of a sophisticated communications interface. BiDAT is a very inexpensive alternative to IEEE 1394, giving speakers the same bidirectional communications capabilities as any other Digital Harmony audio device. For example, a BiDAT speaker with an IR window could be placed in a bedroom, allowing the consumer to use an IR remote control to manipulate a stereo system in the living room.

The essential features of Digital Harmony's BiDAT transceivers are:

- Transparent—data signal does not interfere with audio signal
- Full duplex—bidirectional signal up to 56 Kbps
- Low cost—transceiver component costs are less than $5 (U.S.)
- Small—modest space requirements
- Line-powered—option eliminates power supply in existing installations
- Compatible—supported by Digital Harmony Protocol Suite

A block diagram of a typical Digital Harmony BiDAT amplifier is shown in Figure 12.4.

WireFree Transmitters and Receivers • Digital Harmony's wireless audio transmitters, developed in partnership with Music Sciences Inc., use a revolutionary digital transmission technology—WireFree (U.S. and foreign patents pending). The WireFree digital wireless system brings eight independent CD-quality digital audio signals to home theaters. WireFree is a feature-rich alternative to hard-wired IEEE

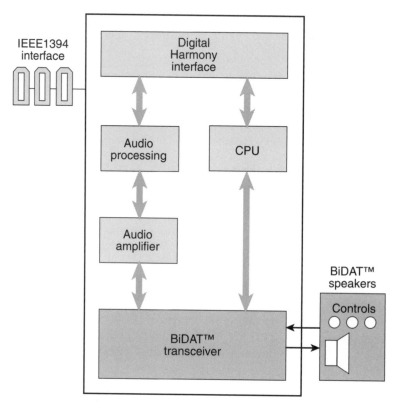

Figure 12.4
BiDAT amplifier

1394-powered speakers, providing transmission links of up to 20 meters—standard IEEE 1394 copper cables can only be used at lengths up to 4.5 meters. WireFree technology is compatible with the Digital Harmony protocol suite.

PAWS Watermarking Codecs • The PAWS audio watermarking system (including U.S. Patents 5,473,631 and 5,404,377; foreign patents pending) is a watermarking method based on perceptual coding, allowing data (PAWprints) to be hidden in an audio signal. This technology is used by software companies to mark a recording with a unique code, allowing each copy to be tracked after it is sold.

The essential features of Digital Harmony's PAWS system are:

• Discreet—does not perceptibly interfere with audio signal

• Robust—data integrity and extractability survives "low-fi" conditions

• Secure—PAWprints can not be removed or altered

- Accepted—approved for use by multiple television broadcast networks
- Proven—currently in use by a major media research company
- Compatible—supported by Digital Harmony protocol suite

REALM Codecs • REALM (U.S. Patent 5,612,943; foreign patents pending) Codecs allow the recording of data along with audio, using standard Red Book audio recording methods. The encoded data can be retrieved from the analog outputs of any audio player such as a portable CD player. The essential features of Digital Harmony's REALM Codecs are:

- Easy—REALM encoding tools used to create content
- Simple—data easily retrieved from analog outputs of any audio player
- Low-Cost—low decoder component cost, less than $5 (U.S.)
- Consumer-Friendly—works with any portable CD player
- Transparent—data signal does not interfere with audio signal
- Synchronous—allows data delivery to be synchronized with audio
- Compatible—supported by Digital Harmony protocol suite

SUMMARY

The Digital Harmony protocol suite was created with the consumer in mind. By actively participating in the standards process from the beginning, Digital Harmony hopes to be instrumental to the success of IEEE 1394 as a consumer electronics interconnect. While some aspects of their business model are similar to Dolby Labs and Lucasfilm/THX (e.g., device certification), Digital Harmony hopes to be for IEEE 1394 interfaces what C-Cube was for MPEG, and what Novell was for Ethernet. The growing list of Digital Harmony partners, as well as numerous public demonstrations of working entertainment systems over the past three years, has established Digital Harmony as a provider of interoperable IEEE 1394 solutions.

13 UPnP

In this chapter...

Industry forecasts indicate explosive growth in the number of homes with multiple PCs, and many homes soon will be geographically served by commodity broadband Internet access (cable, xDSL). Set-top boxes, networked entertainment appliances, and other smart devices are evolving with the growth of the Internet and improved bandwidth availability to the home. Moreover, anticipating the increased demand for new services, PC manufacturers are beginning to ship computers with built-in support for Ethernet, IEEE 1394, radio frequency (RF), powerline carrier, or phoneline connectivity that makes it possible to add home networking without adding new wires. As these trends converge to create a requirement for home networking, simplicity of installation and usage, low cost, security, and reliability all become critical elements of any solution that addresses this market. It is against this background that Microsoft is sponsoring a cross-industry initiative called Universal Plug and Play (UPnP).

ABOUT UNIVERSAL PLUG AND PLAY ....

UPnP is at the heart of Microsoft's home networking strategy and uses open Internet communication standards to transparently connect consumer electronic devices to standard PCs. UPnP makes it possible to initiate and control the transfer of files and A/V streams from any device on an in-home network.

UPnP is an extension to the plug-and-play initiative that was introduced by Intel, Compaq, and Microsoft back in 1992. A high-level overview of the architecture of UPnP is illustrated in Figure 13.1.

The architecture defines a set of common interfaces that allows a user to plug a device directly into the in-home network. In other words, a user can begin using a new device without worrying about configuration settings and installing new drivers. UPnP was developed within the context of existing industry standards. For instance, UPnP provides developers with a common set of interfaces for accessing services on a home network. Another advantage of UPnP is its independence of the physical network media in your house. It is compatible with existing networks, such as standard 10 Base-T Ethernet and new networking technologies that don't require costly installation of new wiring systems in existing homes—HomePNA and HomeRF. Rather than concentrating on one particular device type, UPnP interconnects all types of devices in the home, including PCs, PC peripherals, new smart home appliances, gateway devices, home control systems, and Web-connectable devices. The result of this pragmatic and relatively simple approach is that implementing UPnP on an in-home network requires very little work and human intervention. UPnP is equally adaptable to both dynamic home environments and fixed, configured corporate networks. Other features of UPnP include those discussed below.

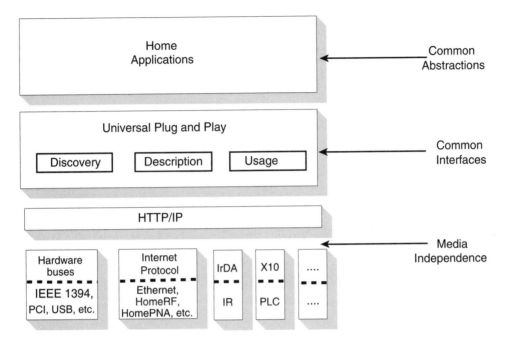

Figure 13.1
UPnP high-level architecture

Open Standards

Relatively simple and open protocols, such as those that have been defined by the Internet Engineering Task Force (IETF) have a proven track record on the Internet. TCP/IP, for instance, allows numerous different types of computing platforms to communicate reliably with each other. As mentioned earlier in our chapter, UPnP is based on a number of these open protocols. Because it is based on standard Internet protocols, UPnP can work with a broad range of devices, from large PCs to small consumer electronics devices. UPnP also eliminates the need for complex testing to ensure devices can work together.

Scalability

UPnP normally functions in small network environments; however, it is possible to scale upward to larger networks.

Plug and Play

Most home users want to just plug it in and have it work immediately with no hassles. UPnP is based on straightforward, innovative mechanisms for discovery and connectivity that provide a basis for enabling device services.

Low Footprint

Unlike traditional PC-based solutions, consumer electronic appliances have radically less systems resource at hand. Typically, they are based on a low-cost micro controller, Application Specific Integrated Circuits (ASICs), and some 200 to 1000 Kbytes of RAM and Flash memory. Implementing UPnP requires very little development work and requires only a very small amount of system resources and footprint.

Multivendor and Mixed-Media Environment

Analysts are predicting that mixed-media, multivendor in-home networks will be a common scenario in the future; consequently, UPnP has been explicitly designed to accommodate these environments. The architecture of this type of home networking environment is shown in Figure 13.2.

Smooth Integration with Legacy Systems and Non-IP Devices

Although IP internetworking is a strong choice for UPnP, it also accommodates home networks that run non-IP protocols such as IEEE 1394-based entertainment networks. A standard home network, for example, could use a Windows PC to host several different types of legacy devices and use the UPnP mechanism to make these devices discoverable to other peers on the network.

Non PC-Centric Architecture

The configuration of a UPnP based network can be based on a peer-to-peer network architecture, which means that home networks can function without a PC. This doesn't however mean that the PC has no role in a UPnP-based network. The PC's general-purpose nature and substantial resources will make it a valuable part of any network where it is present.

To drive and promote UPnP technologies, Microsoft announced the formation of the UPnP forum, and later the formation of the UPnP forum steering committee. The

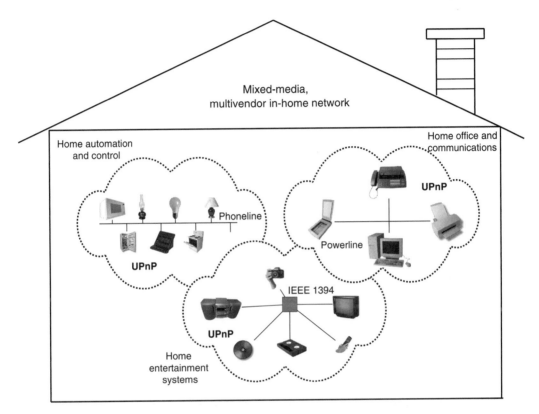

Figure 13.2
Mixed media, multivendor home network

main function of this forum is to identify and establish a number of working committees that will define the manner in which home appliances communicate with each other.

About the UPnP Forum

UPnP forum is an industry initiative designed to enable easy and robust connectivity among stand-alone devices and PCs from many different vendors. It comprises a wide variety of individuals and companies who are authoring specifications and services for UPnP-enabled devices. More than 120 hardware, home automation, computer software, and consumer electronic companies have joined the UPnP forum, and 15 of these companies, indicated by an asterisk, are members of the UPnP forum steering committee. The listing that follows gives a snapshot of the UPnP forum members:

3Com

Actiontec

Advanced Micro Devices, Inc. (AMD)

Agranat

AMX/Phast

AT&T

ATI Technologies

* Axis

Canon

Casio

Cisco Systems Inc.

* Compaq

Conexant Systems Inc.

Dell Computer Corp.

Diamond-Multimedia

Eastman Kodak Co.

* Echelon Corp.

Efficient

ELSA

Epigram

Fore

Fujitsu Limited

Gateway

* Hewlett-Packard Co.

Hitachi Ltd.

* Honeywell

* IBM

* Intel

Intellon Corp.

Iready

Kawasaki

Lexmark International, Inc.

Lucent

Micron

* Microsoft

Minolta

* Mitsubishi

Motorola

* Matsushita Electric Industrial Company

National Semiconductor

NEC

NeoMagic

* Panja Inc.

Peracom

* Philips Electronics N.V.

OKI Electric

Proxim, Inc.

Qualcomm

Quantum

Samsung Information Systems America (SISA)

Sanyo

Sega

ShareWave, Inc.

SHARP Corp.

* Sony

Symbol

* Siemens AG

Texas Instruments

* Thomson

Toshiba Corp.

The steering committee has established a number of technical working groups to cover the following home networking areas:

- Traditional PC usage
- Printing on a home network
- Internet gateways
- Home lighting
- Home security
- Home HVAC
- Home energy management

The steering committee also plans to define and create a new working group in the area of A/V device interoperability.

As part of its home networking strategy, the forum has developed a Web site at http://www.upnp.org for posting information about its activities and achievements. Members of the forum can also use the site for downloading specifications, source code, and implementor's guides. Member companies of the forum are developing a new generation of easily networked devices and services, and evolving sophisticated technologies implementing home networks.

UPNP CORE TECHNOLOGIES ....

As mentioned earlier, UPnP is an open standard home networking technology that can be used by appliances such as telephones, televisions, printers, and game consoles to exchange and replicate relevant data between themselves and PCs on the network. Central to the UPnP forum's strategy of developing a specification for networking in-house appliances was to use existing standards wherever possible and to minimize the creation of new standards. Consequently, the foundation blocks for the UPnP standard are based on the following standard Internet specifications:

TCP/IP

TCP/IP forms an integral part of the Web software infrastructure. UPnP are using this suite of protocols to support the entertainment services that are expected to run on the home networks of the future.

DNS

Short for Domain Name System, an Internet service that is used by UPnP to translate domain names into IP addresses. DNS was created to serve as a hierarchical and delegated database for Internet host names and their mappings to IP addresses. All devices and computers connected to the Internet have a domain name and a corresponding IP address. Domain names and IP addresses are stored and managed on computers known as domain name servers. Prior to DNS, all hosts and addresses were maintained in a canonical list usually called "HOSTS.TXT." As the Internet grew, management of this list became cumbersome, and DNS was created to effectively manage this growing namespace. For more information, see http://www.rfc-editor.org/rfc/rfc974.txt.

HTML

HyperText Markup Language, or HTML as it is commonly known, is a platform-independent language used to format pages for the World Wide Web. UPnP allows devices on your in-home network to view this content.

HTTP

Short for HyperText Transfer Protocol, HTTP is the underlying protocol that is used by the Web to transfer data between browsers and servers. In the context of UPnP, *server* refers to an HTTP server. When a request is received, the server opens a connection to the client and sends the requested file. After servicing the request, the server returns to its listening state, waiting for the next HTTP request. UPnP includes full support for this method of accessing data across a home network.

UDP

Short for User Datagram Protocol, UDP is an IP-based *connectionless* protocol. The term connectionless refers to a network protocol in which a sending device can send a message without establishing a connection with the receiving device. For more information, see http://www.rfc-editor.org/rfc/rfc768.txt.

LDAP

Short for Lightweight Directory Access Protocol, LDAP is used by UPnP-based appliances to access various types of directories. For instance, home networking users could use a digital set-top box in conjunction with LDAP to obtain information such as e-mail addresses and security levels from servers located on the Internet.

XML

XML is an abbreviation for eXtensible Markup Language, a new specification being developed by the W3 consortium. It enables Web designers to create their own customized tags to provide functionality not available with standard HTML. For example, XML supports links that point to multiple documents, as opposed to HTML links, which can reference just one destination each.

XSL

Short for eXtensible Stylesheet Language, XSL is a styling standard that is currently being developed by the W3 consortium.

IP Multicast

An IP multicast is a special form of broadcast where copies of a data packet are delivered only to a subset of all possible destinations. Every receiver that is listening for that particular IP address then receives the data packets. This keeps bandwidth consumption relatively low and reduces the processing burden on the server to a small fraction of that found under conventional TCP/IP one-to-one communication. IP multicasting is especially useful in a UPnP-based network for discovering new services.

AutoIP

In a home networking environment, devices need to be able to operate without access to advanced configuration services such as DHCP. AutoIP, a proposal to the IETF by Ryan Troll of Carnegie Mellon University, allows a UPnP service to obtain an address in a network without a DHCP server. It should be noted that autoIP is only applicable to devices that are running the DHCP client service.

The easiest way to understand how autoIP operates on a home network is to look at an example. Suppose your games console needs to obtain an IP address for connection to the Internet. The following steps follow the sequence of events for auto-configuring an IP address on a UPnP-based games console.

The allocation of IP addresses works as follows:

1. Your games console uses the DHCP protocol to request a home IP address.
2. A DHCPDISCOVER message is sent out.

3. If after a specified period of time, no valid IP addresses are received, the games console is free to autoconfigure an IP address.

4. Once your appliance has determined that it must autoconfigure an IP address, it uses an algorithm for choosing this address. The autoconfiguration algorithm must use the 169.254/16 address range, which is registered with the Internet Assigned Numbers Authority (IANA) as the LINKLOCAL net.

5. Once an address is chosen, the console tests to see if the address is already in use. If the network address appears to be in use, the console must choose another address, and try again.

6. Even though your game console has been assigned a new address, it keeps on checking the home network for an active DHCP server. This allows a network to operate in isolation, be connected to the Internet with DHCP support, and then to be returned to isolation. This type of scenario will be common in homes that use dial-up access.

The Windows 98, Apple Mac OS 8.5, and Windows 2000 operating systems currently support autoIP. You can see the full autoIP proposal that was submitted to the IETF at the following Internet location: http://www.ietf.org/internet-drafts/draft-ietf-dhc-ipv4-autoconfig-04.txt.

ARP

Short for Address Resolution Protocol, ARP is a member of the TCP/IP family of protocols that is used to convert IP addresses into physical hardware addresses. In the context of UPnP-based home networks, ARP is often used by autoIP to determine whether or not a particular IP address is in use. For more technical information, see ftp://ftp.isi.edu/in-notes/rfc826.txt.

Multicast DNS (Name Resolution)

Multicast DNS is a proposal to the IETF on rules for making normal DNS requests using multicast UDP. IP addresses are difficult to remember, and hard-coded IP addresses reduce administrative flexibility on IP networks. The Internet domain name system is a mapping system that translates human readable domain names, like set-tops.com, into their equivalent IP address. Most corporate intranets implement an internal version of the same technology to provide the same services. In small networks, such as at home or in small business, DNS servers may not exist. Multicast DNS allows DNS requests to be multicast. This allows a machine to see requests for its own name and respond to them. Like autoIP, multicast DNS is only used when a DNS server is not available. Multicast DNS is currently being proposed for IETF standardization. Microsoft is actively involved in that effort. For more technical information, see http://search.ietf.org/internet-drafts/draft-manning-multicast-dns-01.txt.

Simple Service Discovery Protocol (SSDP)

SSDP provides a mechanism whereby home network clients, with little or no static configuration, can discover network services. It enables devices to learn of the existence of potential peer devices and the required IP details needed to establish TCP/IP connections. The successful result of an SSDP search is a URL. The following URL illustrates the format of an SSDP-based address: http://device.local/description/path/description.xml. In this example, the *device.local* is the hostname of the controlled device and the *description/path/description.xml* element of the URL is the path and name of the description document on the device.

The SSDP specification has been submitted as an Internet draft to the IETF. For more technical information, see http://search.ietf.org/internet-drafts/draft-cai-ssdp-v1-00.txt.

UNDER THE UPNP HOOD ....

UPnP is a distributed, open networking architecture that leverages TCP/IP and the Web to enable seamless proximity networking in addition to control and data transfer among networked devices in the home, office, and everywhere in between. It comprises the following types of logical nodes:

- **User control point**—A set of software modules that facilitates communication between itself and a number of controlled devices on a home network. Examples of devices that could function as a user control point include a standard PC, a digital set-top box, and high-speed broadband modems.

- **Controlled device**—A set of software modules that facilitates communication with a user control point. The primary difference between a user control point and a controlled device is that the user control point is always the initiator of the communications session. Examples of devices that could function as a controlled device include VCRs, DVD players, security systems, and automated light controllers.

- **Bridge**—A set of software modules that allows legacy devices to communicate with native UPnP devices.

- **Legacy device**—Any non-UPnP-compliant device.

- **Bridged device**—A device that cannot participate in UPnP at the native protocol level, either because the device does not have sufficient hardware resources or because the underlying media is unsuitable to run TCP and HTTP protocols. Examples of devices that could be bridged devices are power line-controlled A/V equipment, light switches, thermostats, wristwatches, and inexpensive toys.

In order to achieve interoperation among these devices on a home network, UPnP is based around five key mechanisms. Understanding these mechanisms is the key to gaining a glimpse of the potential of UPnP technologies. The mechanisms are

- Device model
- Addressing
- Discovery
- Schema
- Rehydrator

The next sections of this chapter present an overview of these UPnP home networking mechanisms and looks at how they work together in practice.

Device Model

The UPnP device model was designed to be general and flexible. It comprises a number of elements for a controlled device or bridge that is emulating native controlled devices. Figure 13.3 shows the main elements.

Every device includes:

- **Optionally one or more home networking services**—A service is defined in UPnP terms as a controllable entity. Every running instance of a service includes:

  Service state table (SST)—A table of data that consists of rows of information on the current, electrical, mechanical, and logical state of a specific service. The SST for a set-top box could represent the tuner frequency, video decoding format, and current channel selection. The SST for a clock would likely represent the current time.

  Service command set—A set of commands that can be invoked by a UPnP service.

  Event subscription server—An event is an unsolicited message generated by a controlled device and delivered to one or more user control points.

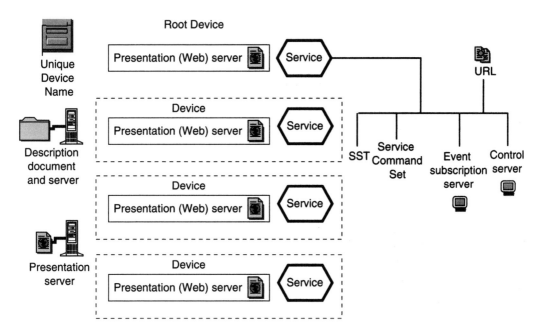

Figure 13.3
UPnP device model

Events are used to maintain a consistent view of the state of service across all interested user control points. A software module called an event subscription server that runs in a controlled device or bridge is used by UPnP to respond to requests from user control points.

Control server—This server accepts incoming commands and passes these commands to the service's native command processing logic and waits for command completion. When the command is completed successfully, the SST is updated, an event is generated, and a successful response is returned to the user control point. In the event of an illegal command or unsuccessful command, no changes are made to the SST and a failure response is returned.

Uniform resource locators—They identify the control and event subscription server.

- **One or more device types**—In relation to the device model, a device represents a container for home networking services. From the perspective of a home networking user, a device generally models a physical entity such as a game console, but can also represent a logical entity. A digital set-top box emulating the traditional functions of a PC would be an example of a logical device. Devices can contain other devices. An example would be a TV/VCR packaged into a single physical unit. A device may also be a logical container of other devices. The top-most device in a hierarchy of nested devices is called the root device. A device with no nested devices is always a root device. All devices, including root devices, belong to one or more device types. A device type is a relatively high level classification of devices with common functionality. An example of a device type is a "DVD player." Similar to the DNS system on the Internet, UPnP also supports human-friendly names for devices connected to a home network. A typical friendly name for a device will contain the manufacturer and model information of the UPnP device.

- **Optionally a presentation server**—A presentation server is a Web server that runs in a controlled device that responds to HTTP-based requests or presentation URLs and returns a graphical Web interface.

- **A globally unique identifier called the Unique Device Name (UDN)**—The UDN is a globally unique address that is used to unambiguously identify a device on a home network. It is a permanent address, even across power cycles and physical location changes.

- **Description document and server**—A description document is a structured unit of data that is used by a user control Point or UPnP bridge to learn the capabilities of a controlled device. Description documents are retrieved from the description server on a UPnP-controlled device. A description server is a standard HTTP server that responds to description document requests from various devices on the home network.

There is one description document for every root device that describes the root device and all nonroot devices. Description documents adhere to the grammar of the XML standard and to the UPnP Architecture Reference. It is also important to note that devices that are described as being a root device also include the description document and description server for all devices under and including itself.

Addressing

UPnP is built on top of the HTTP protocol and leverages the address format of the Web—Uniform Resource Locators (URLs). Every item of information on the Internet has a unique address called a URL. An example of a URL is as follows: http://www.set-tops.com.

This particular URL addresses the home page at set-tops.com. All URLs have two main parts: the protocol identifier and the resource name. In this example, HTTP is the protocol identifier and www.set-tops.com is the resource name. You will notice a colon (":") is used to separate the two components. In the context of a UPnP-based home network, the resource name part of the URL can represent a file or simply an identifier of a local software module. The various types of addresses that are used by UPnP-based home networks are described in Table 13.1.

Table 13.1 UPnP Address Formats

URL	Function
Description URL	Points to the description server and document path on a root device. This URL is returned by the description server as part of the discovery process.
Presentation URL	Points to a presentation (Web) server on a controlled device. There is one presentation URL per device, including root devices. This URL can be entered into the address bar of a Web browser to navigate to the root web page of a device. This URL is returned in the description document.
Control URL	Points to the control server implementing a service on a controlled device. There is one control URL per instance of a service. This URL is returned in the description document.
Event Subscription URL	Points to an event subscription server on a controlled device. This URL is returned in the description document.
Event Sink URL	Points to an event sink (an HTTP server) on a user control point.

Discovery

Discovery is the process by which UPnP applications and services find each other. The first part of the discovery process takes place when a device plugs into the home network. It sends out a small multicast packet to other appliances on the network. The multicast packet essentially says, "I am here, I am a DVD player (for example), and you can reach me at this address or URL." Once the device has established itself on the home network, it is then capable of discovering new services. The main elements of a discovery system include:

- **Discovery server**—A software module on a controlled device or bridge that responds to queries.

- **Discovery client**—A software module that runs in a user control point that initiates queries.

Universal Plug and Play uses the SSDP protocol for the discovery of devices on IP networks. SSDP is based on profiles. A single identifier specifies a profile that defines a contract between the client and service. By identifying itself with the profile, the service advertises compliance with the associated contract. Using a single identifier makes it possible to implement an extremely simple discovery system. Clients send out a UDP multicast packet containing the identifier of the desired service on some standard channel. Services listen on the standard channel, read the request, see whether they provide the service, and respond if so. Discovery questions can be very specific, such as "Is there a printer on the home network?" Furthermore, UPnP-based discovery systems can also restrict a discovery search by IP address. For instance, a requesting device can send out a message that only integrated TV's can answer.

Directories provide a mechanism to allow discovery to scale—to the entire Internet if needed. When present, a directory will read all incoming service requests and respond to them itself. This requires that all services register with the directory so that the directory is able to properly answer on their behalf. The directory is also responsible for communicating with other directories in order to determine whether the service is available within the local home network and potentially the Internet.

To simplify the discovery protocol, directories are treated as proxies. A proxy is a service that accepts requests and takes responsibility for finding the proper response. When a client comes online, it will perform discovery for the proxy. If the proxy is present, then the client will send all future discovery requests to the proxy. If the proxy isn't present, then the client will send all discovery requests to the reserved discovery multicast channel. Regardless of the presence of a proxy, the client's request format and procedures will always be the same. The only difference will be the address to which the client sends its requests.

For services, the difference between a proxied and unproxied network is their need to answer discovery requests. On a proxied network, services need do nothing once they have registered with the proxy. On an unproxied network, they answer discovery requests directly. SSDP uses UDP- and TCP-based HTTP to provide for service discovery. SSDP also will provide support for proxies. These proxies, which are really just fronts for directories, redirect discovery requests to themselves. It is the proxy's job to collect announce requests (see next section) in order to determine what services are available as well as to communicate with other proxies in order to provide for scalable service discovery.

Schema

The discovery process returns only the basic information needed to connect to a device. Once a service has discovered its peers, the service often needs to find out more information in order to work best with them. The description process returns a schema providing descriptive data about the service.

A schema is a structured data definition that defines a set of structured values that provide descriptive information about a service. Universal Plug and Play will use eXtensible Markup Language (XML) for schema, because XML's self-describing structured data format provides the level of expressiveness and extensibility needed by a universal schema and data format.

Rehydrator

Any service that is exposed by a UPnP-based control device or bridge can be remotely controlled and managed. Controlling these services normally involves the exchange of messages between a user control point and the particular device. This exchange of messages happens according to a specific service control protocol (SCP). In-home appliances use this protocol to invoke commands and return results.

A rehydrator is best described as a software module that exposes a suitable API to home-networked applications. The primary job of the rehydrator is to map between API calls and the SCP sequence that invokes the initial command. The success of this operation is dependent on the presence of a service control protocol declaration (SCPD).

BROWSING A UPNP HOME NETWORK ....

So far in this chapter we have explored the main elements and protocols of the UPnP standard. Now it is time to look at a typical browsing protocol sequence on a UPnP-based home network. The process is illustrated in Figure 13.4.

Basically, the user control point sends an SSDP discovery request to the controlled device on the network and waits for a response in the form of a URL. Once a response has been received, the discovery client software module will then send a HTTP GET command to the discovery server that is located on the controlled device. The server will then respond to the request. The device description service on the user control point will now take over and send a number of GET commands to the description server. The server responds by sending the user control point an icon, a name, and an SCPD. The visual navigation subsystem will then allow a home-networking user to select the device icon on the display system (for instance, a television).

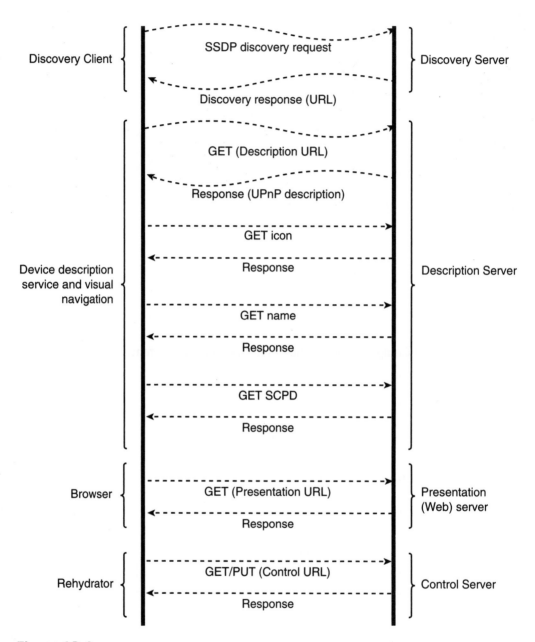

Figure 13.4
UPnP browsing

Visual navigation is term used by the UPnP standard to describe the display of device icons that are connected to a home network. If, for instance, the user control point is running Windows, the visual navigation could be implemented as a folder of icons. The final stages of the process consist of standard HTTP calls to the Web server on the controlled device. The embedded script in the requested Web page displays the device user interface and calls the rehydrator module to interact with the controlled device.

UPNP PRODUCTS..

At the 1999 Windows Hardware Engineering Conference (WinHEC), eight companies provided prototype hardware and software to demonstrate some of the many applications that can be brought together on home networks through Universal Plug and Play. Let us take a closer look at one of these UPnP implementations—a Web-enabled camera from Axis Communications.

Based on its thin server technology, Axis has a line of smart objects featuring print servers, scanner servers, storage servers, and camera servers. Implementation of a smart object in the form of a Web-enabled camera available from Axis Communications is described here. The device incorporates an embedded minimized Reduced Instruction Set Computing (RISC) design that provides all the functions required for the camera to function as a stand-alone network device directly attached to a network. Unlike other networked camera solutions, the Axis camera is a self-contained smart object that connects directly to an Ethernet network. It has its own IP address and built-in Web server for application integration and management. Compressed images can be streamed from the camera to an application (e.g., browser, application server), or be retrieved from the application. It also has built-in scripting capabilities to enable connection and handling sensor-triggered events, such as taking pictures at a certain event, storing images on a file server, and sending an e-mail to an operator with a link to the images. Main application areas for this camera are remote surveillance, where traditional CCTV-based systems can be replaced with more efficient and intelligent networked solutions. This camera uses UPnP protocols, XML descriptors, and XSL style sheets to demonstrate some of the many applications that can be brought together on home networks through Universal Plug and Play. The first UPNP-enabled products are not expected to hit stores until 2001.

HOME API ....

In the early days of writing this book we devoted a complete chapter to a working group called Home API, which was defining and developing software infrastructures for in-home appliances. Toward the end of 1999, Home API announced that it had decided to merge its efforts with those of the UPnP forum to ensure a unified specification for development of home-control, software, and products. Consequently we removed our Home API chapter and decided instead to include a new section in the UPnP chapter to briefly describe the group's background and achievements.

The founding members of the Home API Working Group were Compaq, Honeywell, Intel, Microsoft, Mitsubishi, and Philips.

The final result of the group's work, the Home API Specification and Software Development Kit (SDK), was targeted at independent software and hardware vendors that develop software or hardware for home PCs and controllable home devices. The specification was a set of programming interfaces that enabled software applications to discover and control home devices such as TVs, VCRs, set-top boxes, lights, security systems, and thermostats. The initial release of Home API included support for a variety of existing home networks, devices, and control protocols, and it was easily extensible to support others as well.

Home API supported multiple home-networks and was designed to allow application programmers to access home devices in a protocol-independent manner. By shielding applications from the underlying heterogeneity of home networks and providing standard APIs for controlling home devices, Home API helped get applications that use home devices developed quickly and easily. Home API allowed applications control and query the status of home devices. For example, an application could use Home API to query the current temperature of an outside thermometer or change the channel on a television. Home API did not support data streaming such as sending a video stream from a PC to a digital VCR. Other APIs would be used in conjunction with Home API for that purpose.

SUMMARY ....

The opportunity created by the steep price drops in networking and computing power of recent years is enormous. New technologies will combine information and processing power seamlessly, presenting customers with the right information at the right time and place. In many ways these new technologies hark back to the original promise of mechanical computing devices—devices that would serve to augment our abilities and intelligence and free us from burdensome tasks, just as the steam engine augmented humans' physical strength during the Industrial Age.

The transition from a world of stand-alone devices to networked devices, from appliance users to information users, will not happen overnight. It will certainly not happen any time soon if a costly, winner-take-all API battle is waged. Universal Plug and Play is an open initiative to take existing standards, existing technologies, and existing knowledge, repurpose it, and deliver on the promise and opportunity of the networked world. Standards-based, simple enough for the smallest appliances to implement, powerful enough to scale to the global Internet, and based on the proven approach of explicit protocols, UPnP is an incremental approach, but an approach that has been proven to work. UPnP is defined as an enabling technology for connecting multiple devices throughout a home to the Internet. Universal Plug and Play initiatives are being developed to support key existing industry standards such as TCP/IP, HTML, XML, HTTP, DNS, LDAP, autoIP, DHCP, SSDP and others. The Home API SDK planned for December 1999 was not shipped because the efforts of Home API were merged with the interests of UPnP that same year.

14 Jini

In this chapter...

Now that we have looked at Universal Plug and Play home networking technology, it's time to see Sun Microsystems' home networking protocol—Jini. The Jini vision is simply this: You can walk up with any Jini-enabled device—be it a digital camera, a new printer, a PDA, a set-top box, or a mobile phone—plug it into a TCP/IP-based home network, and be able to automatically see and use the variety of other Jini-enabled devices in your vicinity. Any resource available on the home network is available to your Jini-enabled device, as if it were directly attached to it, or the device had been explicitly programmed to use it. In this chapter we'll look at what Jini is in terms of the six key concepts that the technology introduces into the home networking industry. We'll describe the benefits of Jini-based home networks and explain the synergies between Java and HAVi.[1]

ABOUT JINI CONNECTION TECHNOLOGIES ....

Jini is Sun Microsystems' home networking software solution. It is a layer of Java software that allows devices to plug directly into a home network without the hassle of installing drivers and configuring operating systems. In some ways the history of Jini is the history of Java—Jini is really the fulfillment of the original Java vision of groups of consumer-orientated electronic devices interchanging data and bits of code. This vision requires mechanisms that we don't typically associate with desktop computers.

- The software infrastructure for these consumer and in-home appliances must be incredibly robust. Toasters and washing machines simply cannot fail with a message asking "Abort, Retry, or Ignore?" The software must not only allow, but also encourage, the development of reliable systems.

- In-home devices have to support true, effortless "plug and play." For all intents and purposes they should be the in-home equivalents of the Internet. You plug them in and they just work. There are a couple of requirements that this desire for plug and play imposes. First, devices must be easy to use. Much like a standard telephone, typical consumer appliances may have only a limited number of interfaces. Certainly not every device at home will have a mouse and a high-resolution display. In fact, most consumers will not want such interfaces for these devices—if they require a mouse or keyboard, chances are they're too hard to use. Second, in-home devices need to be easy to administer. Most people would like to plug them in and use them, without having to configure IP addresses for them,

---

1. Portions of this chapter are adapted from *Core Jini* by W. Keith Edwards, ©1999. Reprinted by permission of Prentice-Hall, Inc., Upper Saddle River, NJ.

set up gateways and routers, install (and possibly) remove drivers, and so on. Upgrades of software are an important issue here—if an IT professional needs to be called in to upgrade all appliances on a home network, chances are the appliances simply won't get upgraded.

- Software systems for the Internet age need to be evolvable. While creating software for stand-alone devices, such as a CPU for a microwave, is challenging enough, the potential problems are multiplied by the fact that networked devices on your in-home network must be able to communicate with any number of peer devices on the Internet.

The vision of legions of devices and software services working together simply and reliably had been espoused by a number of researchers and computer industry leaders before. Mark Weiser of the Xerox Palo Alto Research Center called this vision "ubiquitous computing," a term meant to connote the ready availability and usability of devices connected to a network. With this vision in mind, a group at Sun set out to provide the infrastructure that would bring Java full circle—this project became known as Jini. The creators of the system chose the name Jini because it is an energetic and easy-to-remember word that begins with "J" and has the same number of letters as "Java." The Jini project went on at Sun, hidden from public eyes, until *New York Times* technology reporter John Markoff broke the story in a front-page article in 1998. On January 25, 1999, the technology was officially made available to the public with a host of licensees already on board. These partners are building Jini-enabled services and devices, including hard drives, digital cameras, handheld computers, and much more. For its part, Sun is rapidly aligning behind Jini, in much the same way it aligned behind Java back in 1995. At the time of this writing, Jini has already been licensed by nearly 40 companies that run the gamut from home device vendors to enterprise software companies. These include disk drive manufacturers such as Quantum and Seagate; cellular phone manufacturers Nokia and Ericsson; printer vendors including Xerox, Canon, Epson, and Hewlett-Packard; camera manufacturer Kodak; networking vendors Cisco and 3Com; software producers BEA Systems, Novell, and Inprise; and a huge number of consumer electronics companies including Sony, Sharp, Philips, and Toshiba. Jini has also been licensed by companies as diverse as AOL and Kinko's.

UNDER THE JINI HOOD....................................

Jini software can run on anything with a digital heartbeat—cellular phones, digital cameras, PDAs, alarms, televisions, and even smart cards. As illustrated in Figure 14.1, Jini software is an infrastructure that runs on top of a Java platform to create a federation of virtual machines. Each virtual machine sits on top of an OS that sits on

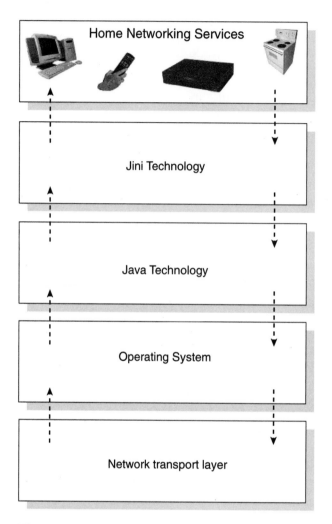

Figure 14.1
Jini software architecture

top of the network. It is based on a simple model that devices with microchips should connect and work together in *communities*. The formation of these communities requires:

- No device drivers
- No operating systems
- No new cabling systems
- No human intervention

Each device on the home network provides *services* that other devices in the community may use. These devices provide their own interfaces, which ensures reliability and compatibility. Sun Microsystems is currently working with a number of manufacturers to integrate the Jini home networking technology into the next generation of digital appliances. Jini technology uses a lookup service with which devices and services register. When a device plugs in, it goes through an add-in protocol, called discovery and join-in. The device first locates the lookup service (discovery) and then uploads an object that implements all of its services' interfaces (join). To use a service, a person or a program locates it using the lookup service. The service's object is copied from the lookup service to the requesting device where it will be used. The lookup service acts as an intermediary to connect a client looking for a service with that service. Once the connection is made, the lookup service is not involved in any of the resulting interactions between that client and that service. It doesn't matter where a service is implemented—compatibility is ensured because each service provides everything needed to interact with it. There is no central repository of drivers, or anything else for that matter. The Java programming language is the key to making Jini technology work. Devices in a network employing Jini technology are tied together using Java Remote Method Invocation (RMI). RMI is best described as a set of protocols being developed by Sun's JavaSoft division that enables Java objects to communicate remotely with other Java objects. The discovery and join protocols, as well as the lookup service, depend on the ability to move Java objects, including their code, between Java virtual machines. Jini technology not only defines a set of protocols for discovery, join, and lookup, but also a leasing and transaction mechanism to provide resilience in a dynamic networked environment. The underlying technology and services architecture is powerful enough to build a fully distributed system on a network of workstations. And the Jini connection infrastructure is small enough that a community of devices enabled by Jini connection software can be built out of the simplest devices.

All of Jini's ability to support home networked-based services is based around six key concepts. The concepts are:

- Communities
- Discovery
- Lookup
- Leasing
- Remote events
- Transactions

Communities

A Jini community is a group of services on a home network that are available both to each other and to the consuming applications. All of the members of a community are available and visible to all other members of that community, and to any application that looks at that community on a Jini enabled in-home network. Each community on a home network has a unique name. All communities are put together without any planning, installation, or human intervention.

Discovery

Before a Jini-aware entity on a home network—either a service or an application—can take advantage of other Jini services, it must first find one or more Jini communities. The way an entity does this is by finding the *lookup services* that keep track of the shared resources of that particular community. A lookup service is basically a name server. The next section of this chapter explains the functionality and features of a lookup service in more detail.

This process of finding the available lookup services is called *discovery*. The Jini discovery protocol is the means by which Jini-aware home appliances find Jini communities on a typical in-home network. There is not just a single discovery protocol—Jini supports several, useful in different scenarios.

- The *multicast request protocol* is used when a home networked application or a service first becomes active, and needs to find the "nearby" *lookup services* that may be active. Figure 14.2 demonstrates the communication flow of the multicast request protocol in a live environment.

- The *multicast announcement protocol* is used by lookup services to announce their presence. When a new lookup service that is part of an existing community starts up, any interested parties will be informed via this protocol. Figure 14.3 shows the communication flow of the multicast announcement protocol.

- The *unicast discovery protocol* is used when a home-based application or service already knows the particular lookup service it wishes to talk to. The Unicast discovery protocol is used to talk directly to a lookup service, which may not be a part of the local home network. Figure 14.4 shows the communication flow of the unicast discovery protocol.

The end result of the discovery process is that the entity—the object doing the discovery on the home network is handed one or more references to the lookup services for the requested communities. Broadly speaking, there are two basic forms of dis-

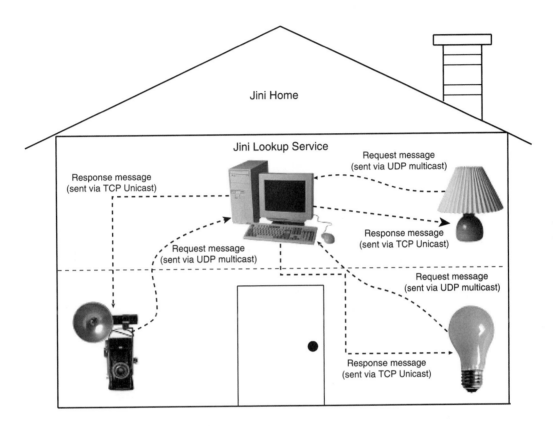

Figure 14.2
Communication flow of multicast request protocol

covery. One form is used to support "serendipitous" interaction between services and lookup services. Serendipitous interaction means that the lookup services and Jini services find each other without any previous configuration or advance knowledge of one another; they discover one another without being explicitly told to search for one another. The second form of discovery is used to "hard wire" a Jini service to a lookup service. Unlike the serendipitous forms of discovery, where services find any and all lookup services in their vicinity, this "direct" form of discovery allows home network services to use lookup services that they may know about ahead of time. This form of discovery uses its own protocol and has a URL-based naming scheme for specifying lookup services.

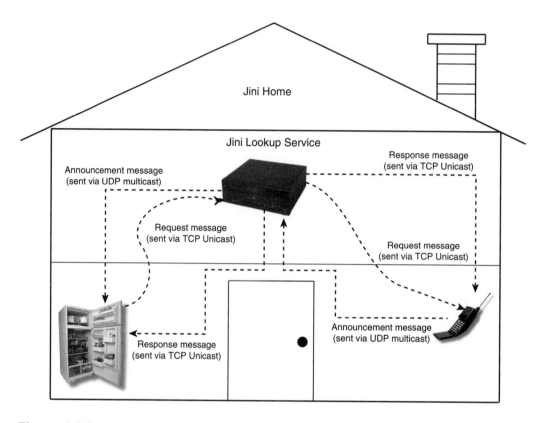

Figure 14.3
Communication flow of multicast announcement protocol

Lookup

To make use of the community services, an application program must first locate a
Jini technology lookup service by using the discovery protocol. It can then use the
lookup service to locate a device offering the desired type of service. The application
then downloads a Java object from the lookup service that can be used to interact with
the selected device. This object handles any device-specific details; the machine running the application does not need to have a driver for the device. We can think of the
lookup service as a name server—it's essentially a process that keeps a track of all of
the services that have joined a Jini community. But unlike a traditional name server,
which provides a mapping from string names to stored objects, the Jini lookup service supports a richer set of semantics. You can, for example, search the Jini lookup
service for particular types of objects. After discovery has successfully found a look-

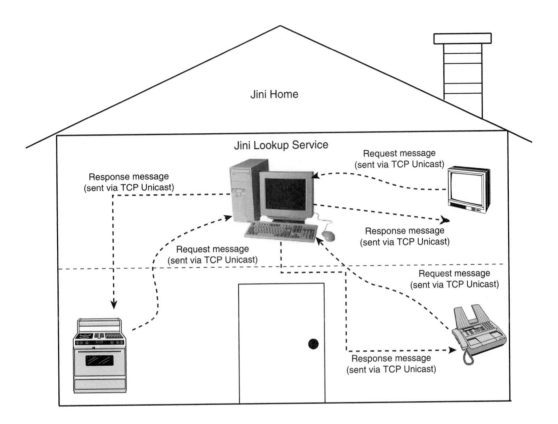

Figure 14.4
Communication flow of unicast protocol

up service for a home networking user, it returns a reference to an object that implements the lookup interfaces. This interface is commonly called the *service registrar*. How the internals of the lookup service are actually implemented is hidden from consumers who use a Jini-based home network. Devices on a home network often use lookup to publish their own and find new services.

Publishing a Service

A lookup service maintains a list of service items. Each service item contains a proxy object that other participants in the community can download and execute as well as attributes that describe the service. The idea of downloadable service proxies is the key idea that gives Jini its ability to use services and devices without doing any explic-

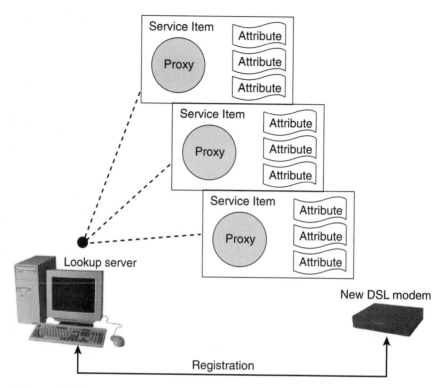

Figure 14.5
Publishing Jini services

it driver or software installation. Figure 14.5 illustrates the concept of a lookup server maintaining a list of service items. If, for example, a new DSL modem was plugged into your Jini home network and wished to publish its services (that is, making its services available to all other devices in your home), it needs to register with all lookup services returned from the discovery process.

Finding a Service

We've seen how home networking devices join communities to publish their services. Now we can look at how consumers of services find and use the services of other members in the community. Once a device on your network has a reference to a lookup service, it can search all the items on the lookup server to find services of interest. Jini provides a number of ways to search—you can search based on the type of the downloadable proxy contained in each service item, you can search by unique identifier of the service, or you can search the attributes contained in each service item.

Leasing

So far I've talked about discovery and lookup, the aspects of Jini that allow communities of services to spontaneously form and interact with each other. But I haven't talked yet about how to ensure that these communities are stable, self-healing, and resilient in the face of (inevitable) network failures, machine crashes, and software errors. The issue of reliability is important when software systems are intended—as Jini communities are—to be long-lived entities that can stay running and responsive over a period of months or even years, with little or no intervention from the user of the home network. Consider the following example.

Suppose you have a new MP3 player and connect it to your in-home network. In a Jini-based network, the player joins a community by registering itself with a lookup service for that community. The MP3 player publishes the fact that it is available for use, and all is well. That is, all is well until you decide to move the player to another room in the house without turning it off first. What happens to your home network? To the other members of the community, this may look like a classic failure situation—they may not be able to tell if the MP3 player has gone down, if it's simply slow to answer requests, or if the MP3 player's Jini software has crashed. But, regardless of how it was disconnected, it has not had a chance to unregister itself before it disconnects because of the abrupt termination of the player's communication with the network. The result of your disconnecting the MP3 player without shutting down properly—a completely common and understandable occurrence—is that a "stale" registration will linger in the lookup service for the community. Services that wish to use the player will see it registered but will not be able to use it. To get around these problems, Jini uses a technique called *leasing*. Leasing is based on the idea that, rather than granting access to a resource for an unlimited amount of time, the resource is "loaned" for a fixed period of time. Jini leases work much like leases in the real world. The grantor of the lease may deny Jini leases. They can be renewed by the holder. Leases will expire at a predetermined date unless they are renewed. They can be cancelled early (and unlike in real life, Jini imposes no penalty on early lease cancellation). Finally, leases can be negotiated, but, as in real life, the grantor has the final word on the terms of the lease that is offered.

Leases provide a consistent means to free unused or unneeded resources throughout Jini: If a service goes away, either intentionally or unintentionally, without cleaning up after itself, its leases will eventually expire and the service will be forgotten. In the case of our MP3 player, the leasing mechanism allows you to move the player around the house without causing problems on your in-home network.

Remote Events

Jini services—like many software components in a system, whether distributed or local—occasionally need to be notified when some interesting change happens in the world. For instance, a software component on a digital set-top box may need to be notified when a consumer uses a remote control to close a window on the television screen. An event is best described as an object that contains information about some external state change that a Jini software component may be interested in. Let's look at a practical example of how events are used in a Jini-based home network.

Take the example of a digital camera that connects to a home network and wants to be able to use any printers that are available in its Jini community. The camera contacts all the lookup services it could find, and then searches for services that implement the *printer* interface. In this example, we are assuming that the printer is already connected to the network and available for use *before* the digital camera. What if the inverse was true? In this case, there are no printers available when the camera first connects, although a printer in the home office may come on line later. Certainly the owner of the camera would still like to print pictures, regardless of the order in which we plug in the devices into the home network. Consequently, the digital camera needs the ability to be notified when any services that it might be able to use appear in a community. It's easy to imagine the user interface to the camera. The print button on the LCD is grayed out. You plug a printer into the home network, and suddenly the print button comes alive! The camera has just received notification (via an event) that a printer is now active on the network. This is only one example of how events are used in Jini.

Transactions

It's now time to deal with the last of the six key Jini concepts: *transactions*. Devices on a home network regularly contact each other for computational purposes. At some point midway through the computational process, one of these devices may crash or the network itself may become unstable This can result in a device continuously trying to contact an unreachable component on the network. This is where transactions come to the rescue. Transactions are a way to group a series of related operations so that there can be only two possible outcomes: Either all of the operations succeed, or all of the operations fail. In either case, the system moves to a known state in which it is relatively easy either move on if the transaction succeeds, or try again later if the transaction failed. The idea of transactions is to ensure data integrity on a home based network.

JINI BENEFITS ....

Device Agnosticism

Jini is agnostic with regard to devices. What does this mean for users of home networks? Essentially it means that Jini is designed to support a wide variety of entities that can participate in a community. These "entities" may be devices or software or some combination of both. If a hardware device is connected to a home network, Jini is flexible about how much computational power it needs to have. Jini can work with a full-blown multimedia computer capable of running multiple Java Virtual Machines connecting with each other at gigabit speeds. It can also work with such devices as PDAs and cell phones that may have only limited Java capabilities. In fact, Jini is actually designed to accommodate devices that are so simple they may have small amounts or no computational intelligence—a light switch for instance. Furthermore, and this may be somewhat surprising, Jini doesn't even require that the home networking service be written in or understand the Java language. All that is required is that some Java-speaking device on the home network is willing to act as a proxy on behalf of the Java-challenged device or service.

Simplicity

Jini technology is all about simplifying interactions with a home network. The Java platform started it, now Jini technology furthers it. Simplification means improved productivity, cost savings, and ease-of-use. Jini technology will allow you to use the network as easily as using a phone. Sun has portrayed Jini as a simple way for devices to find and use each other over a network. Plug a Jini-enabled digital camera into a network, for example, and it sends a Java agent to the network's lookup service and announces itself. The camera is now an object, and a user interface pops up on your PC or television set. Take a picture, and you can store it on the Jini-enabled disk drive you've just plugged into your digital set-top box. No configuration hassles or device drivers is one of Jini's principles.

Reliability

I have already said in a previous section that Jini provides the infrastructure that allows services to find and use one another on a home network. So is Jini simply a name server like the Internet's DNS? As it turns out, Jini does have similarities with a name server; however, there are two essential differences between what Jini does and what simple name servers on the Internet do.

1. Communities of Jini services are largely self-healing. This is a key property built into Jini from the ground up; Jini doesn't make the assumption that in-home networks are perfect, or that software never fails. Given time, the system will repair damage to itself. Jini also supports redundant infrastructure in a very natural way, to reduce the possibility that services will be unavailable if key A/V or computer devices fail.

2. As mentioned, Jini supports serendipitous interactions among services and users of those services. That is, services can appear and disappear to other Jini participants in a very lightweight way. Jini supports what might be called "spontaneous networking"—services that are close to one another that form a community automatically, with no need for explicit user involvement. This means that users of home networking technologies do not have to edit configuration files, shut down or restart name servers, or configure gateways to use a Jini service. You literally just plug it in and Jini does the rest.

Taken together these properties ensure that home based Jini communities are virtually administration free.

Making Life Easier

Jini technology gives users a unique, more convenient option for accessing the services in their neighborhood and the world at large. With Jini software, a laptop or home computer can join the local community of services offered by neighborhood retailers. Rather than drive to your local instant-copy store, you might simply access its services application from your home computer that has joined the local Jini technology network. You tell it what you want copied and where to deliver the job; it takes care of the rest.

Reduced Cost of Ownership

Self-managing devices reduce further the need for expert help, and this should lower the total cost of ownership for Jini-connection-technology-based systems.

Ease of Development

Because Jini technology is based on the Java platform, any existing development tool that can be used for Java software development can be used for Jini software development. In addition, utility classes and implementations are being developed that will be freely available, which will ease the development of services and clients using Jini technology.

Small Footprint

The code required to implement Jini technology is so small that all types of home appliances can use it, from lamps and coffee makers to dishwashers and water heaters.

LICENSING TECHNOLOGIES ....

Jini technology is operating-system-independent and is controlled by the Jini software user community, which has free access and the right to extend and modify the Jini technology source code.

Sun provides access to Jini source code under what they call the Sun Community Source License (SCSL). This license is designed to provide virtually free and easy access to all the Jini source code by developers, while allowing Sun to ensure that Jini products remain compatible with one another and that the Jini source does not splinter into incompatible versions. The community license model allows very open access to source code, while promoting compatibility among the developer community. And yet it does not require companies or developers to hand their Jini home applications back to Sun. Now, let's take a closer look at how to license Jini technologies. The SCSL defines three levels of usage of the source code, with increasing responsibilities for each. At the first level, you can obtain the source code for *research* use. This allows you complete access to the source for personal, research and educational uses, or to evaluate the source for possible deployment. The license itself is just a "click through" page on the Sun download page. At this level, you are free to learn about the technology, modify the source, and try it out on your home network. At the next level is the *internal use* license. If you've been using the Jini software under the research arrangement, you can move to this level of access and responsibility without any extra legal overhead—there is nothing to sign, and you do not need to notify Sun of your use of the technology. The only requirement of this level is that Jini naming conventions need to be followed. This requirement has been designed by Sun to ensure that home network applications will have complete interoperability and compatibility with third-party Jini applications on the Internet.

Finally, if you run a development house and want to sell new home networking products based on Jini source code, you must graduate to the *commercial use* arrangement. Unlike the two previous usage models, which are free, selling a home application based on Jini requires you to sign the commercial use community source license with Sun. This licenses still imposes only minimal requirements on you, though: your responsibility for maintaining compatibility increases. Sun intends the community licensing approach to be the best of both worlds—easy and relatively unfettered access to source code, while still ensuring some degree of compatibility and co-evolution of the code. The SCSL process is still evolving, and Sun is actively soliciting feedback on their licensing strategies. Full details of Jini's community licensing model are available from Sun's Web site at: http://java.sun.com/products/jini/licensing/.

JINI AND HAVI ....

Home audio and video consumer appliances are rapidly moving to the digital world, giving rise to new technologies for connecting diverse components into an integrated home A/V environment. Every person dreams of needing only one remote control for the stereo, VCR, television, and DVD player. HAVi, a specification for home audio/video interoperability, allows consumers to build a home environment to coordinate the control of several devices, simplify operations, and deliver content wherever it needs to go. As described in Chapter 11, the HAVi specification uses Java technology, so it works well with any services based on Jini technology. Add a high-speed cable modem and a set-top box with Jini software and a HAVI-to-Jini technology bridge, and you have instant access to a whole range of high-bandwidth services, such as video-on-demand or live broadcast viewing. Download a movie to the living room television set, and then transfer it to the TV in the kitchen so you can make popcorn without missing a single minute of action. Use the TV remote as a control for your home security system, or to turn off the ringer on the telephone. In addition, you can use Jini technology and the Internet to upgrade the software in your HAVi-compatible devices. Earlier this year Philips, Sony, and Sun announced plans to collaborate in connecting the HAVi architecture with Sun's Jini technology. The companies aim to provide a solution that links HAVi-compliant digital electronic appliances in the home to services provided by Jini technology over a network.

SUMMARY ....

The six basic ideas of Jini were introduced in this chapter:

- A community describes what happens when two or more devices using Jini technology come together to share their services. Jini software lets all devices work together, so you can create your own personal network or community any time, anywhere.

- Jini devices receive their instructions through the network via a lookup server, a device that tracks all the Jini devices on a network and makes sure they can communicate with all the other devices.
- Discovery is the process by which Jini in-home applications find the lookup services that serve their community.
- Jini technology uses a mechanism called leasing to detect when a service becomes unavailable. When a device registers with the lookup service it receives a lease that it must periodically renew. If the lease is not renewed, then the lookup service removes the device from the list of services offered. Removing a device does not interrupt the state or services offered by the remaining members of the community.
- Remote events are used by Jini to inform interested parties about changes that occur on a home network.
- Transactions are an important tool for building reliable Jini-based home networks.

Jini has a number of benefits that improve productivity, cost savings, and ease-of-use for consumers. Jini technology source code is available at no cost to any licensee who wishes to evaluate it, improve it, repair it, and use it internally, as long as you adhere to the community guidelines outlined in the SCSL. The SCSL is a license model designed for distributing source code among the developer community. Toward the end of 1999, Sony and Sun announced plans to collaborate in bridging the technical divide between HAVi and Jini home networking architectures.

15 HomePnP

In this chapter...

In the early days of home automation, the systems that were been promoted by manufacturers lacked the technical standards needed for uniformity and cost efficiencies. In recent years, a number of efforts have been made to establish a common in-home networking standard. One of these industry efforts has resulted in the development of a specification called "Home Plug and Play," commonly known as HomePnP. The specification provides consumer-electronics manufacturers with a set of clear guidelines for transforming stand-alone products into interactive home entertainment devices. Its main goal is to transform the home control industry from a niche market to a mainstream consumer retail industry with vastly expanded markets. The main features of this standard include:

- Nonproprietary and open technologies
- Modular architecture
- Interoperability across multiple manufacturers
- "Mix and Match" of PCs and electronic devices
- Simple implementation

In this chapter we first examine the evolution of the HomePnP specification, then explain the main features of this home networking technology, and then conclude with a description of the main technological components that comprise HomePnP.

ABOUT HOMEPNP...

The evolution of the HomePnP specification commenced in 1995 with the formation of a group called the HomePnP task force, comprised of individuals from Honeywell, Intel, Microsoft, and Thomson Consumer Electronics. Shortly after its inception, Smart Interface, AMP Incorporated, and Interactive Media Systems joined the task force, and have substantially contributed to the specification's development. In early 1997, the task force announced it had selected the CEBus Industry Council (CIC) to complete the development of the HomePnP specification and promote its adoption by manufacturers of electronic product for the home. CIC is an industry-based, nonprofit, membership organization established in 1994. CIC's end objective is to establish a thriving home networks industry for its members. The organizational structure of CIC is shown in Figure 15.1.

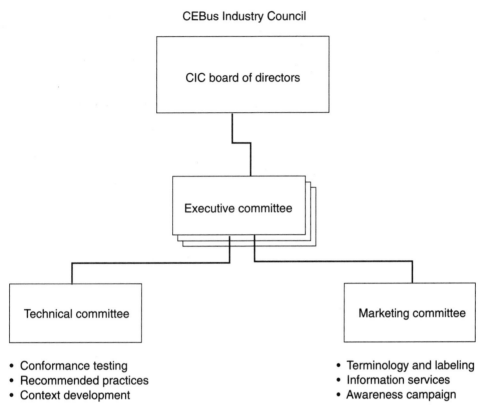

Figure 15.1
CIC organizational structure

HOMEPNP BENEFITS ....

Wide Range of Functionality

When traditional home electronic products are outfitted with HomePnP "network features," they can work together to offer a new generation of functionality.

- Consumers could save on utility costs by having their homes automatically respond to variable time-of-day pricing by utility companies.

- Security systems could display a home's floor plan on a bedroom TV to show trouble spots as they happen.

- Household appliances could offer self-diagnostic options that notify residents when maintenance is due, and call to schedule a repairman's visit if so desired.

- Multitasking home PCs could monitor conversations between other household products, and let the home's resident tell products what they want done.
- Household clocks could always keep the right time, even after power outages.
- Security system occupancy sensors could let the home's lighting and temperature-control equipment know when the home, or individual rooms, are occupied.
- Other home applications that have not yet been dreamed about.

Interoperation of Subsystems in the Home

In today's residential market, home control is typically achieved through stand-alone subsystems (e.g., environmental control, security, and lighting). Although the environmental subsystem may maintain a home-and-away schedule, and the lighting system may have the ability to provide a lived-in look, interoperation between these subsystems is generally nonexistent. Each subsystem is installed by different trades people, with no way to be part of a larger integrated home control system. This is illustrated in Figure 15.2.

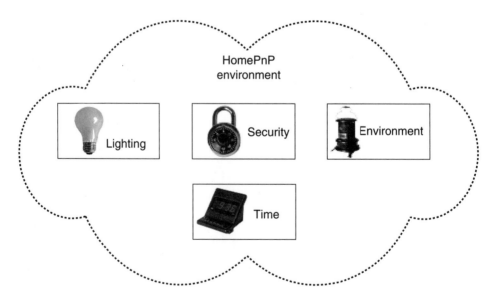

Figure 15.2
Individual subsystems, no interoperation

For homeowners, the installation of a home control system can be highly complex. Typically, a home control system is installed in a phased basis: Individual subsystems (environmental, lighting, security, etc.) are installed by separate teams of contractors who have little knowledge of the entire home system design, potentially few tools, and little training for the integration of their subsystem into an overall home control system. Although each subsystem vendor may have detailed knowledge of their own subsystem, it would be unusual for an individual tradesperson to be cross-trained on other subsystems or on the total system operation. Exceptions to this environment are provided for high-end customers via professionally installed home control systems. Homeowners who desire highly customized behavior may contract with these vendors to install and program these systems. With the lack of interoperability standards, these professionally installed systems typically use proprietary networks and interfaces. One of the visions of the HomePnP specification is that stand-alone subsystems may be delivered today and through other distribution channels. These HomePnP subsystems have the additional feature of being easily integrated into a single home control system that is harmonized with the activities of the occupants and other subsystems present in the home. This is illustrated in Figure 15.3.

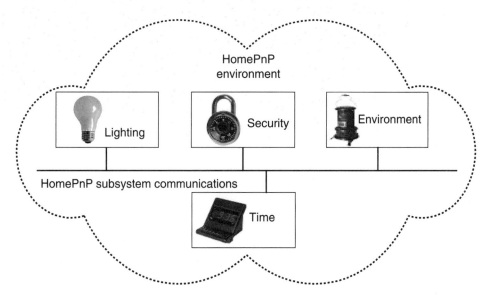

Figure 15.3
Interoperation using HomePnP subsystem communications

With the HomePnP subsystem communications capability available on the major subsystems in the home, standardized state information is shared among all subsystems. This allows a security subsystem, for example, to notify all other listening subsystems that it is in an "armed" state. In response, a lighting subsystem may go into a lived-in-look mode, and a windows control subsystem will not allow opening a window without authorized user intervention. This level of cooperation among subsystems provides a basic level of integration. It can supply benefits to the homeowner in the form of convenience, peace of mind, and savings. Additional interoperation can be provided using the HomePnP specification with professional installation tools

Upgrading Home Control Systems

The installation of home control subsystems can be separated by a multiple of years. For each new subsystem within the home, the owner chooses from a variety of vendors and installers as well as subsystem complexity and cost. For example, one homeowner may desire a simple heating subsystem with a single setback. Another may prefer a highly sophisticated environmental control subsystem complete with heating, air conditioning, multiple zones, air filtration, multiple setback modes, and energy-saving features. Both of these environmental subsystems must operate consistently within the same home control system with little or no installer reconfiguration of the existing subsystems in the home. To support both customers, HomePnP subsystems are expandable and upgradable. This allows the homeowner to purchase and easily install new functionality when it becomes available. It also permits vendors to compete in a larger market, providing unique functionality while still being able to interoperate with both new and legacy subsystems (see Figure 15.3).

Vendor-Specific Features

Although available for the upscale market for many years, home control in the mass market is still evolving. Many new applications, features, and devices will evolve over the next few years. Therefore, any attempt to provide an industry specification in this market must allow for vendor-specific adaptations and evolution of the standard itself. To further enable the home control market, it is important for each vendor to be able to provide features that differentiate their product in the marketplace. The HomePnP specification allows vendors to add vendor-specific information for unique functionality.

HOMEPNP CORE TECHNOLOGIES ....

The HomePnP specification details a set of behavioral characteristics for products and systems within the home that will allow them to take actions based on the state of the home. HomePnP is not a programming language. It is however, a set of implementation rules that utilize a programming language called CAL (Common Application Language). The standards we described in earlier parts of this guide focussed on low-level communication protocols and device-level product models.

The HomePnP specification does not concentrate on these protocols; instead, it establishes a common application level control protocol that enables devices on disparate home networks to interoperate. The specification itself contains details about how manufacturers products should behave in a HomePnP based network. Additionally, the specification details a set of behavioral characteristics for devices that are connected to your network. For instance, the standard identifies different conditions within your home such as "occupants away" or "occupants home and asleep." Thus, if your network is operating in "occupants away" mode, then the HomePnP appliances would initiate appropriate actions, such as arming the security system and turning on exterior lights. The components of a HomePnP-based device are described in the following sections.

EIA-600 CEBus Standard

CEBus is an open standard for home automation that is been developed by the Consumer Electronics Manufacturers Association (CEMA), a sector of the Electronic Industries Association (EIA). The CEBus standard gives manufacturers from multiple industries a uniform way to link household products. It defines a set of rules for transporting messages between CEBus-compliant products throughout a home. These rules are applicable to a number of different transmission mediums, including:

- The home's powerline wiring
- Telephone wire (4 pair)
- Video wire (dual coax)
- Wireless options such as radio frequency (RF) and infrared (IR) signals

CEBus solves the problems of integrating products, systems, and services from different manufacturers by standardizing a plug-and-play physical interface.

Manufacturers using CEBus to develop products for home networks can give their products CEBus compliant features during the manufacturing process. They also have the option of creating an add-on module that gives their product the ability to send and receive CEBus-compliant messages via the in-home network.

As mentioned, five different transmission mediums are supported by CEBus; therefore, it can handle many more messages per second than standards utilizing powerlines only. The CEBus standard provides uniform speed on all media. The signalling speed for control channel messages is the same on the powerline, twisted pair, coaxial wire, radio frequency and infrared. No buffers are required. In addition to supporting a variety of different mediums, CEBus allows two-way, high-speed communications between digital appliances on your network. It allows in-home appliances to share information time, temperature, status of devices, and so on. As mentioned, CEBus uses a peer-to-peer connectionless service called CSMA/CDCR communication protocol.

For more technical information on this protocol and the CEBus standard in general, see ftp://ftp.gci-net.com/pub/trainingdept/eia600 for the latest versions of the EIA-600 documents.

Common Application Language (CAL)

A/V devices and PCs communicate with one another using a common language. The CIC's HomePnP specification provides these devices with the common language they need, plus the "grammar" rules to be followed when using this language. CAL is a universal communications language for home network products. CAL is not a formal programming language like C or Pascal, but rather a command language consisting of two parts:

1. The definition of a data structure that models product operation
2. The description and syntax of the messages that operate on the data structure

By establishing a common product model and common set of commands, residential devices can communicate with other products without knowing how each product operates, who built it, or what's in it. As with other home networking languages, CAL uses a set of identifiers to allow unrelated products to communicate with each other. These identifiers are based on a method that looks at the context in which messages are sent between source and destination appliances. Thus, the identifiers used by the EIA's CAL are known as "contexts." The HomePnP specification has organized contexts into groups, or "subsystems," that apply to specific industry categories. The following is a list of the existing CEBus contexts:

- **Audio/visual group**—These contexts define the basic functional units necessary to control the full range of residential audio and video equipment as well as related audio and video functions of other consumer devices.

- **Lighting group**—These contexts define the basic functional units necessary to control a full range of residential lighting equipment as well as related lighting functions of other consumer devices.

- **Environmental group**—These contexts define the basic functional units necessary to control the full range of residential HVAC equipment (indoor temperature, humidity, ventilation, air quality, dampers, and fans) as well as related HVAC functions of other consumer devices.

- **Utility/energy management group**—These contexts define the basic functional units necessary to operate a full range of residential utility equipment, appliances, and energy use oriented devices.

- **Security group**—These contexts define the basic functional units necessary to control the full range of residential security equipment as well as related security functions of other consumer devices.

- **Computer group**—These contexts define the basic functional units necessary to control the full range of consumer personal computer equipment and peripheral devices as well as related computer functions of other consumer devices.

The design of CAL is based on the assumption that all electrical appliances and products in homes have a hierarchal structure of common parts or functions, and that the basic operation of the common functions is the same from device to device. It was designed to be understandable by most home electronic devices.

Originally, CAL was only available as an integral component in the CEBus standard. However, as various industry sectors examined how they might offer whole-house network features, the need for a common application language that can be transported by multiple carriers surfaced as essential to the success of home networks. After studying the options, many industry sectors found that CAL as used in the CEBus Standard could serve their needs, if it was available outside the CEBus Standard. In April 1997, the CEMA agreed to publish CAL as a separate EIA Standard, known as 721. With this move, EIA's CAL truly becomes the common application language for controlling home network devices around the globe. Many companies have also adopted CAL, spanning a number of different industries. Interested parties can order EIA/CEMA standards through Global Engineering Documents at the following Web address: http://global.ihs.com.

SUMMARY ....

The "plug-and-play" concept is key to establishing a broad consumer-based market for home networks. It is critical that consumers be able to purchase network-ready products at familiar retail outlets, take them home, plug them in or have them professionally installed, and immediately be able to enjoy the benefits of the product. It is also important because it allows the consumer to upgrade or add products to their in-home network as time and budget allow—one product at a time. The HomePnP specification intends to bring these benefits to the mass market by providing manufacturers of home electronics and home controls with the information necessary to build products that will work together without custom installation or programming. Until now, the entertainment, convenience, comfort, safety, and security benefits of home networks have only been available through very expensive, custom designed and installed home control and entertainment systems. The limitations of these systems can be overcome by deploying the HomePnP standard on your network. This chapter explored the architecture and technologies associated with the HomePnP standard.

16 VESA

In this chapter...

In the future, data for audio, video, telephony, printing, and control will be transported through the home over a digital network. This network will allow connection of devices, such as computers, digital TVs, digital VCRs, digital telephones, printers, stereo systems, and remotely controlled appliances so that they may all interoperate and talk to each other. The Video Electronics Standards Association (VESA) home network committee is developing an interoperability standard for the following components:

- Physical media
- Data link layers
- Midlayer protocols and associated services such as directories, control, network management, and security

The standard uses a long-distance version of IEEE 1394 as the digital backbone and Internet Protocols for internetworking. External access networks, such as telephone, cable TV, broadcast TV, and direct-broadcast satellite, will interface with the VESA Home Network (VHN) via access devices such as residential gateways, xDSL modems, or cable modems.

This chapter begins by giving you some background on the VESA group, then explains the technical architecture and features of VESA.

ABOUT THE VESA GROUP.....................................

VESA began in 1995 as an outgrowth from an effort to standardize functions within set-top boxes. The group issued a call for proposals and received several responses. The input received was evaluated, and allowed the VESA group to develop its standardized architecture and ultimately acted as a catalyst for the group to choose IEEE 1394 as the backbone in the home. This choice was controversial at the time but is since better understood and accepted in the home networking community. After the group agreed on the lower-level layers and media, they began to work on higher levels. The IP protocol was chosen as the internetworking layer because of its ubiquity and flexibility. Shortly thereafter, Web browsers and servers were chosen as the interface of choice. VESA has defined an architecture and a set of protocols that will enable this vision to be realized. The committee goals are:

- To provide an interoperability specification that will allow the transfer of information from any device to any other device in the home
- To allow interoperability between all home networks, regardless of their individual physical and data link technologies and bandwidth capabilities

- To provide a common interface on the home side for access devices, such as the residential gateway
- To provide a migration path from analog distribution to totally digital distribution
- To provide directory services for all networked devices in the home

VESA ARCHITECTURE AND TECHNOLOGIES ....

The VHN architecture is based on a digital baseband home network common to all intelligent devices in the home. An external network is terminated at an access device that demodulates, decodes, and decrypts according to the external network specification on the outside and interfaces to the common home network on the inside. User devices also on the baseband network in the home may access the external services or data through the access device. Thus the external services are shared and equipment replication is unnecessary. As well as physical layers, standardized information and control protocols are essential factors to ensure interoperability of home network devices. No one physical layer technology is perceived to satisfy all cost, bandwidth, and mobility requirements, so a network layer approach is used to allow seamless operation across different physical layers and, by using IP, also the Internet. IEEE 1394 is used for the main backbone of the home network because of its high bandwidth and inherent quality-of-service for multimedia delivery. Devices capable of accessing MPEG video streams attach directly to the IEEE 1394 network, while other devices may use technologies such as Ethernet, powerline, and RF. In the future, wireless 1394 may provide a no-new-wires option for the backbone. The VESA Home Network Committee has developed network, device, control, and network management models with interoperating standards based on existing specifications where possible. Work is progressing to make a complete IP-network-layer-based interoperability specification. The VESA home network will:

- Allow complete interoperability for all devices in the home independent of the component network on which they reside
- Provide an open, transparent interface for all access providers and for connecting multiple networks together
- Accommodate all proposed residential gateway architectures
- Simplify implementation of the residential gateway for all devices on the home network by providing a single-protocol interface on the IEEE 1394 home network backbone

VESA is working with many other standards groups to ensure compatibility with all emerging network and multimedia standards. Let's now examine the technical architecture of the VESA standard.

Technical Overview

Today, most houses have a copper-wire telephone network and a coaxial cable TV network. These networks will stay in the home for a long time, and new digital networks will be put in place to supplement them. The VHN architecture has the benefit of allowing low-bandwidth, low-cost devices to remain on their own network, while high-bandwidth devices are accommodated by high-speed networks. The VHN architecture, shown in Figure 16.1, allows the integration of these networks, and full connectivity between devices.

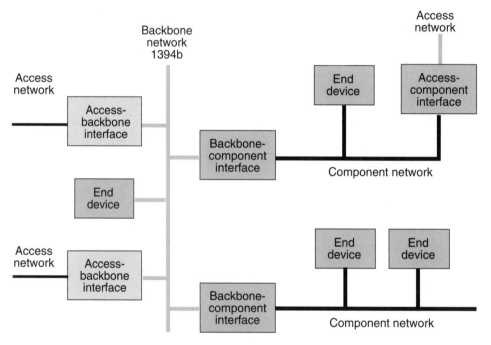

Figure 16.1
VESA home network architecture

The backbone network spans the whole house, so those devices located on *component networks* anywhere in the house can communicate with each other. The backbone provides sufficient bandwidth and QoS for the applications and devices that communicate over it.

The component networks enable devices connected to them to communicate with each other, perhaps over a relatively short distance such as within a room. The choice of a component network is dictated by the communication needs and cost points of the device. Examples of important component networks are IEEE 1394-1995 (known as FireWire), Ethernet, Powerline CEBus, phone line, and RF wireless LAN. An access-backbone interface connects an external access network to the home network. An access-component interface provides a similar function for an access network to connect to a component network. A POTS modem, an ISDN adapter, a cable modem, residential gateway, and a set-top box are all examples of devices containing access-component interfaces. An end device is a digital device connected to a network whose purpose is to provide some utility (other than network service) to the end user. Examples of end devices are printers, TVs, audio speakers, security sensors, and HVAC controllers. A backbone-component interface connects a component network to the backbone network. Backbone-component interfaces may function as repeaters, bridges, or routers, and may be stand-alone, or embedded in an end device or PC. A single physical device such as a PC may act as an end device, and may contain an access-backbone interface and/or a backbone-component interface. Similarly, although the primary purpose of the backbone network is to connect component networks together, it may also have the attributes of a component network (connecting end devices and access-backbone interfaces together) because the VHN architecture allows end devices and access-backbone interfaces to connect directly to the backbone network. A residential gateway is a unique kind of device because it may terminate multiple access networks and may have connections to the backbone network as well as to component networks.

Shown in Figure 16.2, the devices connected to the backbone and component networks or access networks are examples of devices containing access-backbone interfaces that facilitate interoperability between networks. The telephone network, powerline network, and IEEE 1394 network are examples of component networks. The set-top box is acting as a residential gateway. The telephone, power outlets, PC, camcorder, and TV are end devices. Notice that the TV is acting as an end device, but also contains a backbone-component interface. The VHN hub is at the center of the star wiring. The home network, consisting of backbone and local physical technologies, is united by the network layer. For example, in Figure 16.2, the camcorder, although on a component network, is accessible by the TV or PC, which is shown directly on the physical backbone. A VHN backbone device will connect directly to the backbone and be able to control, or be controlled by, all VHN-compatible devices. A VHN device might not be connected to the backbone, but would support all Web-based control and user control schemes required for VHN compatibility. End devices not capable of talking to the VHN are not VHN-compatible. A non-VHN device may act as a VHN device by using a proxy service in an interface device.

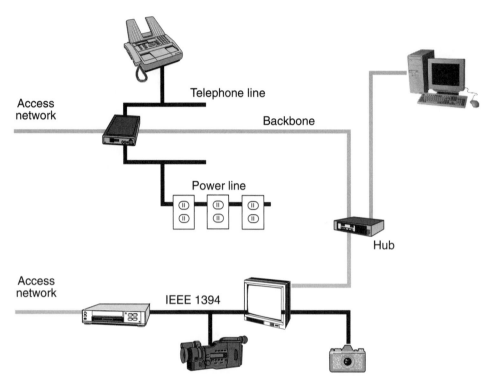

Figure 16.2
VESA home network example

Topology and Media

The VHN physical backbone topology will be a star configuration to preserve bandwidth on the IEEE 1394 home network backbone. With this topology, data can be isolated within individual segments in order to increase the total system bandwidth. The
backbone network will transport data from room to room. Within the rooms, a component network may be used. The standard IEEE 1394 technology is a high-performance
serial bus that is designed to provide communications over relatively short distances
(maximum 4.5 meters between nodes). To obtain the advantages of the IEEE 1394
bandwidth allocation, support for isochronous multimedia streams, and bus management, VESA Home Network member companies have been developing a long distance
version of IEEE 1394 with the goal of achieving 100 Mbps speeds over distances of 100
meters, using Category 5 UTP. Glass optical fiber (GOF) will also be used and various
forms of plastic optical fiber (POF) are being considered for the transport medium. The
majority of this work is taking place in the IEEE 1394b work group. Each segment of

the home network backbone will extend to each room in the home from a central location. In compliance with the National Electric Code, there will be no active electronics inside the wall. It is anticipated that adapters to the in-room network may be wall-mounted, deriving electrical power either from a nearby AC outlet, a component network cable (such as IEEE 1394), or from the home network itself.

Network Protocols

A typical home network will probably consist of several heterogeneous component networks connected to each other on a backbone network to form an IP-based network. VESA considered several strategies for providing addressing and data connectivity between heterogeneous networks and has selected the IP family of protocols to enable communication among devices in the home. The use of IP will ensure that any device in the home will be able to exchange messages and data streams with any other device and can access any service available over the home network. Additionally, devices that connect to the Backbone Network can use IP services to communicate among themselves.

The use of IP also ensures that higher layer protocols can be specified independent of the underlying networks and their data link layer protocols. It also enables incorporation of new physical communication technologies into the home network without disturbing the existing networks and devices.

If a DHCP server is present on the home network, it will assign IP addresses to devices. Many consumer electronics manufacturers intend to include DHCP servers, as well as other network and Internet tools, in their digital video products. If one is not present on the home network, an autonomous addressing scheme is used.

Data and Control Protocols

The VHN is a hybrid protocol model where the IP is used for control and asynchronous data, and IEEE 1394 protocols are used for the video and audio streaming to take advantage of the isochronous channel capability. Access to high-bit-rate digital audio or video streaming is done by direct hook-up to the IEEE 1394 network.

User-to-Device Control

User-to-device control occurs when the consumer interacts with a user interface device, which generates a command that is sent on the network to a controlled device. This control is based on the Web paradigm. Device controls are represented graphically by HTML user interface documents, the top one called the d*evice homepag*e. Con-

trolled devices, such as a digital VCR (DVCR), have an embedded HTTP Web server.
A Web browser remote from the DVCR, for example, in a high-definition television
(HDTV), PC, or wireless PDA, is used to access the device homepage and render and
present the DVCR graphical user interface (GUI) to the user. The user begins by calling up a browser window on the television screen, perhaps using only a portion of the
screen, or a partially transparent display. In the window is the top-level *Home Network Homepage* GUI of available devices on the home network, which is dynamically
generated to include an icon and name text for each device. This GUI could include
external Web-based services. When the user clicks on an icon, the corresponding device home page is retrieved from that device. The device home page may contain buttons or icons for controls, such as "play," "record," "volume up/down," and so forth.
When the user clicks on an icon, hyperlink messages are sent as control commands to
the controlled device. The controlled device may issue an updated GUI document
showing the new status of the device, for example "play" or "rewind." This control
model is designed for the operation of networked intelligent consumer electronics devices without a keyboard. These devices can be accessed and controlled from locations inside or outside the home, via the World Wide Web.

Device-to-Device Control

Device-to-device control occurs where application software in one device discovers
and controls application software in another device to effect some action without human intervention. The VHN device-to-device control architecture is also based on the
Web paradigm to provide a method compatible with the user-to-device control mechanism. Web technology XML with standardized vocabulary is used to describe the device interface and generate the control messages. The XML device interface
represents the interface of the controlled application in the device. It describes device
commands, capabilities, and properties, e.g., the function name "record" and its parameters "channel," "start time," "duration." Controllers can access the interface of
controlled devices to learn the functionality and generate control messages, which are
described in the format of an XML-based Remote Procedure Call (RPC). Device messages are "carried" using XML tags to identify them. Thus CAL, X-10, or AV/C syntax may be embedded in Web pages and sent to, for example, a CAL network via a
VESA Home Network CAL host without its having to translate.

In addition, existing standard language command messages can be sent in the
"English" text form as XML documents rather than using the compressed syntax
above. Generic CAL messages, for example, follow the CAL message format, but
with XML tags and attributes. This allows Web browsers with XML and scripting language support to interact with devices. RPC is a way to create connections between
procedures that are running in different applications, or on different machines. XML-

based RPC uses XML as the marshalling format. It allows software running on different operating systems in different environments to easily make procedure calls over the network. XML-based RPC uses HTTP as the transport protocol and XML as the encoding format. The device interfaces can be collected and put together to make a middleware layer, Home Network Broker & Interface Repository (HNB & IR), that can be searched or retrieved over the network by other devices. This control model provides standardized access to the device interface information, and a standardized way to communicate between devices. It also offers a high degree of extensibility and interoperability. Common Web development tools are utilized to bring the expressive power of the Web to the home.

Directory Services and Device Discovery

Devices connected to the home network, and the applications operating over the home network, will often need to locate other home network devices and applications. This is a particular concern for the residential gateway. Currently, application-specific or network-specific mechanisms exist to allow devices and applications to locate each other. The VHN network layer discovery mechanisms, including DHCP, interface to the Web control paradigm. The discovery mechanism runs and generates an HTML devices page at a predefined location. The home page of the user control browser is directed to this location. Thus, devices become visible and usable when attached. The devices home page can also be accessed via a standard web browser. Devices on component networks may have similar discovery means that allow for access of component network devices through the user control browser. For example, the HomePnP specification provides a mechanism to locate CAL-based devices with specific characteristics. Similarly, devices connected to an IEEE 1394 network can use IEEE 1394-specific mechanisms to search for devices hosting desired functionality by searching the configuration space of all devices on the IEEE 1394 network. The VHN discovery mechanism is evolving. Future discovery and naming mechanisms will be addressed in the second version.

Device Capabilities

Part of the management system requires linking devices with compatible services. When the devices page is run, the device capabilities are accessed and the user selection is checked.

Event Management

For asynchronous events, such as a broken tape or rewind completion, a device can post a message to another device. If the other device is turned off, then the messages can be stored for the device to access at a later time.

Management User Interface

All device control follows the Web paradigm user interface, including management roles such as setting up gateways.

SECURITY ....

Security of data on the home network is a very important consideration. There are many different types of security needed:

- Firewalls to the outside world
- Security of data from copying, such as movies and credit card numbers
- Security of device access

Basic message-level security is provided in the first version of the specification. Additional security issues will be addressed in the second version of the VESA home network specification.

KEY BENEFITS OF VESA ....

The VESA home network is meant to be a complete system, in that it connects multiple networks. It is the only home network standard that covers layers from applications down to physical and even media. Further, it has the advantage of providing all the tools necessary to connect to the Internet, since it supports Web browsing as a system requirement.

VESA IMPLEMENTATIONS ....

VESA has completed a proof-of-concept trial that is a physical realization of the VHN architecture. The trial was built around an operational long distance IEEE 1394 backbone, and demonstrated the capability of the architecture to support:

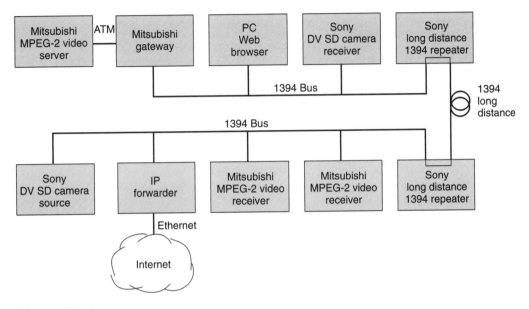

Figure 16.3
VHN proof of concept

1. Multiple simultaneous digital video streams—digital video (DV) and MPEG-2

2. Multiple types of datastreams—digital video and asynchronous data (Web browsing)

3. Multiple types of network segments—IEEE 1394 and Ethernet

The trial used Category 5 UTP as the backbone transmission medium. Figure 16.3 shows the equipment and connections for the proof-of-concept.

Samsung publicly demonstrated the Web paradigm user-to-device control at Comdex and the Western Show in 1998 (see Figure 16.4). The demo consisted of an HDTV, high-definition digital VCR (HD-DVCR), cable set-top box, standard DVD player (SD-DVDP), and a PC connected using IEEE 1394.

The HDTV remote control is used to access all devices. A Web browser is shown on the HDTV to initially access the devices page, which shows icons from all connected home network devices. Clicking on a device icon replaces the devices page with the HTML control GUI from the particular device. User interaction with the device control GUI sends hyperlink commands back to the device. User controls to the HD-DVCR are used to begin playing the HD-MPEG2 video stream to the HDTV. Similarly, the DVDP

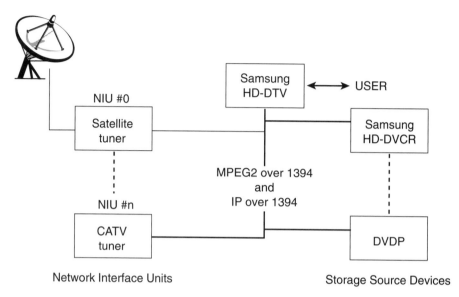

Figure 16.4
Samsung demonstration

GUI is rendered by the browser and used to start the DVDP play of SD-MPEG2. At this point, two video streams are playing simultaneously on the IEEE 1394 network. The user views the control GUI of the HDTV to do source selection and switch between the HD-DVCR stream and SD-DVDP stream.

Motorola has publicly demonstrated the user-to-device, device-to-device control and home network management models in a mixed technology home network (Ethernet and IEEE 1394). The demonstration consisted of multiple PCs, a digital video camera, a DVCR, and DV/analog converters operating in a home network with a cable modem-based access network.

RELATIONSHIP TO OTHER HOME NETWORKING TECHNOLOGIES..

Many home networking technologies have been announced recently. These technologies are primarily data link and physical layer technologies or high-layer APIs. Table 16.1 shows the layers that each technology utilizes.

Table 16.1 Layers Used in Various Home Networking Technologies

Layers	X-10	CEBus	HomePNA	HomeRF	Ethernet	HAVi	UPnP	VESA
Application		CAL				HAVi	UPnP	XML, HTML/ HTTP (CAL)* AV/C)* (X-10)*
Transport				SWAP		IEEE 1394 (TAM)		TCP, UDP, IEC81883
Network		CEBus		SWAP		IEEE 1394 (FCP)	IP	IP
Data Link	X-10	CEBus	802.3	SWAP	802.2 802.3			IEEE 1394b
Physical	X-10	CEBus	Broadcom	SWAP	802.3			IEEE 1394b
Media	PL	PL, IR, RF, UTP, Coax	UTP	RF	UTP 5 Coax Fiber		Phone Powerline Fiber UTP 5	UTP 5 Fiber

*Application language examples
(Source: VESA)

FUTURE PLANS AND STRATEGY ....

VESA is continuing its work on XML, network management, security, and network time support. The group has joined under CEA (Consumer Electronics Association) as the R-7.4 committee and will seek ISO/IEC approval for future versions. By working with both VESA and CEA, the committee will have improved marketing capabilities and be working with a larger group of companies. At the time of writing, the organization announced the creation of a VESA committee for the Japanese home networking market.

SUMMARY ....

VESA is the international nonprofit organization that sets and supports industry-wide electronic standards for the video, audio, and graphics interface of computer designs. It develops open, interoperable, and international standards for the global marketplace, thus ensuring worldwide market growth. It is headed by a board of directors representing a membership of more than 225 companies worldwide. The VESA home network specification allows consumers to connect together their disparate networks in the home, such as Ethernet, HomeRF, and other "no-new-wires" networks. It offers services such as directories, device existence and capability discovery, and network management. Visit VESA's Web site at www.vesa.org.

17 OSGi

In this chapter...

$\mathbf{A}$s discussed in earlier chapters, the next frontier in the networking industry is without doubt the home, and within a few years this market will become a billion-dollar industry. The Internet market has moved from the domain of the technologically literate to a mass market, with many users connecting from their homes. In addition, consumers are increasingly equipping their homes with multiple and other computer peripherals. As well, the non-PC Internet access market (including Internet TV, digital set-top boxes, Web-phones, and gaming consoles) is forecast to grow rapidly. And other household appliances (including consumer and entertainment devices) are starting to have intelligence and networking support built in at the point of manufacture. Furthering the concept of a Web-enabled home, many companies are working on plans for a central device, or residential gateway, that will be needed to network home appliances, PCs, and phone services. This chapter examines a new open standard for connecting the coming generation of smart consumer and small business appliances with commercial Internet services—the Open Services Gateway Initiative (OSGi) specification.

ABOUT THE OSGI GROUP.....................................

The OSGi is an industry group working to define and promote an open standard for connecting the coming generation of smart consumer and small business appliances with commercial Internet services. The group was founded in March, 1999 and has set the following objectives:

- Provide a forum for the development of open specifications for the delivery of multiple services over wide area networks to local home networks and devices.
- Accelerate the demand for products and services based on those specifications worldwide through the sponsorship of market and user education programs.

The group started out with 15 companies that were the founders and original members. At the time of writing this guide, OSGi had grown to more than 30 companies committed to supporting the full incorporation and charter of the organization. These companies are listed below; original members are listed first and are indicated by an asterisk.

*Alcatel	Deutsche Telekom
*Cable & Wireless	Berkom GmbH
*Electricité de France	Domosys
*Enron Communications	Echelon Corporation
*Ericsson	emWare Inc.
*IBM	France Telecom
*Lucent Technologies	Gatespace AB
*Motorola	GTE
*Liberate Technologies	Hewlett-Packard
*Nortel Networks	National Semiconductor GmbH
*Oracle Corporation	Nokia Corporation
*Philips Electronics	ProSyst Software
*Sun Microsystems	Schneider Electric
*Sybase	SA Sharp
*Toshiba	Siemens AG
AMD, Inc.	ST Microelectronics
Coactive Networks	Telia Research AB
Com21, Inc.	Tokyo Electric
Compaq	Whirlpool Corporation

OSGi was incorporated as a nonprofit organization in May 1999 and has since completed the preparation of by-laws and membership agreements, elected initial directors and officers, established expert groups to work on the initial specifications, and engaged resources to support the organization's operational and marketing programs. Unlike other initiatives, OSGi concentrates on complete end-to-end solutions architecture from remote service provider to local devices. Because the OSGi specification focuses on providing an open application layer and gateway interface, it complements and enhances virtually all current local networking standards and initiatives. The OSGi specifications deliver an open, common architecture for service providers, system developers, software vendors, device vendors, and equipment manufacturers to easily develop, deploy, and manage multiple services in a coordinated fashion.

OSGI ARCHITECTURE ....

OSGi is creating a new technical specification that is based on open standards and includes mechanisms for downloading of software from service providers, managing in-home application development cycles, security, remote management, and access to devices that are attached to the residential gateway.

To understand a complete end-to-end OSGi architecture model, you first need to be familiar with the model's main components:

- Services gateway
- Service provider
- Service aggregator
- Gateway operator
- Wide area network (WAN) and carrier/ISP
- Local devices and networks

The relationships between these entities are shown diagrammatically in Figure 17.1.

Services Gateway

The central component of the OSGi end-to-end architecture is the open services gateway (OSG). Service gateways further the concept of Web-enabled homes and facilitate the development and deployment of a wide range of advanced broadband-based services. From a technical perspective, the services gateway is an embedded server that is attached to a broadband Internet connection. It is highly secure and is based on a zero-local-administration management model.

The OSGi specification includes APIs for service cradle-to-grave life-cycle management, interservice dependency management, data management, device access and management, client access, resource management, and security.

Service Provider

Service providers enable the provision of services to their customer base using the services gateway in conjunction with an optional remote server and possibly some in-home client appliances. Services made available to customers are software applications that have been downloaded into the home or residential gateway. Examples of in-home services include:

- Verifying that all appliances on a home integrated network are in working order
- Provisioning of health care and remote monitoring services
- Itemized billing of Pay-Per-View events

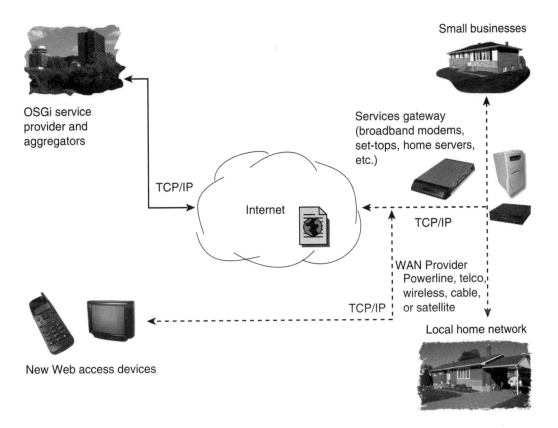

Figure 17.1
OSGi architectural overview

- Using the Web infrastructure to remotely monitor and manage the in-home security alarm system

The aforementioned range of services will only become a true reality when consumers are comfortable with secure download facilities that only allow trusted source code to be installed on their residential gateways.

Service Aggregator

Service aggregators bundle and provision a set of home networking services for their customer base. Additionally, aggregators are responsible for ensuring that delivered services are mutually compatible and do not conflict with devices that reside on the customer's home integrated network.

Gateway Operator

In the context of an end-to-end OSGi system, the terms *service aggregator* and *gateway operator* are often used interchangeably, though strictly speaking the roles are different.

The gateway operator manages and maintains the services gateway and its services. This management responsibility may overlap somewhat with that of the service aggregator and is the reason the terms are often used interchangeably.

Typical functions of a gateway operator include:

- Remotely managing the gateway and monitoring its status
- Initiating, downloading, starting, stopping, updating, and removing home networking services
- Controlling software and driver upgrade versions
- Ensuring that communication channels between the gateway and the service providers are secure from external attacks
- Controlling and managing the logical attachment of devices and local networks to the gateway, including authorizing the download of device and network drivers

Gateway operators may also generate revenue streams from the following business models:

- Renting a residential gateway to consumers
- Online reselling gateway appliances
- Providing professional installation services to consumers
- Entering into hardware maintenance contracts with home networking users

WAN Provider

The WAN provides the necessary communications between the service gateway, gateway operator, service aggregator, and service provider. This service is currently being used to offer speedy access to online information, entertainment, and e-commerce centric applications. Cable and satellite companies, ISPs, and wireless operators are examples of WAN providers who are looking at different ways of integrating their delivery mechanisms with home networking technologies. OSGi makes a clear distinction between WAN providers and gateway operators. Even though a clear distinction has been made between both parties, there will be instances of WAN providers also performing the role of gateway operators, such as the cable TV industry.

Local Networks and Devices

The last major piece of the OSGi architecture is the local home area network and household devices (i.e., Internet-ready PDAs, Internet TV sets, smart phones, and other information appliances) attached to the services gateway. Devices can be directly networked to the gateway using hardware links such as parallel or serial connections or indirectly connected by means of a local transport network, such as Bluetooth, IEEE 1394, HomePNA, powerline, or HomeRF.

UNDER THE HOOD ....

The first release of the OSGi specification is a Java-based application layer framework that gives service providers, network operators, device makers, and appliance manufacturers vendor-neutral application and device layer APIs and functions. The main reason for choosing Java is because it is an open technology that can run on multiple platforms including services gateways, consumer electronics equipment, household appliances, communications appliances, computers, and more. The following sections provide additional technical details on key entities of the OSGi framework.

Java

To ensure a large target market for third-party service developers as well as a large selection of compatible services for gateway operators, OSGi specifies API standards for the gateway platform execution environment. Gateways must support these API standards in order to be compliant with the OSGi specifications. For a Java-based gateway, the APIs are based on the Java 2 package and class definitions. The goal is to allow implementations of service gateways to be based on Personal Java (PJava) as well as on versions of Java 2 Micro Edition (J2ME) and other compatible Java runtime environments. The following sections provide additional technical details on these two runtime environments.

Personal Java

Personal Java, or PJava, is an application development and middleware environment developed by Sun Microsystems. It is designed for a myriad of consumer devices, such as network computers, smart telephones, game consoles, and TV set-top boxes. It executes software written in the Java programming language. PJava comprises a lightweight version of the JVM, a set of core libraries, and optional libraries that may be used as needed.

J2ME

J2ME is a new edition of the Java 2 platform targeted at consumer electronics and embedded devices. J2ME consists of a virtual machine and a minimal layer of APIs targeted at providing only enough functionality to securely and safely download Java classes to a device and configure the Java environment. J2ME comes in two flavors, called configurations, that are targeted at two broad categories of devices: (a) those with 128 to 512 KB of memory available for the Java environment (and applications) and (b) those with 512 KB+ available for the Java environment (and applications).

If you are looking for more technical detail on both of these environments, we suggest visiting Sun's Web site at http://www.sun.com.

Services

A service is a self-contained component, accessible via a defined service interface. In the OSGi model, an application is built around a set of cooperating services. The framework maintains a set of mappings from services to their implementations and has a simple query mechanism that enables an installed service to request and use the available services. After a service is published, other services can use it to accomplish their tasks. From a development perspective, the OSGi specification has decoupled a service's interface from its implementation. This point is critical for the development community because OSGi is designed to run in a variety of different gateway devices. Each one of these gateways will have different hardware characteristics, which could affect many aspects of the service implementation. The availability of a stable interface to developers will ensure the overall stability of the software system running on the device.

Bundles

Service implementations are packaged into *bundles*. A bundle is a file that:

- Contains the resources implementing zero or more services. These resources may be class files for the Java programming language, as well as any other data (such as HTML help files, icons, and so on)

- Contains a manifest file with headers specifying various parameters so that the Java environment can correctly install and activate the bundle

When the OSGi framework is started on the gateway, an initial bundle that usually assumes administrative roles must be created, installed, and activated; it in turn manages the lifecycle of other bundles, which can be installed, started, updated, stopped, and uninstalled. The relationship between the OSGi framework and its installed bundles is captured by the notion of a *bundle context*. Each time a bundle is installed, a unique bundle context is created for it.

Events

The OSGi framework is capable of generating three different kinds of events:

1. The ServiceEvent is used to report registration, unregistration, or property changes for services
2. The BundleEvent report changes in the life-cycle of bundles
3. The FrameWorkEvent reports that the framework itself has started and lists any errors that were encountered during the starting process

For each kind of event, there is a corresponding listener interface.

Java-Embedded Server (JES)

JES is a small-footprint application server for use within remote networkable devices. It allows devices to upload, download, activate, and deploy customized home services and applications on demand. From a technical perspective, JES consists of two primary components: a *servicespace* framework and a number of modular in-home *services* that are executed within this framework. The relationships between these two JES components are shown in Figure 17.2, and explained in the following subsections.

Servicespace

Originally developed by Sun Microsystems, this service framework allows programmers to write Java-based applications as independent components that can be managed independently of one another and can be dynamically added, removed, executed, or updated from within a running application. The framework provides a rich and structured development platform for component-based software architectures and takes advantage of Java's ability to download code from a broadband or dial-up network.

The servicespace framework requires only 100KB of memory and a Java runtime platform such as PJava.

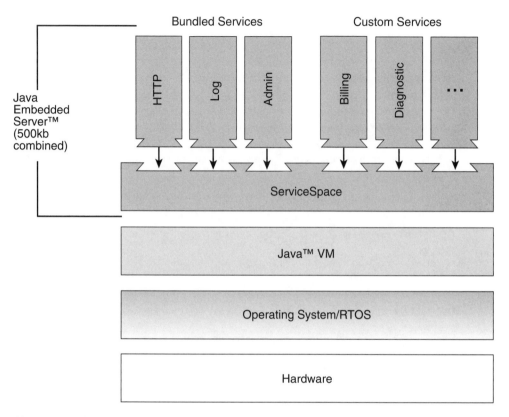

Figure 17.2
JES Technology architecture

Services

Home Applications that run in the JES are called *application services*. JES comes with a set of prebuilt services that address a variety of common requirements for networked homes. Core services include:

HTTP Service • The Internet homes of the future will allow consumers to activate their gateways from anywhere in the world. Such an environment will be based on Web protocols, so an API has been defined by OSGi for an HTTP-based Web server that runs as part of the services gateway device. This lightweight HTTP service provides a complete embedded Web server, which may be used by developers to build a

Web interface to devices on a home network. Additionally, this HTTP API provides consumers with the ability to publish content on the Web.

Servlets • Servlets can be thought of as server-side versions of Java applets that extend the functionality of Web servers. JES provides support for execution of Java servlets.

Remote Management • The remote management service supports remote management of application services resident on the device. The remote management service can be integrated with enterprise management systems, such as IBM Tivoli and CA Unicenter.

SNMP • The Simple Network Management Protocol (SNMP) agent service facilitates management and monitoring of the gateway device.

Scheduler • The time-based scheduling service can be used to automatically activate an application service to run at a particular time of the day or night.

Logging • The logging service defines a standard API that allows OSGi home networking services to write events to a log file on the gateway. The facility of a log file helps developers and service providers to resolve gateway problems. Following are some of the features of the OSGi:

- Records the current system time in the log entry
- Records a severity level in the log entry
- Records a text message in the log entry
- Records an optional Java object in the log entry
- Records the identity of the Java program running in the service framework that created the log entry
- Listens to Framework events and creates log entries representing these events
- Reads past log entries via an enumeration
- Notifies listeners of log entries as the entries are created

Gateway implementers are free to construct the log service in a variety of ways depending on the capabilities of the gateway, including spooling to a local log file on a hard disk or transferring to a remote management server.

Remote Method Invocation (RMI) • RMI is a set of protocols being developed by Sun's JavaSoft division that enable Java objects to communicate remotely with other Java objects.

Console • The console service provides an administrative console for JES. This console could appear on any type of display unit such as a television screen or a standard PC monitor.

Device Access Systems

The OSGi device access system has a number of goals, including:

- It must support plugging and unplugging of home networking devices at any time
- It must cope with device technologies that do not support automatic detection
- It must be capable of loading new device drivers on demand with no prior specific knowledge
- It needs to support mixed network technologies
- It needs to support multifunction devices and devices that have multiple configurations

The device access system consists of a set of drivers and a device manager.

Device Drivers

The OSGi device access system is independent of home network infrastructures and in-home devices. New devices or network topologies will simply require new device drivers. Device drivers are third-party software and are typically provided by device manufacturers. Device drivers fall into two different categories: (a) those that directly manage native hardware on the gateway, and (b) those that connect to other device services.

When a driver is started by a gateway it immediately registers a service and remains registered with the OSGi framework for as long as the driver is running. Each device driver has a unique identification number.

Device Access Manager

One of the device access manager's primary functions is to dynamically load services for appliances that are connected to the services gateway. In addition to controlling drivers, the device access manager, where possible, is able to detect the addition of new in-home devices, and then locate and load supporting software modules with a minimum of user interaction. Finally, the device manager can be configured to support devices that do not contain OSGi specific functionality (i.e., appliances that were designed prior to the OSGi specification release). It is also worth noting that the device access system is an optional component of OSGi. The easiest way to understand how the device access manager works is to look at a short example. Let's take a simple device discovery system, such as attaching an IEEE 1394-enabled camera to the gateway. In the following scenario, we can assume that the 1394 driver is fully operational. When a consumer attaches their IEEE 1394-enabled camera to their gateway the following sequence of events takes place:

1. The camera is connected to the gateway and the IEEE 1394 detects the new hardware device
2. It queries the camera to obtain a 1394 descriptor
3. It registers a 1394 device service together with the properties describing it
4. The device manager detects the camera through its service listener
5. The device manager then queries all running drivers trying to identify a driver that matches the digital camera
6. The level of suitability is collected by the device manager and selects the driver that returned the highest value
7. The new driver than calls the camera service and attaches to it

If no driver is available for the camera, the device manager displays a message informing the user that the gateway does not support connectivity with the digital camera.

Optional Services

In addition to the required services, OSGi is also defining a number of optional services. We briefly explore these forms of communication in the following subsections.

Client Access Service

In a live home networking environment, there will be occasions where family members will need to interact with the gateway. The client access service API provides developers with a framework for managing these interactions. Typical interactions between a home network user and the gateway range from viewing operational information to making modifications to configuration parameters. This advanced API supports URL name space management, which goes beyond the basic facilities provided by the HTTP service. Other features include full support for negotiation of different types of data formats ranging from mobile phones to standard PC browsers.

Configuration Data Service

Many of the services loaded and running in a gateway need additional information to perform their day-to-day tasks. This information can be as simple as a list of authorized appliances or as complex as personalized user profiles. To access this information, OSGi has defined a common service API for services to store and access this data. This allows the gateway operator or service provider to remotely change the configuration of the in-home gateway.

Persistent Data Service

Many of the services running on a gateway will need to store and retrieve information that persists beyond the life of the service and that can be shared with other services. So rather than developing code for reading and writing information to the file system for each in-home service, OSGi provides a common persistent data service that can be used by other services to store and retrieve data. This API has a number of features, including:

- A high-level query language to search the persistent information store
- Recovery from partial updates
- Ability to synchronize the data with databases located on servers

OSGI SECURITY ....

Security for OSGi gateways is based on the Java 2 specification. Full details of the security features are available from Sun's Web site at: http://java.sun.com/products/jdk/docs/guide/security/spec/security-spec.doc.html.

KEY BENEFITS OF OSGI ....

The following list is a high-level summary of the key technical benefits associated with the OSGi specifications.

Platform Independence • The OSGi APIs can be implemented on a wide range of hardware platforms and operating systems to tailor the services gateway to the unique needs of a particular vertical market.

Application Independence • The OSGi specifications focus on defining common implementation APIs, making it suitable for services gateways for a variety of applications in different markets. While initially focused on the requirements of the residential gateway market, OSGi services gateways can be used in telematics applications, embedded in PDAs and cell phones, and supported on PCs and other consumer electronics devices.

Security • The OSGi specifications incorporate various levels of system security features, ranging from digital signing of downloaded modules to fine-grained object access control.

Multiple Services • The OSGi specifications support hosting multiple services from different providers on a single services gateway platform. This flexibility allows a gateway operator to offer a wide array of services to their customers.

Multiple Local Network Technologies • A variety of wired and wireless, data, and audio-video local transport standards are emerging. The OSGi specifications are designed to complement and enhance local network and device attachment technologies such as Bluetooth, the HAVi standard, HomePNA, HomeRF, IEEE-1394, Lon-Works, powerline communication systems, Universal Serial Bus (USB), the Video Electronics Standards Association (VESA) Home Network, wireless systems, and other local network technologies.

Multiple Device Access Technologies • By concentrating on the service implementation aspects of the platform, OSGi supports a variety of device access technologies, such as UPnP and Jini, as a part of the device access API. These device access technologies let users control devices from many different places and diverse client devices. The standards define the discovery process of devices on the network, how commands can be issued to other devices, and how events from devices can be received. OSGi and device access technologies such as UPnP and Jini are very complementary, solve very different problems, and are a natural fit to cooperate.

Coexistence with Other Standards • OSGi service gateways can use narrow-band Internet access approaches as well as the faster DSL and cable modem technologies. OSGi gateways may also be compatible with market-specific device and network management schemes, such as DOCSIS and SNMP.

Future-Proof • OSGi preserves consumer investments in future smart home devices. For example, today, when a consumer switches from one home security provider to another, the entire internal network has to be replaced. By choosing devices compatible with the OSGi specification, consumers can switch between various vendor offerings without having to replace virtually any of the networking infrastructure.

OSGI APPLICATION EXAMPLES...................................

As new Internet-based appliances are introduced over the next few years, the Open Services Gateway will directly benefit small businesses and consumers in many ways. Below are three real-world examples that illustrate the potential impact of the OSG initiative.

Energy Services

Power companies leveraging OSGi-based products can deliver not only energy measurement but also energy load management throughout the home. Consumers can buy services such as a specific daytime and nighttime temperature or balancing the load so that the HVAC systems do not operate at the same time as washers/dryers or other high-consumption equipment. This reduces service costs for the consumer and makes load management more intelligent for the utility, reducing peak loads and investments required to support these services.

Security Services

There are a variety of building systems you rarely think about (e.g., fire alarms, employee security and access systems, and in-building climate management). Many are monitored from remote locations but maintained through field visits. The OSGi specification allows providers of these systems to standardize the software gateway used to manage, upgrade, and administer these systems, while leveraging the Internet to connect them to the data center. So when the area code used to call the fire department changes, or when new security policies are implemented, the system can be upgraded via the Internet without requiring a field visit. Furthermore, home security systems will no longer require proprietary communications systems and you can buy services that let you know through your cell phone or pager if your kids did not return from school at the normal time. You can get a message to your cell phone or pager the minute your house is broken into—the same minute the alarm company or the police learn about it. Or, you can get a notification that the temperature in your home office has fallen below the freezing point.

Remote Home Healthcare Services

Consumers caring for an elderly parent or relative will be able to avail themselves of low-cost patient monitoring devices that continuously transmit critical care or emergency information through the services gateway to hospitals, physicians, or paramedical services, reducing costs and increasing the sense of safety and security. The likely services for this segment are monitoring and sensing devices (such as motion detectors), personal alarms, assistance tools (simplified Internet home shopping), and communication (e.g., e-mail and video conferencing).

SUMMARY ....

The OSGi specification provides a common foundation for ISPs, network operators, and equipment manufacturers to deliver a wide range of e-services via gateway servers running in the home or remote office. The OSGi specifications are designed to complement emerging standards in local device connectivity and in WAN access. OSGi is compatible with physical local transports such as Bluetooth, the HAVi standard, HomePNA, HomeRF, and USB. The device access architecture of OSGi is compatible with several different logical device access technologies, such as Jini and UPnP. From a technical perspective, OSGi is best described as a collection of APIs that define standards for service gateways. Where possible, the OSGi is leveraging existing Java standards, such as Jini. Where there are standards that apply that are not Java-based, the group work focuses on integrating with these standards. The services gateway uses JES to connect the Internet to devices on a home network. JES software is 100% Java technology.

18 Copyright and Watermarking Technologies

In this chapter...

When you buy a DVD player and connect it to your home network, the DVD you insert into the drive is capable of storing around 5 Gbytes of data. In other words, it can accommodate three hours of a standard motion picture. This is great; however, there are valid fears within prominent industries associated with the home networking industry that the prevalence of casual piracy could destroy this emerging industry. Realizing this, a number of working groups and committees have been established to develop various methods of safeguarding copyrighted material. This chapter describes these organizations and the emerging technologies that are been used to protect digital content.

ABOUT CONTENT PROTECTION............................

Original copyrighted content is delivered to your home network from a number of sources. It may be transmitted via satellite, terrestrial, or cable systems or recorded on various formats of digital media—CD-ROMs, DVDs, and hard drives. To protect this content from unauthorized copying, a number of different technologies are being developed. The development of these protection technologies is driven by the movie industry, which fears that the proliferation of digital technologies will encourage people to illegally copy content. For instance, it is relatively easy to download a new movie from your cable operator's broadband network and use your in-home network to make several copies of this film. The level of content protection that is used in a home networking environment will largely depend on the type of person that is running the system. Table 18.1 categorizes the different levels of danger that are associated with people who actively copy digital content.

Table 18.1 Copyright Threats

Groups of People	Threat to Content Revenue Streams
Casual copier	Low—The individual may record a film on their VCR for personal viewing.
Hobbyist	Relatively low—The individual may purchase or develop a device for storing Internet content.
Small-scale hacker	High—Operates a bank of recording devices (e.g., DVD players, VCRs, and CD-ROM drives).
Professional pirate	Very high—Well funded and very knowledgeable of the digital security systems.

Much of the copy protection technology has been developed to "keep honest people honest." That is, it is aimed primarily at the first group identified in Table 18.1. All the technologies that have been proposed or developed so far have been breakable, and the breaches have become accessible to the casual copier as upgrades to consumer A/V products.

An important part of the strategy behind copy protection is legal prosecution. Legal means are used against the latter two categories. It is clearly impractical to initiate legal action against average consumers. The use of copy protection technology is partly to force the copier to buy pirate equipment to make illegal copies. The distribution of pirate technology is illegal. Again, this gives the industry a means to prosecute those in the latter two groups who would make a business of distributing this technology.

For honest people, an in-home copy protection system must provide a number of features:

- It must not degrade the quality of the signal that is used by our in-home appliances.
- We should not need to know about a complex protection system running on our network unless we decide to make pirate copies. In other words, any content protection system that runs in our home is transparent.
- It does not add significantly to the cost of appliances.
- All content protection systems must be designed to work with other computing and A/V devices.

Over the past year, a couple of factors have accelerated the need for a standard copyright protection system. Television producers are not overly excited about releasing digital content that can be easily pirated. Consequently, the drive for copy protection systems has largely been from the movie industry.

In addition, all DVD players with a IEEE 1394 interface port that are manufactured today are required by law to comply with an industry-wide digital-protection scheme. These factors have acted as a catalyst in developing new standards that address the copyright protection of video, audio, and data in a digital format. The remaining sections in this chapter will explain in detail the groups, proposals, specifications, and technologies that are associated with these new global protection standards.

STANDARDS GROUPS, PROPOSALS, AND TECHNOLOGIES ....

Copy Protection Technical Working Group (CPTWG)

The CPTWG is an ad hoc group of experts from computer, consumer-electronics, and movie-studio industries that was formed in 1996 to assess the technical merits of competing copy-protection proposals for movies, video, and other content on digital media. Figure 18.1 is an illustration of the major industries and organizations that are working with CPTWG to stop the unauthorized copying of digital content.

CPTWG is the frontrunner in developing standards for the protection of digital content. One of its main accomplishments was the launching of an encryption approach called Content Scrambling System (CSS) in 1997. CSS is a technology that prevents unauthorized copying from prerecorded DVD disks.

Digital Watermarking

Current read-only DVD systems prevent unauthorized copying from prerecorded DVD disks by using licensed technologies, such as the digital content scrambling system (CSS) from CPTWG. The content scrambling system is a form of data encryption to discourage reading media files directly from DVD disks. But with the advent of digital recording equipment such as recordable DVDs, digital tape recorders, and personal computers with large disk storage capacities, additional copy-protection features are needed to prevent unauthorized copies of the copyrighted digital content. The solution is the creation of invisible electronic watermarks for digital movies and video. The use of watermarking technologies is becoming a popular method of protecting video content from unauthorized copying and/or playback.

These watermarks are embedded in the video content during the processing and digital compression of the content. For this method of content protection to be effective, the watermark must always be added to the content before the content is distributed via DVD, cable, satellite, broadcast, or MMDS. Watermarking technologies make life difficult for counterfeiters because they are difficult to erase or alter. Although invisible to the user, electronic watermarks contain information that can be recognized, for example, by a detector chip in consumer digital set-top boxes, or special detection software running on compliant PC systems as instructions for enabling or disabling its ability to make a copy. In addition to being invisible to users, electronic watermarks must survive through normal processes such as digital-to-analog conversion and repeated digital compression/decompression cycles while still remaining

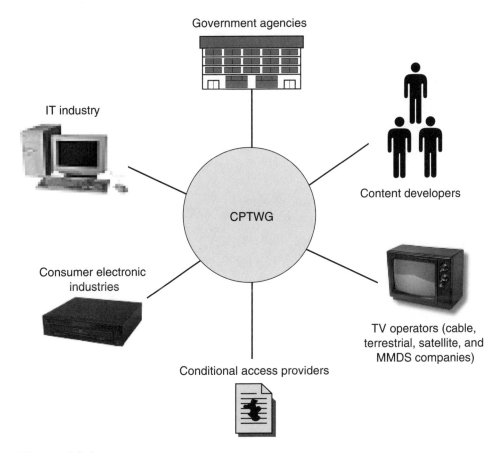

Figure 18.1
Principal players in the content protection industry

detectable by the digital recorder system. The addition of a watermark to video/audio material does not interfere with the quality of service for home networking users.

In theory, the idea of having detection built into the PC or player sounds really good. However there are two problems. There is no reason why anyone needs to include watermark detection in equipment that they manufacture or software that they develop. Given that absence of copy protection technology is a big selling feature for any equipment, one can only guess that there will be no rush to include the technology from equipment providers and software developers. Second, if you know how to detect a watermark, you know how to remove it. If the watermark algorithm is in every player and piece of software it will be very quickly reverse-engineered, and before long there will be watermark removal utilities.

A subgroup of the CPTWG called the Data Hiding Subgroup (DHSG) was formed in May 1997 to assess the technical merits of competing copy-protection proposals for movies, video, and other content on digital media. In July of the same year, the DHSG issued a call for proposals (CFP) for a data-hiding system that could be used to protect high-value content from unauthorized copying and recopying.

The CFP defined a set of requirements, ranked as either essential or desirable. The essential requirements are as follows.

- Transparency—The presence of watermark should not affect the quality of the digital signal.
- Low-cost method for digital detection.
- Digital detection domain—The digital detection can be made at source data (uncompressed digital video), MPEG-2 compressed elementary data, a multiplexed stream (program/transport), and/or logical sector data.
- Generational copy control for one copy.
- Reliable detection of piracy.
- Watermark will survive normal video processing in consumer use.
- Licensable under reasonable terms.
- No restriction in export/import.
- Technical maturity (proven technology).
- Data payload—Three states ("never-copy," "no-more-copy," or "one-copy").
- Minimum impact on content preparation.
- Data rate of at least 11.08 Mbps

In September 1997, eleven proposals were submitted in response to the CFP. In May 1998, DHSG issued the interim report on the results of its analysis of the eleven proposals. Following the release of this report, several companies sought to strengthen their independent proposals by joining forces. IBM and NEC combined their efforts to jointly develop a powerful method for automatically creating and embedding robust watermarks that are invisible to viewers. At about the same time, Hitachi, Pioneer, and Sony focused their extensive expertise in consumer products and watermarking technologies behind a separate proposal that featured critical technical elements for maintaining the high visual quality of authorized copies and for meeting the more demanding requirements of future high-definition television (HDTV) content. Macrovision, Digimarc, and Philips also joined forces to develop their own proposal on how to deter unauthorized copying of digital content.

At the end of 1998, the IBM-NEC group and the Pioneer-Hitachi-Sony group held a series of meetings to evaluate the possibility of merging their two proposals together. As a result of these meetings, IBM, NEC, Pioneer, Hitachi, and Sony announced the formation of the Galaxy team. The Galaxy team merged watermarking proposals for DVD copy protection and submitted a unified proposal of video watermarking to the DVD Watermark Review Panel (WaRP) on March 2, 1999. WaRP was formed at the December 1998 meeting of the CSS licensees to define and execute the final evaluations of the remaining proposals for video watermarking.

At the time of writing, only two proposals remain for evaluation by WaRP: the unified Galaxy proposal and the one submitted by Philips, Macrovision, and Digimarc.

Protecting Digital Content

As mentioned previously, high-speed digital interfaces allow consumer A/V electronic devices to interoperate with PCs. This is very exciting for home network users; however, it poses some serious challenges to industries that are worried about the pirating of digital content. To confront these challenges, copy protection systems are being developed to:

- Protect content in transmission from one A/V device to another
- Protect content that is stored on digital tapes, DVDs, CD-ROMs, and hard disks

At the time of writing, digital video sources such as DVD players, set-top boxes, and PCs were not permitted to exchange digital entertainment content with CE devices such as TVs and VCRs through any external digital bus. In an effort to overcome the legal and technical restrictions associated with the transfer of digital data within our homes, the consumer electronics industry has developed the following protection systems.

Digital Transmission Content Protection (DTCP)

The CPTWG formed a subgroup in April 1997 called Digital Transmission Discussion Group (DTDG) to work on the standardization of copy protection tools for digital interfaces (IEEE 1394). A number of companies submitted proposals to the subgroup over a twelve-month period. Figure 18.2 shows the companies that are involved in the protection of 1394-based content.

From the diagram we can see five of the companies (Sony, Hitachi, Toshiba, Matsushita, and Intel) merged their proposals into one, referred to as 5C. The proposal

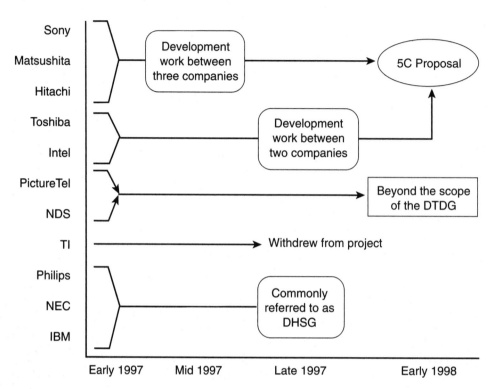

Figure 18.2
Timescales of DTDG proposals

uses a cryptographic protocol called digital transmission content protection, common-ly called DTCP, to protect A/V entertainment content from illegal copying, intercep-tion, and tampering as the content traverses such high-performance digital buses as IEEE 1394. The technology is available for licensing in two forms. The "use license" is for system OEMs and the "development intellectual-property license" is for semi-conductor companies. Semiconductor divisions of Japan's two consumer electronics giants—Sony and Matsushita—have each launched their own DTCP-enabled IEEE-1394 chips. Designed for use in digital set-top boxes and other home networking ap-pliances, these chips support the secure, two-way transmission of digital content across the IEEE interface at speeds of up to 200 Mbps. Both chips encrypt and de-crypt digital content in real-time with no load on the consumer appliance's micropro-cessor. In August of 1998, NDS announced an initiative to broaden the approach of 5C. The new initiative was called *C.

The *C title is fashioned after the 5C, replacing the number 5 with a wildcard. *C covers all the areas covered by 5C and goes beyond. The *C proposal has been submitted to various standards bodies, including CPTWG.

*C is fair, open, secure, flexible, extendable, and involves no nondisclosure agreements (NDAs). To content owners and distributors, *C architecture offers ultimate security as well as powerful and secure support for a wide range of distribution and business models. *C allows consumer electronics manufacturers to shift the bulk of security burden and associated responsibilities to the security provider companies. It also allows them to offer/support a number of consumer features, such as anti-theft protection, flexible and secure parental control and customization, and others. Consumers would enjoy the benefits above—the more convenient and attractive distribution options, anti-theft protection and parental control.

Extended Conditional Access (XCA) Approach

Original copyrighted content is delivered to a home network from a number of sources. Under the XCA approach, content can be identified as "never-copy," "copy-once," and "free-copy." These three states are represented using the Copy Generation Management System (CGMS) bits. The A/V devices on your home network should obey "playback control," "record control," and "one-generation control" rules, as summarized in Table 18.2.

Table 18.2 Device Response to CGMS Bits

Device Type/ Content Type	Never-copy	Copy-once	No-more-copies	Free Copy
Player	Play	Play	Play	Play
Recorder	Do not record	Record and change content type to "no-more-copies" in the new copy	Do not record	Record

Zenith Electronics and Thomson Consumer Electronics are heading a group of manufacturers that favors a smart-card-based renewable encryption scheme called XCA. There are several reasons why this was seen as being advantageous.

First, it decouples the security system from the manufacture of the player. This is important as player manufacturers can come under market pressure to short-cut security as the lack of it is a selling point. (One consumer electronics manufacturer received significant pressure from its distributors to make the ability to remove country codes and macrovision from its DVD players easier. The competition had done so and this had helped their sales).

Second, security is never static. Security systems have a significantly shorter life span than consumer equipment. The breach in the CSS system has become unrecoverable because there is a large base of DVD players that cannot be upgraded. Every security system gets broken. Good system design means that you can recover from the breach. The use of security models goes some way to achieve this.

XCA protection involves two steps:

1. Content scrambling—Different parts of the content are scrambled with a symmetric algorithm under different keys. For robustness, the key is changed every few seconds.

2. Key protection—The scrambling keys are derived in a number of ways. They can be generated randomly or derived from Entitlement Control Messages (ECMs). Randomly generated keys are protected using a public-key algorithm or any other method.

Scrambling and key protection take place at the source (i.e., broadcaster head-end or publishing house). MPEG-2 defines Entitlement Control Messages (ECMs) for carrying the scrambling keys (control words) together with A/V content. ECMs are then used by the smart card to decrypt the relevant program. In XCA, the ECMs are extended to contain the CGMS bits and access rights as well as control words. Every time copyrighted content (e.g., a movie) is recorded, the extended ECMs (XECMs) are modified through a one-way, irreversible transformation to distinguish copies from the original.

Further information about current XCA activities can be obtained through NDS's Web site at http://www.ndsworld.com/cmp/cmp_docs/xcav5.doc.

SUMMARY ....

The dramatic rise in popularity of home networking products has raised concerns—first within the motion picture industry and then among the entertainment, electronics, and broadcast industries—about unauthorized copying of copyrighted digital content transmitted between digital electronics products. The flotation of digital signals around a home network is a hacker's dream come true. Consequently, an organization called Copy Protection Technical Working Group (CPTWG) was formed to protect entertainment content during all stages of production and distribution.

Digital watermarking technology is seen by content providers as critical to controlling unauthorized copying of content with future digital recording equipment. Data Hiding Subgroup (DHSG) was set up by the CPTWG to establish a standard mechanism for watermarking electronic content.

Since September 1997, when the DHSG began considering ways to check illegal copies of digital-video contents, 11 proposals by 11 companies had been squeezed down to three by groups composed of IBM/NEC, Hitachi/Pioneer/Sony, and Digimarc/Macrovision/Philips. Now the first two groups have allied under the Galaxy banner, leaving only two coalitions to champion opposing digital watermarking standards. Content management and protection systems should ensure that only authorized actions (uses of content) are performed with the content.

Index